Through the Lo

Richard Idemon
(1938–1987)

Through
the
Looking Glass

A SEARCH FOR THE SELF IN THE MIRROR OF RELATIONSHIPS

SEMINARS IN PSYCHOLOGICAL ASTROLOGY, VOLUME 5

——by——

Richard Idemon

——Edited by Howard Sasportas——

SAMUEL WEISER, INC.

York Beach, Maine

First published in 1992 by
Samuel Weiser, Inc.
Box 612
York Beach, Maine 03910-0612

02 01 00 99 98 97 96
10 9 8 7 6 5 4 3 2

Library of Congress Cataloging-in-Publication Data:

Idemon, Richard.
    Through the looking glass: a search for the self in
  the mirror of relationships / Richard Idemon.
        p.   cm. - - (Seminars in psychological astrology ; v. 5)
      1. Interpersonal relations — Miscellanea.   2. Astrology.
  I. Title.   II Series.
  BF1729.P8I34 1992
  133.5'81582- -dc20   91-43165
                                                               CIP

ISBN 0-87728-721-X
CCP

Cover illustration is "The Baleful Head" (1886-87) by Sir Richard
Burne-Jones (1833-96). Staatsgalerie, Stuttgart/The Bridgeman Art
Library, London. Used by kind permission.

Typeset in 10 point Palatino

Printed in the United States of America

The paper used in this publication meets the minimum requirements of the American National Standard for Permanence of
Paper Printed Library Materials Z39.48-1984.

I want to thank Lynn Kaufmann and Steve Pincus for their help with this seminar. I want to extend a very special thanks to Gina Ceaglio, who coordinated the seminar and who is a blessing not in disguise. And I want to thank all the members of the seminar group, for they made this book possible.

Seminars in Psychological Astrology series

CONTENTS

PART ONE
The Basics of Relating

PART TWO
Realizing the Self

PART THREE
Practical Applications
of Synastry

PREFACE

Richard Idemon's untimely death on February 22, 1987, shortly after his forty-ninth birthday, left a significant void in the astrological community and we are enormously grateful that his unique contribution lives on in this and other presentations. Richard's insights bring added depth and dimension to our understanding of the human condition and his method of integrating Jungian psychology and myth with astrology demonstrates his capacity to correlate other disciplines with astrology's symbolic language. Extremely bright and well-read, he was conversant in many fields; a literary pundit, history buff, thespian, gourmet, world traveler, bon vivant, and connoisseur of life, all of which contributed to his charismatic style as a teacher and anecdotal story-teller, and to his objectivity as a psychotherapist.

The hundreds of students Richard taught at his School of Astro-Psychological Studies in San Francisco and the countless people he reached in the years he lectured throughout the United States, Europe, South America, and Africa continually beseeched him to set down his observations and wisdom in book form. Shortly before he fell ill, he made a commitment to himself to fulfill these requests and was in the process of gathering together his research and material to actualize that pledge. However, during his long illness he came to know his condition was incurable and there would not be time for him to do the writing himself, so he set up The Richard Idemon Literary Trust, which he endowed with the responsibility to publish his life's work.

We, the three trustees Richard appointed to bring his request to fruition, all knew and loved him well: Michael McCloskey, his trusted attorney and devoted student of many years; Jeff Jawer, a fellow astrologer and loyal, sensitive ally; and Gina Ceaglio, his confidante and vigilant friend who tried with loving care to ease the pain in his final months of life.

The Richard Idemon Literary Trust

FOREWORD

Richard Idemon invited me to run an astrology seminar with him in 1982, when he first spoke to me about his dream of teaching astrology in a "retreat" setting of beauty, tranquillity, and historical interest. Although I had heard him lecture at various conferences in America and Europe, and was always inspired and delighted by his rare ability to bring astrological symbolism alive in the imagination as well as in the intellect of his audience, I had never worked with him before. He wanted to organise a programme of yearly seminars with me under the auspices of his School of Astro-Psychological Studies, with each year's residential location being different but equally exciting; and we discussed with enthusiasm the various places in the world which might provide the kind of ambience he was looking for. We agreed that participation needed to be limited, to preserve a group rather than a lecture hall atmosphere and to encourage questions and discussion. The first concrete product of this developing partnership was born in 1983—a week-long seminar given in Orvieto, a medieval hill-town in central Italy. Its theme was "The Hero's Journey," and all the vast mythic panoply of the planets and the signs sprang to life against the backdrop of La Badia, a 12th-century monastery transformed into a luxury hotel that overlooked the ancient towers of the town and the Etruscan tombs below. The pleasure and stimulation of working with Richard was such that I had no reservation about committing myself to the next year's project, and the next year's after that.

Since my home was in Europe and Richard's in America, it seemed logical to alternate continents. For our first American venue he chose a wonderful resort hotel in the Green Mountains of Vermont, with all the timeless charm of an old New England hostel—the Sugarbush Inn. This conference, "Through the Looking Glass," with the complex drama of human relationships as its theme, was the result of a year's careful planning. Because the number of participants in this seminar, given in August 1985, was much smaller than at most residential astrological conferences, we were able to work with a relatively intimate and informal group atmosphere. Richard was at his very best—a magical blend of wit, warmth, and honesty, with the personal charisma of the accomplished actor (which he had once been) and the profound insight of the trained psychotherapist blended to produce his unique and powerful style of teaching.

By the time we had organised and arrived at our third conference, called "The Magic Thread" and held in the Blue Ridge Mountains of Virginia in 1986, Richard was already fatally ill—although few people knew it, and his energy and presentation seemed as exciting and dynamic as ever. But there would be no more of these extraordinary seminars which embodied his ideal of how astrology should be taught, with techniques and locations that spoke to the soul as well as the mind and provided visual and imaginative food as well as intellectual stimulation. In 1987, Richard died, leaving behind him his school and a rich legacy of taped lectures, seminars, and workshops, but no published book. He had told me that he had always wanted to write a book, but had somehow never sat down and done it—more a tragedy for the astrological world than for him personally, since he was perpetually busy generating new ideas through his teaching and received his rewards, like any truly dedicated actor, from the immediate and inevitably positive response and participation of his audience.

The book which follows is a transcription of Richard's lectures and discussions from our joint seminar given in Vermont. Howard Sasportas has done a superbly sympathetic job of editing this material, and Richard's ironic humour and deep understanding of myth and metaphor shine through without any sense of another person intruding on his personal style. His death is a terrible loss, not only to those of us who knew him well, but to the whole field of astrology, because he ws one of the most original, gifted, and insightful astrologers I have ever met. He was also great fun to listen to, since he had the rare grace of being able to laugh—not only at life but also at himself. I am grateful that his work has found its way into print at last.

Liz Greene
London, December 1991

Editor's Note

Although I met Richard several times on his various visits to London and always enjoyed our contact and exchanges, I never had the chance to attend any of his classes or workshops. Having finished editing these transcripts, I now realize just how much I missed by not studying with him. He was a brilliant astrologer with a remarkably brilliant and original mind. While working on this material, I can honestly say that I gained many rich and valuable insights into myself and into astrology in general; and I want to assure the reader that I remained as faithful as possible to Richard's language and highly entertaining teaching style. It gives me genuine pleasure to know that this book will allow a wider audience the opportunity to benefit from Richard's knowledge, experience and expertise, and it gives me even greater pleasure to know that he will live on in our memories in this way.

Howard Sasportas
October 27, 1991
London, England

INTRODUCTION

I'm very pleased to see that we have people here from twenty-eight American states, twelve countries and five different continents, and I'm looking forward to meeting as many of you as possible during the week. At another conference I conducted in Italy, I used an analogy or metaphor that seemed appropriate to the occasion. I had just done some touring through Italy, and any of you who have traveled around in that country will probably know that many of the churches are kept dark, so when you visit them, you have to put a 100 lire piece into a little machine and turn the knob in order to illuminate the frescoes and any other interesting works of art that happen to be there. The analogy I made then was that this procedure was *nothing* like learning in the kind of situation we are in now. This conference isn't about dropping a coin into a machine and getting enlightenment. I promise that you will leave here in five days without all your questions answered. All I can hope for is that your questions will have become more refined. To be honest, you will have some of your questions answered, but so much of what's going to happen for you here depends upon you and what you put into it.

We'll be dealing with the theme of relationships, and it's a heavy one. Relationships remind me of a castle under siege: Everybody inside wants to get out, and everybody outside wants to get in. Only you know where you stand on that one! A lot of people believe that we are going through an important time of social change and transition, and that this is putting a great strain on our relationships. I've been an astrologer for 20 years, and over these 20 years my clients, my students and my fellow astrologers have been asking, "What's going on out there? Everybody I know is in a state of flux, and everybody's relationships are going through big tests and changes. What kinds of transits are making this happen?" Well, my friends, I imagine that people were asking the very same questions in the 12th century. The question in my mind is: Are our relationships currently going through more difficulty than they ever have before, or does it just seem as if this is so? My answer to this question is a very clear yes, and a very clear no. I think that we would have to say that relationships have always been difficult, and that in some ways they're no more difficult now than they've been at any other time in history. Nor do I think that the reason for our current relationship problems can be attributed solely to the fact that Pluto has recently been transiting through Libra and Scorpio, although I'm sure Pluto and the other outer planets have something to do with it. But having said all this, I also believe that we are living through a time of tremendous change. We seem to be at a watershed or a crossroads, on the verge of a new age (I hate to use the word "age"), on the edge of a new way of being, and this is reflected by the enormous upheavals and changes happening to the social structures throughout the world, East and West. We see it politically, we see it in terms of the Church and established religion, we see it in terms of the communications media, the entertainment media, and the unprecedented changes that family life has been going through in the West. The last 50 years have seen a tremendous shift in what we call the family, and this is a topic we'll be talking a great deal about during this week.

So I think that relationships have always been challenging, but I also believe that we *are* going through an exceptional period of crisis right now. The guiding posts which have steered us for so many years are now gone, or, at the very least, they're no longer in the same place as they used to be, and people are very confused as a result. I'm sure there isn't a person in this room who has not come to this conference with major questions about relationship. When we talk about relationship, I hope you realize that we are not just talking about love relationships or sexual relationships, although we will be spending ample time on these subjects. But please remember that there are other important relationships we also should be thinking about – the relationship with our parents, the relationship with our children, with our brothers and sisters, with our bosses and coworkers, and with our friends. If you're practicing as a therapist, counselor or astrologer, then you have your relationships with your clients to consider. All of these are important. There's also our relationship to the collective, to the greater world we live in. And most fundamental, the bottom line as far as I'm concerned, is the relationship we have with ourselves, because we can't bring into our relationships anything more than what or who we are.

I'm excited about this conference. I'm *very* excited about this conference. Relationships, synastry and issues to do with sexuality are all areas in my astrology work that I find extremely exciting and interesting. There's a lot of chemistry happening in this room, a lot of really incredible energy circulating. I'm sure it's going to be a powerful course, and I don't want you to overdo things. I may sound like daddy here, but I'm telling you in a kindly way to take care of yourselves this week. Get plenty of rest, because it's going to be a long, long week, and a lot of stuff is going to happen. I can promise this. Be prepared for surprises and serendipities, for things happening that you didn't expect. Some of you may even find that you've come here looking for one thing, and that you end up by going away with something else entirely.

I encourage all of you, if you wish, to mix with and meet one another during the week, and to share your particular interests and fields of study and work. You could even form a Virgo knitting group or a Sagittarius archery group, if you really wanted to.

Audience: What about an Aries boxing group?

Richard: Yes, and a Taurus eating club.

Audience: I want to start the Capricorn Monopoly Game club.

Richard: Should we continue and do all the signs, or can I get on with tonight's introduction? I already can see that this course is going to be fun. Several people have asked me to talk about the program in more detail, to give you an idea of what specific topics I'll be covering, and when. The answer is, I don't know. Well, I do know, but I won't tell. Actually I can't tell you, because I haven't come with a precooked meal, that's not the way I work. But I promise that you'll get all there is to get. I can't quite say what order it will come in, but I can say that tomorrow I'll be beginning with the parent-child relationship, because, in my thinking, all relationships begin at that point. The plan also is to give you time during the week to break up into smaller group workshops to process the material from the lectures in a more personal way.

You know me, I'm a real storyteller. I love stories, and just before we end tonight I have to squeeze one in. Most of you will know the story of *The Wizard of Oz*,[1] which I consider to be a classic, and probably the most famous, most archetypal American fairy tale. It's also a story about the pathway toward consciousness. You realize that what you have in it is a little girl who has lost her home. She ends up going to this magical place, and along the way she meets the scarecrow who's looking for a brain, the tin man who's looking for a heart, and the cowardly lion who's looking for courage. For me, this is a beautiful astrological, as well as psychodynamic, metaphor, because what we really have is a journey about the Moon longing to return to its home. The Moon is Dorothy, the little girl who's lost her home and family and wants to get back to them. Then we have the scarecrow, Mercury, looking for his mind; the tin man, Venus, wishing for a heart; and the cowardly lion, who, of course, is looking for his Mars. The Moon, Mercury, Venus, and Mars all go trotting down the Yellow Brick Road, in search of this magical wizard who is omnipotent and who's going to fix everything up. If you remember the story or the film, you know that they have many adventures along the way— very specific, important adventures. And when they get to the Emerald City, what do they find? What kind of wizard is this wizard? He's a humbug, he's no wizard at all. He stands behind a screen and makes images and illusions happen by cranking wheels. Naturally, this is a great disappointment to Dorothy and her three traveling companions. They feel cheated. This wizard they thought had all the answers, has none at all, and they're very crushed and wounded by this.

As you probably remember, the wizard sends them off to destroy the wicked witch. You could say that, essentially, they are on a hero's quest, that the story of *The Wizard of Oz* is a true American hero's journey. Strange and wonderful things happen to them all along the way. And when they return to the wizard's palace

---

[1] L. Frank Baum, *The Wizard of Oz* (New York: Putnam, 1956).

after completing their task, they discover that it was the journey itself which has given them what they needed and wanted. It wasn't the wizard after all. I want to point out to you that the same is also true of astrology and psychotherapy. There is no wizard up here on the podium. There is no sorcerer sitting up here with all the answers, no sorcerer up here who has it all together. The thing that will give you what you are looking for is the journey itself. What you experience along the way is what will lead you to greater understanding and personal transformation. Greater understanding and transformation won't magically come from my giving you the right answers, although I can promise you that I'll certainly provoke a lot of good questions. I also see that there are quite a few different schools of astrology represented here, as well as various schools of psychotherapy. I'm not setting myself up as having the only right and true approach. I can be quite positive and strong in the way I express my feelings, but I'm not saying my way is right and your way is wrong. Take from me what you find useful and helpful. I am not preaching dogma.

The Moon is still full, and I can see that this is going to be a very wiggly week. Mercury is retrograde right now as well. Everybody must be thinking why in the world did I choose to put on a conference with Mercury retrograde; but I believe that the period when Mercury is retrograde is a very good time for turning the mind inward and backward—something we'll be doing a great deal of this week. So I apologize for any airplane connections you may have missed as a result of the retrograde Mercury, but you'll see that it will pay off in terms of the quality of this conference.

PART ONE

THE BASICS OF RELATING

YOUR PERSONAL MYTHOLOGY, BASIC GROUND, AND HIDDEN AGENDAS

My main topic today is the parent-child relationship, but I want to begin by exploring some ideas and concepts that apply to all relationships in general. First of all, I'd like to describe a very important part of my thinking about astrology, which I call "The Einsteinian Theory of Astrology," based on Einstein's view of reality. Before Einstein, scientists viewed the world according to Newtonian physics, and the Newtonian world was essentially a place where everything was linear and given. The story goes that Newton had a sudden flash of inspiration when he saw an apple falling from a tree. He realized that the apple was pulled to the earth by the force of gravity, and proceeded from there to formulate very exact and precise laws of motion for all bodies affected by gravity. As Newton saw it, the universe was a vast mechanical system, which operated according to set mathematical formulas. So Newton's world was very fixed, with set ideas, expectations and absolute laws that could account for everything that happened in the physical world. In many ways, traditional astrology is Newtonian, in that traditional astrologers believe that a chart describes certain events which are going to happen (or which, at least, are liable to happen) according to where the planets and signs are placed in that chart. Now, I prefer to view astrology according to Einstein's perception of reality, which says that what we observe depends on the position of the observer rather than on fixed mathematical rules and laws. So what is the position of the observer when looking at an astrological chart? By the way, I have two types of observers in mind here. One observer is you, the astrologer, because every astrologer will interpret a chart from the point of view of his or her own complexes and subjective experiences (what I call "collections of *mythos*"). The other observer is the person whose chart it is, because every individual mythologizes their own chart in their own way. Astrological counselors, therefore, have the tricky job of interpreting the way in which a person mythologizes the material in his or her chart. I'll try to make this clearer.

I should start by explaining what I mean by the words "myth" and "mythologize." Some people think that a myth is a fable, or a fantasy, or an untrue story, but I assure you that this isn't the case. A myth is the way that an individual or a group illustrates and makes a metaphor out of something observed as a natural phenomenon in their universe. The myths we remember and use, and which are so potent for us today, are still with us because they describe universal facets of human nature, regardless of time or place. The myths about Oedipus, Electra, Perseus or Medea, for example, are as alive and familiar to us today as they were for the Greeks. Myths are very, very living things, and the same can be said about the astrological chart. The astrological chart is a living *mythos*, a living process. The task of the astrologer or the astrological counselor is to bring the mythical content of the chart out into the open.

Reality is in the eye of the beholder, and this is certainly true of relationships as well, because our relationships are basically derived from the pictures we have of ourselves and the pictures we have of the world around us. How do we see ourselves? How do we envision the other people around us? What are our expectations? I believe that the answers to these questions form the *basic ground* of our being—a concept fundamental to my work, and which I'll be discussing in greater depth with you as the course goes on. Let me give you an example of what I mean by the idea that reality is in the eye of the beholder. For instance, if Joan of Arc were here today and were to announce that she was told by St. Michael and St. Catherine to dress up as an man and lead the French army into driving the English out of France, she very probably would be diagnosed as an adolescent schizophrenic, and taken immediately to the nearest state hospital, where she would be doped up to the eyeballs on thorazine. And most of the French real estate would still be called England. So what is truth? Most people believe that what is truth and reality for them, and what is accepted as truth by the majority of people, is indeed the truth. I call this "the Saturn system of truth," and I don't think this way of defining truth and reality is very useful to the psychologically oriented astrologer. Maybe we need to look at all this in a slightly different way. I'll illustrate what I mean with a story. Let's say you're walking down the street in the city, and on the opposite side of the street you see a friend of yours hurrying by, whom you haven't seen for some time. You're sure that your friend has caught sight of you, so you wave to her and shout out "Hi!" Just at this moment, your friend puts her hand up over her face and hurries along down the street. Now, the question is, what happened? Actually, the question is not so much what happened—it's more a question of how you observed what happened. And the way in which you make observations about what happened depends an awful lot on the mythology that you are carrying around about yourself and about relationships in general. You might be thinking, "Oh, well, there goes old Sue with a toothache rushing off to the dentist." Or you might be thinking, "Look at that bitch, snubbing me in that way. I'm never going to speak to her again. She's obviously ignoring me because she's angry about my not inviting her to a dinner party I gave six months ago. That's it, that finishes my relationship with her!" Or maybe you think, "Ah ha, I bet she's sneaking off to a rendezvous with a lover. I can't wait to call her up and tease her about it."

Do you see what I'm saying?—there are endless ways of mythologizing a given situation. And the same thing is true in astrology—there are endless ways of mythologizing any given placement in a chart. Saturn in Leo in the 5th house, for instance, could be mythologized in as many ways as there are minutes in the day. I could sit here with you and right away rattle off at least fifty different ways of mythologizing that placement. However, from the point of view of pure astrology, there is no way of knowing what Saturn in Leo in the 5th indicates mythologically to the person who has it in his or her chart. The point I'm making is that every person carries around their own system of myths, and that every person's reality is founded and based on their mythical system. I don't believe you can tell a person's mythical system solely by looking at his or her chart. A person's chart is the door opening us into their mythical system, but the chart alone doesn't tell us what we need to know to define someone's mythical system. The chart is a little like Ariadne's thread which allows us access into and out of the heart of a labryinth, but the chart itself is not actually the thread. The real thread is the process of consultation that leads the astrologer to the living myth symbolized and created by that person's chart. In other words, by talking and dialoguing with clients, we find out the ways in which they mythologize their chart and their lives.

I'll come back to this point later, but right now I want to ask another question: Where do our myths come from? Myths can be divided into three basic categories. Firstly, there are *collective myths*, which are myths about being born and dying, about falling in love and getting married, and myths about things like sorrow and loss. Our great myths and our great dramas are based on very basic and universal human experiences, shared by everyone who is alive or who has ever been alive. The great myths of every culture have similar themes—the melodies may be slightly different, but the themes are the same. So the first category of myths are the collective myths, and all of us are sensitized to them in one way or another. The second category is what I would call *social myths*. All of us live in a particular time and place, all of us live within a particular society, and there are myths derived from the society in which we live and the society in which we have been raised. Jung once said an interesting thing (actually he said more than one interesting thing, but this is the interesting thing at this moment), which was that people who are not individuated, people who are still heavily projecting their stuff all over the place, tend to feel that everybody is either like them, or ought to be like them. Remember this, because it's a key factor to consider when we start analyzing the whole area of relationship, and specifically, it's a very key factor in the relationship between parents and children. In other words, what a person believes is normal and usual is what is normal and usual for *that person*. I don't think there is any such thing as normal. What is normal? I know a Viennese Jungian analyst who was asked that question at a lecture she was giving. She insisted that there was no such thing as normal, but the audience kept pushing her to give her definition of it. Finally she said, "I'll tell you how I define normal . . . if I do it, it's normal; if I don't do it, it's abnormal." End of subject!

At any rate, we all live within a particular society, and our society has what we call mores, and these mores could be called social myths. Every person must find a way of living not only with universal, collective myths (myths about birth, death, love, aloneness, togetherness, etc.), but every person must also find a way of making peace with, or an adjustment to, the social myths engendered by their particular society. And when we, as astrologers, do someone's chart, we need to know something about the societal myths that person carries around. Did you hear the story about some Harvard students who sent the birth details of a goat into one of these computer chart-reading services? The chart service wasn't told it was the birth data of a goat; they thought they were doing the chart of a man. The Harvard students received back a very elaborate reading—you know, this person has great managerial tendencies, and he'll graduate from college and find good work, and he will have multiple relationships (well, at least that was probably true!). It's essential to know the social setting of the person whose chart you are doing. Is it somebody living in 20th century America? Is it somebody who is black and living in South Africa? Is it somebody living under a socialist government in China? Is it somebody born into a very devout Catholic family and background? All of this is part of the social mythos that we live in. To really understand someone's astrological chart, we have to know something about the social myths he or she carries around.

Finally, there are family myths, and I'll be talking at length about these in later lectures. Every family has its own mythical system, its own drama it's acting out. Depth psychology involves probing into the psychological myth we've inherited from our family background. Pinning down your family myth doesn't automatically change things for you, but it brings it into the light of consciousness where it can be seen and examined. These three types of myths—collective, social and family—combine to make up what I call our *personal myth*. Different people's personal myths are derived from their interaction with collective myth, from their interaction with the social myth of their particular society, and from their interaction with their family myth. Built upon the symbol system of your astrological chart is the overlay of your personal mythology. You can't define how somebody mythologizes his or her life just by looking at that person's chart, but you can do it by dialoguing with the person. Dialogue is a wonderful word stemming from the Greek word *dialogos*, which is a combination of two words—*logos*, which means mind, reason and structure, and *dia*, which means across. Astrology is also a logos, or at least it ought to be; however, as it is often practiced, astrology tends to be an astromancy, a divination art, rather than a logos art. Dialogue between the counselor and the client can give us clearer insight into how the client mythologizes his or her chart, and his or her life in general.

Let me give you an example. Take the case of a woman born with Sun conjunct Mars conjunct Jupiter in Aries in the 1st house. We'd say that by nature this woman would be a very assertive, dynamic, competitive, *yang* type of person. But I ask you, how does this fit into the social milieu into which she was born? It's one situation if she's from a well-to-do New York City family, or from California, or almost anywhere in the United States or western Europe. But it's a completely different situation if she's living in a peasant commune in China, or if she's living in a tribal situation along the Amazon. You see how vastly different her experience will be according to the nature of the culture in which she lives. Even though there's been a lot of switches and changes in the consciousness of women lately, it is still difficult for a woman who is strongly yang and assertive to live out totally who she is. And the reason for this comes down to the general social expectations about the way a woman should behave. It's the same problem for a man who is predominantly watery, or very lunar, or very Piscean, or who has a strong Neptune in his chart. He's a natural mystic, he's tremendously sensitive, he wants to write poetry and dream rather than go out there in the world and compete. Immediately he's going to get messages from his family or from society saying that there's something terribly wrong with him. As far as I'm concerned, it's this kind of dilemma between our true inner nature and what our family or society tries to put onto us, that gives rise to many of our personal problems and complexes. We will be examining all of this in great depth throughout the conference.

What I'm asking you to explore this week is the way in which you have mythologized your astrological chart. And when you start using other people as mirrors, it's amazing how you can begin to see yourself and your life in a different way. I recently had a visit from my brother, and, as we always do when we get together, we got around to discussing our mother. To hear us talk, you would think that we had completely different mothers, or that she was two completely different people. I listened to him describing his view of our mother as a certain type of person. And then I said, "I don't know who you're talking about, because my mother behaved in a totally different way with me." So here's another myth that I think we're going to have to puncture: The myth that all parents treat all children in the same way. Have you ever heard a parent say, "I love all my children equally?" Not true, at least in most cases. I call these kinds of generalities "frame statements," and they're the kinds of statements we all like to make. Another frame statement is that all parents always love their children. Not true. Another one is that all children love their parents. Again, not true.

Let me ask you a question: What do you think is the most basic and fundamental need within a relationship? The vast majority of people answer this question by saying things like love, security, nurturing, companionship, closeness or trust, but I wouldn't agree with any of these answers. *I believe that the most fundamental need in relationship is the revalidation of our basic myths.* I believe that this, more than anything else, is what we look for in relationship. Isn't it interesting? This explains why we tend to get into patterns in our relationships. Have you ever noticed your patterns? And I'm not just talking about your patterns in an intimate or erotic love relationship; I'm also talking about the friends whom you pull into your life, the coworkers, bosses and assistants you draw into your world, the people who you might end up sitting next to at dinner tonight, or anyone you connect with during this conference. We all want to maintain and preserve our basic ground, we all want to keep re-creating through our interaction with others the myths we have about ourselves and about life in general.

I'll illustrate what I mean by a little nature lesson. All animals have territory, I'm sure you know that. It varies, of course, from species to species, but I'll give you an example specifically of the good old American jackrabbit. The jackrabbit has its own territory, and it will only live within that territory. Now imagine that a jackrabbit is being chased by a predator, a coyote, let's say. And let's say that the coyote chases the jackrabbit to the limits of this jackrabbit's territory. Even if it knows it will end up being eaten, the jackrabbit will double back from the edge of the boundary of his territory right into the jaws of the coyote, rather than go beyond what he knows as his territory. Astrologically, I connect this with the archetype of Taurus. When I'm speaking archetypally about a sign, I don't mean to say that all Taureans are like this, but I do mean to say that safety is the essence of the Taurus archetype—safety on the material level, and security, comfort, and life-sustaining nurturing are all primitive needs I associate with the sign of Taurus. These needs are a basic necessity for all of us, or more precisely, for the Taurus part of all of us. Taurus is the sign I would associate with Eden—with a safe refuge where there is plenty for us. Now, you might think that Eden is a wonderful place to be in, and that you wouldn't want to leave it ever, but this isn't necessarily the case, because many of us live in very poisonous Edens from which we need deliverance. The opposite of Taurus is Scorpio; the opposite of this Edenic world of security is death, or the fear of death. Let's make a transition here from the physical world of the jackrabbit into the psychic world of the human being. Like the jackrabbit who stays within his basic territory no matter what, we humans also live within a psychic basic ground, and to leave or go beyond the boundaries of our basic ground carries with it the implication of death and dying, which is why we have deep resistances to change. Otherwise, everybody would be living out their Scorpio side, burning old letters, doing away with worn-out relationships, moving and changing whenever we felt the inclination. New job? Sure, I don't mind. I'm getting older? Great, fine, I love it. You want to leave me to go off with another man? Yeah, that's great, you do that and I'll find someone else. No problem.

Audience: But isn't it true, Richard, that if you had this attitude, then it would no longer be Scorpionic? If it was that easy to accept change, then it wouldn't have the drama and crisis and the charge we normally associate with the Scorpio archetype.

Richard: Yes, I agree. There is a dynamic tension between Taurus and Scorpio, and archetypally, I define Taurus as the basic ground of security that we establish in order to keep us at one with ourselves, and Scorpio as the urge to die and be reborn in a new way.

Let me give you another example of what I mean by basic ground. Take the case of the person who says, "Golly, I never can find a relationship with anybody who loves me and treats me right." As I always say, if you think you're advertising for a poet and you keep getting truck drivers, you had better check your advertisement, because the chances are that you're getting what you're advertising for, but it's what you're *unconsciously* advertising for as opposed to what you say you want. My theory is that your basic ground is what you equate with survival and therefore is the most fundamental thing you want to hold onto. So if your basic myth (or your basic ground of reality) says that no one could ever love you because you are unlovable, then the only people you can accept into your life are the people who are guaranteed to revalidate the myth that you are unlovable. If somebody came around to offer you genuine love, you would probably say, "Well, he's too short," or "Well, he's too fat," or "He's too old," or "She's got strawberry blond hair and I prefer auburn" because you need to find a way of rationalizing and explaining why this is not a suitable relationship for you in order to hold onto your basic ground. Trying to hang onto our basic ground is the main reason we get stuck in an endless repetition of patterns. Or maybe when you were growing up, you had alcoholic parents you had to care for, and this experience contributed to you forming a basic myth that says that you are the strong one, here to take care of all the poor wounded creatures of the world. If this is the case, then the only people who need apply for relationships with you are the ones who fit into the category of poor and wounded—in spite of the fact that you may be moaning and whining about what weak and helpless people you keep attracting.

Psychotherapy, depth psychology and psychoanalysis focus on trying to bring your basic myth into consciousness so that you can be aware of it, and perhaps change or transform it in a way that broadens you or opens up your world. In this respect, the psychotherapist plays the part of Lucifer tempting you to leave the Garden of Eden—an archetypal story that I associate with the leaving of your basic ground. This story from the Bible (which, of course, is derived from an earlier Babylonian tale) is all about leaving a familiar place where you feel safe and secure in order to go out into the world and be born again. Notice it's the serpent—an ancient Scorpio symbol—who comes into the garden to tempt Eve into doing something that will eventually take her (and Adam as well) away from their Eden. The name Lucifer means the light-bearer, and it is Lucifer who awakens Adam and Eve to their humanity, making it possible for them to relinquish the safe, protected animal consciousness they were living in Eden, and thereby venture out into the greater world. Virtually every myth I can think of that is about changing and transforming your basic ground has a Plutonic flavor to it. One of these is the rape of Persephone. Here's the classic mama's girl, still tied by the umbilical cord to Demeter, the archetypal possessive and narcissistic mother who doesn't want to let her daughter go. This constellation between the mother and the daughter summons Pluto up from the depths to force a separation. Breaking the basic ground is, in many cases, breaking what I call "the psychic umbilical"—the psychological tie that connects us with our family myths and our family of origin. Even though you may have moved all the way across the continent, or even to another continent, to distance yourself from your parents, it's still possible to be linked to them by the psychic umbilical. The psychic umbilical cord can remain in place even after they have died. To cut your psychic umbilical is, in a way, to move out of your basic ground. As I see it, the psychotherapist can be an ally on the side of the hero within us, encouraging us to take up our swords and face the dragon. The worse thing that can happen to you by taking up your sword and facing the dragon is death, or perhaps, madness . . . good Pluto and Neptune stuff. But taking up your sword and moving beyond your basic ground also holds the promise of greater individuation, greater self-realization and self-fulfillment, and greater freedom from old patterns and complexes that have inhibited and trapped you. So how do you feel about exploring your basic ground, and eventually venturing beyond its borders and parameters?

The first thing you need to do is to explore what your basic ground is. Once we know the territory, we open up the possibility of stepping beyond it. Something has always bothered me. This certainly doesn't apply to anyone here, of course, but I know many people who have studied astrology for 25 years or have been in psychotherapy or depth analysis for 15 or 20 years, and, although they have learned an awful lot about themselves as a result, they still don't change. Yes, they have much better rationalized explanations of why they do what it is they do, but still they don't change. So, what is the missing ingredient that enables people to change? Number one, it's a mystery. Secondly, it's that point in time when we have enough courage to take our first step over the inner psychic boundary that has hitherto meant safety for us. And maybe the only way you can really tell that you've begun to change is to look and see what is happening in your relationships. Relationships are our mirror.

For example, let's say your myth has been that you only get involved with bad guys, and, as a result, you keep falling for bad guys in order to revalidate your myth. Now, if you've worked hard to break free of your basic ground, you may find that you meet the kind of bad guy to whom you would normally be attracted, and, lo and behold, you don't experience the same powerful pull toward him which you always used to feel in that situation. You meet a new bad guy and you say, "Oh my God, nothing's happened to me. I can't believe it!" This is a classic one for many people. He's got all the wrong ingredients to make you fall right in love with him, and yet there's no magic—nothing happens. This kind of experience indicates that you have changed, and although you may not have totally shifted your basic ground, you have begun to grow beyond it. You've glimpsed another world outside the known and familiar Eden of your basic ground, and, as the strongly Cancerian writer Thomas Wolfe once said, you can't go home again. Once you've bitten into the apple, there is no turning back. And, as I've said earlier, it's the Scorpio part of us that urges us onward, that compels us to bite the apple. Scorpio says, "Try it, you'll like it—bite into the apple, break the umbilical cord, and leave home." Even Christ invites his followers to do this: "He who would follow me must have no father or mother, brother or sister, husband and wife, but must be alone and follow me." This is his way of saying break the umbilical cord and leave your basic ground. Now, this is not something that just happens suddenly. It's a lifetime process. The astrological chart can be a tremendously helpful indicator of the nature of one's basic ground, but what it can't tell us is how we've mythologized it. And another thing it can't tell us is whether we're still stuck in the ground or whether we have taken our first adventurous steps outside of it to explore the rest of the world. How can you find out these things? *Dialogos*. As an astrologer, you need to talk to your clients to fathom how they've mythologized the basic ground shown by their charts, and to discover if they've taken their first steps outside of it. When somebody comes to you for a reading, you should begin by finding

Table 1. The Qualities of the Two Types of Relationship.

STATIC	EROTIC
1. No Risk	1. Risky

2. Safety & Security
    (Prime Goal)
	2. Intimacy & Growth
	    (Prime Goal)

3. Sameness	3. Variety
4. No Change	4. Open to Change
5. Limited Communication	5. Open Communications
6. No Anger—No Passion	6. Assertive—Passionate
7. Deceit	7. Trust
8. Defined Roles—Projections	8. Varied/Shifting Roles
9. Dependency	9. Independence
10. Parent—Child—Symbiosis	10. Adult—Adult
11. Vertical	11. Horizontal

out *why* this person has come. This knowledge, coupled with what the chart tells you, is your way into someone's mythical system.

I believe there are basically two kinds of relationships— relationships which are static, and relationships which are erotic (see Table 1). In actual fact, most of us have relationships that are a mix of the static and erotic. Firstly, I'd better explain what I mean by erotic, because it's a word often misunderstood. I don't mean erotic in a sexual sense, but I do mean erotic in the way the ancient Greeks used the word. There are many Greek myths about the god Eros, and it's only in one of them that he's portrayed as the little son of Aphrodite who goes around shooting arrows into people. In the earliest myths about this deity, Eros represented the primal force who took matter and chaos and brought them together through passion to create the universe and to create life. My definition of eros is that it is a force that brings two or more separate entities together in such a way that they are totally transformed. It's true that sex can be erotic, but unfortunately very little of it is. Which possibly is why we're so obsessed with and addicted to sex in this country—we are caught in a constant search for the kind of erotic sex that will truly recharge and transform us. But sex isn't the only thing that can be erotic. If it's working, the relationship between a therapist and client can be an erotic one. Of course, anything erotic will also feel risky and dangerous, because true eroticism involves hovering around the border of your basic ground, which isn't a place where you feel all that safe. And the really great love stories—I mean ones like the story of Tristan and Isolde, or the story of Romeo and Juliet—are erotic, because there is always something dangerous and potentially tragic about them. In itself, romance isn't necessarily tragic, but it's the erotic component of romance that leads toward the tragic. I have much more to say about this later. It's also perfectly possible to have an erotic relationship between a parent and a child. I'm not talking about incest or child abuse here. Because we tend to automatically sexualize eroticism in our linear Judeo-Christian world, we assume that anything that invokes really deep feelings must be sexual. But this is not necessarily the case at all.

I believe that at least 90 percent or more of most people's relationships are static rather than erotic. (Remember, I'm not just talking about lovers and spouses, but any relationship in which intimacy is the goal, and this can be with our children and our friends as well as with our lovers, husbands and wives.) I don't know anybody whose relationships are entirely erotic, because it's virtually impossible to maintain the erotic state constantly in a relationship. I would say, however, that there are a certain number of people in our culture, maybe 10 percent, who have a sufficient amount of the erotic within their relationships to keep them lively and transformative. The basic goal of the static relationship is safety or avoidance of risk. A static relationship is one where everything is meant to stay in its place: I've been with Old Joe for 20 years, and though he bores me to death, at least I know what he's all about, and I know what he's going to do or say next. I'm sure you've seen couples like this in restaurants: She's sitting there looking at her fingernails, and he's sitting there looking up at the ceiling. The only conversation is, "Will you have coffee or tea?" and most likely they know the answer to that already.

The erotic relationship, however, is risky. There are no guarantees in it. To eroticize a relationship is to bring the element of risk into it. How many people do you know who have been living together unmarried for any number of years, and then after they get married, the relationship falls apart? In a sense, getting married de-eroticizes the relationship, because the erotic always borders on the edge of danger, risk and the unknown. The erotic moves us out of the Taurus world toward Scorpio. But for the person whose relationship is static, the prime goal is safety and security, and this is often the case with parents and children. Parents feel safe and secure when their children are direct replications of themselves, or at least direct replications of how they would like to be. The parent-child relationship becomes eroticized when the parent lets the child go and says, "Be who you are, even if it's totally unlike me, and even if it's in ways I can't support. I love you enough to let you go. Like puffing on a dandelion, I free you to go out into the world." In reality, most relationships between parents and children are not this overtly erotic, which is why children, for their own growth and development, have to go through the terribly painful process of breaking the umbilical cord and wrenching themselves away from their parents. The failure of children to do this means that they will never achieve individuation, and instead are devoured and swallowed up by one or both parents.

To the person in a static relationship, sameness means safety, and this means not allowing anything too different to happen. Watch out for people who tell you never to change, who say you are wonderful just as you are, who want you to stay as sweet and innocent (or whatever) as you already are. These kinds of friends or partners have a hidden agenda for you, which requires that you stay the same (probably because if you change, then they will have to change, and this is not something they're very keen on). Just watch what happens if you do start to make a big change; just watch the people who supposedly are your friends, allies and loved ones, trying to subtly undermine any major change you are going through. If your pattern in relationship is to be the sick one, the wounded one, the alcoholic or drug abuser in need of help, or the one who is constantly overweight, or the one who is always having terrible problems with your lovers, then you'll constellate people in your relationships who play mommy, daddy or therapist for you. The people playing such roles for you may not actually want you to change, because this would take the relationship out of the known and into the unknown, and possibly even cause the relationship to fall apart altogether. These static-loving friends may say things like, "Gee, Richard, I just wish you would change and get your act together and find yourself a nice person to settle down with, and stop drinking so much." But watch what happens if I do start to change—watch how they try to block or undermine my attempts to change.

There's a term in family therapy called "the identified patient." This is the person in the family considered to be the one with the problem—poor mother with her weak heart, poor junior with his juvenile delinquency, poor dad with his drinking, or poor sister with her bulimia. All the troubles the family is having are often blamed totally on the behavior of the identified patient, when, in actual fact, the identified patient is being used as a decoy to divert attention from where the real source of trouble stems within the family, or the identified patient is living out what the rest of the family disowns and rejects in themselves. So, although the family will insist that junior clean his act up or that dad stop drinking, watch what happens if the identified patient actually starts to change: The rest of the family will close ranks in such a way as to prevent the identified patient from changing, because the family's primary goal is homeostasis—that is, to maintain the family system just as it is. Or the family plays a game of musical chairs, and certain members of the family take turns being the identified patient. It's almost as if the family needs one person in it who will carry the family shadow, that is, someone to express and live out drives and characteristics that the rest of the family as a whole deny in themselves. Whole societies also turn certain segments of the population into shadow figures. For the last 2,000 years, women have been cast in this role. Christianity classifies women primarily into three groups: The Virgin Mary type is the good woman who stayed good; the Mary Magdalen type is the bad woman who became good; and then there's Eve (the temptress responsible for the banishment from Eden), who is the good woman who went bad. Or as they say in Italy, there are two kinds of women, *la madonna et la putana*, the madonna and the whore. However you see it, women in the Christian world have been pushed into the role of collective scapegoat. This kind of thing goes on in every society, whether it's the Jews in Germany, the blacks in America or South Africa, or the homosexuals in any largely straight society. Families do the same thing when one member gets cast in the role of the family's shadow or the family scapegoat. When I say family, I don't just mean your blood relationships; I'm also referring to the people you have brought into your life. The family that is meaningful to us is not just our blood relations or our family of origin (what I call "accidents of birth"); there is also the family we've collected around us who usually also serve the purpose of keeping us in our ground in spite of the fact that some of them seem to be encouraging us to change.

Not long ago, I had a case that is a clear example of what I mean about people not really wanting us to change, even if they say they do. A vastly overweight woman came to me for a consultation and pleaded with me to treat her husband, a triple Pisces alcoholic. She told me, "I can't stand living with him anymore; he's been impotent for 20 years, and I'm the one who has to work and support the family. I have six children—five of them are out of my body and I married the sixth. I'm at my wits' end." So I did work with the man for quite some time, and he later went on to some other therapy, and managed to get off alcohol, and he eventually took a very sharp turn into the spiritual path, and even started teaching yoga in mental hospitals. It was after all these changes that he came to consult me again. He told me, "My wife has just left me and I feel terrible." I assumed he must have been hitting the bottle again and that was why she left. But he said, "No, I haven't touched the stuff. The trouble started after I had stopped drinking, when one day I looked at her and told her how overweight she was and how unattractive I found that." And then he told me something very interesting. Although he was a member of Alcoholics Anonymous and not meant to drink a drop again, his wife brought some booze into the house on New Year's Eve and actually tried to make him take a drink. She said, "If you're any kind of man, you can handle a brandy or two." He refused, and soon after she left him.

This story leads me into another subject that I'll be spending a lot of time on: every relationship has a hidden agenda or hidden contract attached to it. I stress that the hidden contract is most often unconscious on the parts of the people involved. I'll give you an example of a common hidden agenda or contract between people, but remember that people don't actually come out openly with these things in the way I'm going to now. The man's contract may be, "I'd like to marry you because you're a poor, wounded, damaged thing, and being with you makes me feel more confident and on top of everything. So I'll marry you, but with the following proviso—that you always stay helpless and damaged, so that I can feel like a much stronger and more capable and together person than I actually am." The woman may then think to herself that this sounds like a pretty good deal, so her part of the contract is, "I promise to stay helpless and wounded, if you promise never to be passive or vulnerable, and that you'll always stay in charge and solve all my problems for me. If you're in agreement, sign here on the dotted line." I call these kinds of relationships "symbiotic relationships." Many of us are deeply involved in symbiotic relationships, without even being very conscious of the fact. Now, what happens when one person breaks the contract? What if, for instance, this helpless and weak woman one day grows tired of being that way, and tells her husband that she is going to go out there and face the world, and get a job and earn a good income. Her husband may outwardly say (through gritted teeth), "What you're planning to do is wonderful. Nothing would please me more than to see you fulfilling yourself." So she does face the world and gets a job and ends up earning more than her husband. What happens then? Well, he'll probably run off with his secretary or something along those lines. Or what if "Mr. Strong, All-Together, I've Got It All Figured Out Man" suddenly gets sick, or has a mild heart attack and decides that he doesn't want to be a high-powered Wall Street broker anymore, but is going to take up raising bonsai trees or petunias for show, or is just going to let himself sit around and dream a lot. In doing so, he has broken his part of the contract, and his wife will probably find some reason to leave him. All the time in counseling work, women come to me and say, "Oh, God, this man of mine has to change. He's such a chauvinist pig, he's so disgustingly macho. I want him to be more aware of and sensitive to my sensual needs, and for him to learn how to be a better lover. I want him to communicate more with me and spend more quality time with me. I want him to help with things around the house and be a better father to our children." So it finally gets to the point where this lunkhead of a man realizes he had better change or he's going to lose his wife and family. Reluctantly he drags himself into therapy and has some big breakthroughs, and gets more in touch with his anima, and begins to show his more communicative, sensitive and compassionate side and helps out with the children more. What happens? His wife leaves him.

Audience: I bet she runs off with her therapist!

Richard: No, not that, because *all* therapists are such incredibly sensitive and compassionate people. No, she runs off with the garbage man. And chances are she'll have the garbage man in therapy in about a year's time. Do you see what I'm saying? What we say or think we want can be very different from what our basic ground really wants. The kinds of contracts we make in our relationships are directly derived out of our basic ground, out of the myths we have about ourselves—myths that we have imbibed without discrimination from our family or the society in which we live. All of this contributes to our having a hidden agenda or contract within a relationship. When I work with couples (when I say couples, I mean a couple of anything—a parent and child can be a couple), my strategy is to get to the bottom line and uncover the contract going on between them. And, I'll tell you, discovering and admitting to the contracts you set up can be a very painful procedure.

To repeat, static relationships are based on sameness; erotic relationships are based upon variety. Often, what we really want is for our relationships to be a little of both, and I personally don't see why this isn't possible. But what we do in many cases is to marry the erotic relationship, turn it into a static relationship, and then feel compelled to go off and find a new lover with whom things are more erotic. Once we find this person, we think that we should get out of our existing static relationship and marry the new erotic relationship, which eventually becomes a static relationship in its turn. And then where are you? You are back saying, "Oh my God, where has eros flown? I must get that magic back into my life somehow." So you go through this process and you become another Liz Taylor or any one of these people who has endless cycles of relationship and who is constantly looking for that magic erotic something which they believe lies outside of themselves.

The static relationship is based on maintaining the status quo, whereas the erotic relationship is open to change. It's very erotic to say to somebody, "Look I can't promise you that I'll be with you until death do us part, because my feelings could change. All I can promise you is honesty and open communication." It's amazing how erotic honesty can be. The static relationship has limited communication—you don't feel safe saying what it is you actually feel or want, because this could upset the relationship, and the primary goal of a static relationship is to keep it safe and secure. One of the hidden rules of a static relationship is to never really say what's on your mind, to never really talk honestly with the other person. So you hold your tongue and sit on your feelings. There's an incredible number of people who live together and don't really know each other; there's an incredible number of parents and children who don't really know one another.

Another rule of the static relationship is no anger. I'll be talking a lot more about anger during this course, but I believe that there can be no passion in a relationship that doesn't allow for the expression of anger from time to time. Watch out for those people who say, "Oh, Grandma and Grandpa had such a wonderful relationship. They never raised their voices in anger to each other," but of course, it turns out that they weren't sleeping with each other either, or hardly ever. Anger is permitted within the erotic relationship, but not in the static relationship, because anger tends to open doors that can lead into the unexpected. Change might happen if anger is expressed. The erotic relationship is both assertive and passionate. Passion, however, is like food. Our eyes may be bigger than our stomach. In other words, we often have more of an appetite for passion than we really have the capacity to endure. And when we really get it, do we really want it? The static relationship is based on quite a bit of deceit. You have to be deceitful, because if you verbalized your feelings, the whole relationship could come crumbling down around your feet—so you feel safer not saying anything. The erotic relationship is based on trust. And I don't mean trusting the other person as much as I mean trusting yourself. It takes a certain amount of trust in yourself to lay things on the line with a partner, to have open communication and talk about what you feel is wrong with the relationship. Doing this is scary, because it could endanger your cozy, comfy, safe, and familiar relationship if it turns out that the other person isn't able to cope with what's been brought out into the open. I call this "the Uranian Humpty-Dumpty effect": All the king's horses and all the king's men can't put the egg together again, but it might make a nice omelette.

I believe that trust in yourself is the mythical system that prepares the ground for potential erotic relationships. The static relationship is based on defined roles and specific projections, whereas the erotic relationship is varied and has shifting roles. There's nothing wrong in my being in a relationship with somebody, and playing different roles at different times. Depending on what's needed at any moment, I might play the daddy at times, or the mommy at other times, or the little sister, or the big brother, or the good friend, or the boon companion to my poor, wounded partner. Changing roles like this is erotic. It's exciting because I don't know what to expect from one day to the next. I could get sick, I could need my partner to take care of me, or I could suddenly become a world-famous celebrity and an extremely powerful person. By comparison, the static relationship is based on very strict, clearly defined roles and projections: I must always be the daddy and you must always be the helpless, little girl, and this mustn't ever shift or change, because then the relationship would no longer be static, but turn into something erotic and uncertain. I've often seen static relationships fall apart entirely when one or other of the partners experiences psychological changes resulting in a major shift of identity—when a hitherto childlike or dependent woman begins to integrate her animus and starts to become an independent and strong person in her own right, or when a hitherto "butch" man begins to integrate his anima and starts to show his more tender, needy or vulnerable side. Should defined roles alter in this way, the contract is violated, and unless the relationship can accommodate these changes, it will invariably break down. This brings us to another rule about relationship, which I call "the ripple effect." If you drop a pebble into a pond, you create ripples that spread far across the water. Similarly, anyone who experiences a major shift or personality change will automatically stir or set off ripples that affect any relationship in which that person is involved.

As I've been saying, the static relationship is based on each person playing clearly defined roles according to what projections are flying around. In other words, the static relationship is based on dependency, because each person is dependent on the other person to express or live out disowned facets of one another's personality. It may be the man who's totally given away his anima and expects his partner to carry his entire feminine function, or it may be the woman who gives away her animus and expects the man to carry her masculine function. Astrologically speaking, women often carry the water function or the earth function for men, while men carry a lot of the air or fire function for women.

Let me give you an example. The last time I was in France, I stayed with a married couple who are both friends of mine. I asked the wife if they were planning to come to the States for a visit. She told me that she really wanted her husband to go to Houston, because he's sick and should be getting specialist medical attention there. I asked how she knew he was sick, and she said that he hadn't told her as such, but that she was sure of it. She also told me that he wouldn't go to a doctor unless she set up the appointment and got him there through some kind of trick or scheme, because he thinks that he's invulnerable and that nothing like a bad illness could ever happen to him. So she set up this elaborate scheme that involved the two of them visiting friends in Houston for a holiday in the near future, but she also had arranged for a specialist to be staying at their friend's home in Houston at the same time that they were visiting there. This was how she was going to trick him into getting a proper examination. Later that day, I spoke with her husband, and mentioned that I had heard from his wife that they were planning a vacation in Texas. He said yes, and then he winked at me a few times, and told me that she had planned the holiday as a ruse to get him to see a doctor. He knew all along what she was up to. So their contract was that his wife was to carry his earthy function and assume the responsibility of looking after his own body. This is the little dance or game they had going. She said things to him like, "Have you taken your bath this week?" or "It's time you got your hair cut" or "Stop drinking so much coffee" or "You smoke too much and should cut down." Their relationship contract called for set roles in this respect. No shifting of roles allowed. Let me tell you something: If you're feeling bored in a relationship, you've probably set up some unspoken contract with clearly stated and fixed rules about who is allowed to play what roles. Therefore it's boring, because both of you always know what the other person is going to do.

The static relationship is based on dependency, whereas the erotic relationship allows for greater independence and variety. For a lot of people in the world, their worst fear is not being in a relationship. The static relationship is largely connected with the re-creation of parent-child symbiosis, something I'll later be going into in much more detail. By comparison, the erotic relationship has an adult-adult quality about it. And there's no reason why you eventually can't have an adult-adult relationship with your grown-up children, or now that you're an adult, why you shouldn't have an adult-adult relationship with your parents. But how many of us do? How many of us say, "Oh my God, I have to go home for Christmas and go through all that usual stuff with Mom and Dad." You say that you're grown up now, but perhaps this is not the case in your mother's or father's mind, or even in your own mind when it comes down to it. The static relationship is a vertical relationship based on hierarchies like top dog/bottom dog, the one in charge and the one who's dependent, a one-up/one-down kind of thing (although in some static relationships the roles are reversible from time to time). By comparison, the erotic relationship is horizontal. It's a relationship of equals, where both partners look across at one another, not up and down at each other. Don't get me wrong, I'm not suggesting that all of you should immediately change all the static tendencies you have, rewrite your contracts and become totally erotic. This is not what I'm implying, even if it were possible. What I'm saying is that you should check to see to what degree your relationships are based on the qualities I've listed as static, and whether or not it's possible for you to change aspects of your behavior in order to begin the process of eroticizing your relationships. A good place to start would be by opening up the lines of communication. You may think this is an easy thing to do, but it isn't. I suggest you start by saying to your partner, "You know, there's something I've been wanting to tell you . . ." and take it from there.

Audience: I was really struck by the point you made about no anger being a rule of static relationships, and that you can't achieve intimacy and passion unless some anger is allowed.

Richard: Yes, I consider Mars to be a key planet in relationship, and later we'll be talking much more about Mars and anger. Briefly, my definition of anger is assertion plus passion. While growing up, most of us haven't seen anger expressed in a healthy way, which means we've never had good role models for it. We're frightened of anger because we have seen or experienced the distortions of anger, rather than cleanly expressed anger. And we're often as much frightened by our own anger as we are about other people's anger being directed at us. Plus the fact that society has told us that it's not Christian to feel anger. So we learn to turn the other cheek, and then get them from behind!

I'd like to talk a little about symbiosis before turning my attention to some of the fundamentals of the parent-child relationship. Symbiosis is derived from two Greek words, *sym*, which means together, and *bio*, which means life. Symbiotic relationships occur fairly frequently in the animal world, and there are also some strongly symbiotic relationships that humans get into as well. There are three basic types of symbiotic relationships. The first category is *commensalism*, which literally means "dining at the same table." Commensalism occurs when two organisms live together in a situation in which they neither harm one another nor benefit from one another. You see it in nature when animals of different species share the same land or the same watering hole, which fits very well with the definition of dining at the same table. Out in the American West, where the bison still roam, you'll find jackrabbits comfortably running around beneath the bison's feet, and the two species don't necessarily harm one another, but they don't help one another either. There are human relationships like this, and these largely fall into the static category. The main rule is not to make waves, which means don't get too passionate, don't ask for anything, just stay as you are. So long as this rule is observed, it's possible to feel safe dining at the same table.

The second type of symbiotic relationship is called *mutualism*, where both organisms (and in some cases, three species or organisms) benefit from being together. One example is the relationship between the rhinoceros and the tick bird. The rhino is annoyed by its ticks, and is more than happy to give the tick bird a free ride on its back on the condition that it eats its ticks. The tick bird loves ticks, and the rhino provides the tick bird with meal after meal of tasty ticks. Bees and flowers have a mutualistic relationship—the bees pollinate the flowers when gathering their honey. I was in Africa a short time ago and had the chance to go on a safari. One of the most interesting things I learned was that the giraffe and the zebra and the wildebeest all like to hang out together. The reason for this (and I hope I get this right) is that the giraffe has tremendously acute vision, the zebra has very sensitive hearing, and the wildebeest has remarkable powers of smell. So the three together make one perfect sensory organism. This is mutualism. Many human relationships are mutualistic as well. She cooks, cleans the house, and raises the children, while he goes out and interacts with the world, makes the money to support his wife and family, and agrees to treat them fairly. Ultimately, this kind of relationship can get very boring. How long can they live like that, and what are they doing about their need for something more passionate and erotic?

The third type of symbiotic relationship is called *parasitism*. In parasitism, the host is subject to varying degrees of injury while the guest benefits. Of course, you all know what parasites are—any of you who have paid a short visit to Mexico will probably have had first-hand experience of non-human parasites. The tourist who visits Mexico and picks up a parasite doesn't benefit at all by this new acquisition, and could even die as a result; whereas the parasite is able to thrive and live happily off his newfound host. Germs and viruses also have a kind of parasitic relationship with us humans. Parasitism is quite common between humans as well. For instance, a chronically weak, helpless and wounded person often lives off the energy of someone bigger, tougher and stronger. In actual fact, weak people usually command the real power in this kind of relationship, because they're exceedingly good at getting others to look after them and to run around doing things for them. I call these people "psychic vampires." What eventually happens is that they devour the host and have to move on to a new host. As soon as all of your blood or all of your psychic energy is drained, they'll leave you to find someone else. There are a lot of people like this, and you should be careful of them, because astrologers and counselors are particularly vulnerable to psychic vampires. Any of you who are strongly identified with Jupiter or Saturn, which means that you may appear to be rather parental, are especially prone to attracting people-parasites.

Audience: Would you classify a parasitic relationship as static or erotic?

Richard: That's a good question. Because the roles are so set and fixed, the parasitic relationship is normally static, and yet, interestingly enough, it can give the illusion of being erotic. This is because any relationship in which there is mutual destruction, or in which one person is getting destroyed, can feel erotic to the people involved. It all depends on how you mythologize what's happening. Some hosts actually look for parasites. I remember one woman telling me that she continually goes for men who steal her money, beat her up, abandon her for other women, or whom she eventually finds out are already married to someone else. She is an example of a host looking for a parasite, and one part of her admits that she finds these kinds of relationships quite exciting. I suggested that there must be nice men in this world whom she might also find attractive. I even suggested Joe So-and-So, a pal of mine, whom I know has been trying to get a date with her for a long time. And she shook her head and said, "Oh no, he's too nice." Nice guys finish last.

Audience: As a counselor, how do you protect yourself from psychic vampires or parasites?

Richard: Counselors need to draw very clear boundaries in order to protect themselves from these kinds of people. It takes two to play the game, and if you refuse to participate, the feeders will have to go someplace else.

Audience: But then you might have no business!

Richard: Actually, you'll probably have better clientele if you make the switch.

Before I talk specifically about parent-child relationships, I first want you to tell me what planet you consider to be the primary planet of love. I hear you saying Venus, right? Oh, you are a shrewd group. Later I'm going to spend time trying to define this thing called love. The Greeks had at least eight different words for love, while we have only one, which suggests that our society is pretty clueless when it comes to knowing what love is all about. (I once heard that the Eskimos have twelve or fourteen different words for snow.) We say things like I love pizza, I love God, I love my child, I love my lover, and in each of these different cases we use the same word. No wonder love is such a loaded and even taboo word; no wonder we are intimidated by it. Somebody walks up to you and says "I love you," which is what mostly everyone would like to hear. But stop and think a minute. Does that person mean that he loves you like he loves a pizza, or that he loves you like he loves God? In my mind, the most basic and fundamental planet to do with love isn't Venus — it's *the Moon*. I say this because the Moon is the archetypal child in the chart, and it's the Moon that is the emotional receiver in the chart. By sign, house, and aspect, the Moon indicates how we go about giving and receiving nurturance.

The Moon's placement (along with the house with Cancer on the cusp) fills us in on the details of what kind of myths we have around nurturing. The first love experience we have is between our mother and ourselves. I say mother, but what I really mean is the person who nurtured us the most when we were infants, and this could have been a mother substitute, such as the grandmother or a nanny or some other caretaker, or even the father if he was the one who mostly nurtured us. In any case, our first experience of love and nurturing comes through the Moon. I also connect the Moon with the *inner mother*. This may seem like a paradox (astrology is full of them), but what I'm saying is that the planet that is the indicator of our inner child is also the indicator of our inner mother. We don't tend to think of nurturing as something that should come from the inside; we tend to think of it as something that ought to be coming from the outside. The process of breaking the umbilical cord is critical if we are to have adult-adult relationships. This process also involves seeing and naming our myths, as well as identifying and reclaiming the projections and expectations we have put onto others in terms of the fulfillment of our nurturing needs. In other words, the inner mother is born through insights we have into ourselves. There's only one Moon that's attuned to the perpetually hungry inner child in us, and that's our own Moon. Accepting this fact means that we must give up the collective myth that somebody out there is going to find us, heal us, cure us, love us, and make us feel okay about ourselves. So cutting the umbilical cord moves you in the direction of individuation, and bestows on you the awareness that the perfect, overflowing breast is inside you, that no matter how old you are and no matter what you are going through, you can find a safe haven, a home, a womb, a breast for you to come back to—because that loving and nurturing place exists all the time inside you.

Astrologically, the process of breaking the umbilical cord connection entails a shift from Cancer to Leo, because when we leave Cancer, we move out of the first four signs, which I call personal, and into Leo, which begins the next group of four signs, which I call social. Jung talked an awful lot about what he called "twice-born" people. To be a twice-born person, you have to break the umbilical cord that not only ties you to your family, but also the umbilical cord that ties you to the particular society to which you belong. Breaking the umbilical cord that connects you to your family involves a shift from Cancer to Leo. Breaking the umbilical cord that ties you to society involves a shift from Scorpio to Sagittarius, the first of the universal signs.

The Moon is the key to understanding the nature of our need to be nurtured. We try to project this outward and look for someone to nurture us in the way we need, but this will not work, because, as I've said, the only person who really knows how to nurture you completely is your inner mother, the nurturing mother inside you. The child in us, which is still lurking about when we are supposedly adult, says, "I know I'm in love when I find the person who automatically and intuitively knows what I need and is able to give it to me." Our inner child also expects the loved one to be responsible for fixing anything bad that happens to us, and may even blame the beloved for letting bad things happen in the first place. The child in us believes that the beloved should know what we want and need to feel good even before we know it—which is precisely what we expected from our mother when we were infants. When we were in distress as a child, we expected mother to know how to make things better. We expected her to figure out the cause of our discomfort. Is it that we need to be fed, is it that our diaper is wet, is it because of wind, is it because a pin is sticking into us? And if she can't soothe our pain, we feel betrayed and get incredibly enraged and angry at her. Similarly, the inner child that is still there in us when we are an adult, expects that the current mother figure in our life should be able to determine what it is that's causing us distress, and exactly how to go about fixing it.

One of my favorite cartoons is by Jules Feiffer, and I have it on my wall at home. The first panel shows a little man sitting in the fetal position, all curled up in a shell, and he's saying, "I live in a shell." In the next few panels, you see that this little man not only lives in a shell, but that this shell is in a box kept in a cave, which is actually part of a castle protected by a fort with thick walls around it, and all of this is under the sea, which he says is his way of keeping himself safe from the world. In the panel after all that, you see a woman in a rowboat on the sea looking around for this little man. And the last panel shows the little man saying something like, "Well, if you really loved me, you'd find me." There is an element in us which is a perpetually hungry child. One of the worst things you can say to a child is that they're acting like a baby; one of the worst things you can say to an adolescent is that they're acting like a child; one of the worst things you can say to an adult is that they're acting like an adolescent, and I guess it eventually comes round full circle, because when you're very old, some people find it cute if you are childlike. In any case, we also carry a social myth that says that being helpless, needy, or narcissistic is bad, and something that we ought to have grown out of. So what happens is that we put all these things into our shadow, which then leaks out in terms of the needs we feel in our supposedly adult relationships. Any questions so far on what I've been talking about?

Audience: It strikes me that when a couple starts to have children, they need to make their relationship more stable so that the children don't have to grow up in a tense, uncertain environment. And by stable, I don't necessarily mean static.

Richard: Although I've presented the concept of static and erotic relationships in a very linear way, this really isn't the case. We all have needs for security and safety and for a certain amount of permanence in our lives. I'm not saying that all our relationships should be entirely erotic, or that the qualities we seek in a static relationship are a definite no-no. It's not going to be very comfortable if you're married to somebody and you don't know whether he or she is going to come home again from one night to the next. Some people might find this situation deliciously erotic, but most of us don't want to put up with such extremes of insecurity and instability. There needs to be a certain balance between the erotic and the static. So I'm not implying that we should all pack our bags and move immediately from Taurus into Scorpio. Taurus is an archetypal, fundamental part of us, and it should be respected and given its place. We need the security and structure that Taurus has to offer. But I do think we ought to try to free other people from our childhood projections, that is, from our expectations that someone should be an artificial parent for us in terms of taking care of our own safety and security needs. Letting other people off the hook in this way is necessary if our relationship with them is to have an erotic content and be more interesting, exciting, and growth-oriented. By the way, this doesn't just apply to you and your lover, or you and your spouse, but it also applies to friendships and other types of relationship.

Many of you will be examining your close relationships more deeply this week, and after this discussion, you may decide that some of them are not so hot. But, remember, I'm talking about relationships in a highly theoretical way. I believe that if it ain't broke, don't fix it. If you and your partner are happy with the relationship you have, then why bother to change it? Astrologers need to be careful, because, as I've said, the chart is in the eye of the beholder. Some astrologers are in danger of looking at a person's chart and telling that person how they think he or she ought to live, which, of course, has to do with the astrologer's own projections. There is no ideal way to make a relationship. What works for one person may not work for another. What works for us at one period in our life may no longer be right for us after we've grown and individuated a bit more. There shouldn't be any strict standards about what is wrong or right for us in life or in relationship. But if you are growing and changing, then you need to accommodate these changes into your life and into your relationships, rather than trying to stifle your growth for the sake of safety, security and keeping everything the same as it has always been. Some of us pay a very high price to keep ourselves safe and secure. Is it worth it, I ask? This is why I emphasize the value of biting into the apple, and breaking away from your basic ground.

THE MOON: NAMING YOUR INNER CHILD

What is your life goal? Is it to stay in Eden and lead an unconscious kind of existence, or is it to bite into the apple and lose your innocence and simplicity? Normally, my choice is to bite the apple. I'm a compulsive apple-biter, and I've had to give up quite a lot of peace and quiet in my life as a result. That's my choice, although I also have to confess that there have been times and places when I chose not to bite into the apple. Nonetheless, one way or another, I think we all take a stand about whether or not we're an apple-biting kind of person.

If you take some time to read the biographies of famous people, you'll see that most of the people who have distinguished themselves in some way — especially those known for their creative talents — are what I would call erotic people. They are risk-takers. If you read the life stories of Beethoven, van Gogh, Mozart, Shakespeare, Dostoyevsky, Tolstoy, Michelangelo, or Abraham Lincoln, you'll soon realize that the lives they led were intensely erotic. Some of us might think that our lives are fated, and it is up to the fates whether or not we live an erotic life — a life in which we are open to change, to risks, to being honest and truthful about who we are and where we stand. I still believe, however, that we do have choice, at least to some extent, at various points in our life. Robert Frost is one of my favorite poets, and I'm especially fond of his poem "The Road Not Taken," which tells of a person standing at a crossroads having to decide which of two paths to follow. And more recently, I was impressed by M. Scott Peck's book, *The Road Less Traveled*,[1] in which he discusses ways we can approach life to achieve a higher level of self-understanding and a richer existence

---

[1]M. Scott Peck, *The Road Less Traveled* (New York: Simon and Schuster, 1988).

in general. I believe that at various times in our lives, we arrive at a crossroads; and if we choose one path, we move in the direction of eros, but if we go the other way, we move in the direction of stasis. I'm not saying that one way is always right and the other way is always wrong—it depends on what's right for you at the time. The question is, "What is the choice that's correct for me now?"

I'll be talking mostly about the Moon today and how it relates to the inner mother and our childhood experiences, but before I start on this, I want to say a word about Venus. In mythology, Venus was often depicted as a whore goddess. Whether we know her as Isis, Ishtar, Cybele, or Aphrodite, she is normally shown as self-involved and narcissistic, and totally obsessed with the pleasures of her own body. Judeo-Christianity found Venus distasteful and evil, and chose to discard her completely, which is why most of us don't really understand or appreciate the living archetype she represents. Modern society doesn't really have an acceptable archetype that conveys the power of the feminine and of female sexuality. Although we've retained the feminine archetypes associated with such goddesses as Demeter, Hera, and Athene, we have thrown Venus out of the pantheon. As I was saying, the goddess of sexual self-indulgence and the pleasuring of the body is unacceptable to so-called Judeo-Christian society. We don't really understand Venus. We think she is a big troublemaker. After all, she was the natural complement to the Greek Ares and the Roman Mars, which is why they were depicted as lovers in mythology. We could say that Venus was in love with and naturally attracted to the war god. In fact, some of the greatest calamities in mythology—including the Trojan War—have been triggered off by Aphrodite (Venus). It is Venus who loves seeing the warrior with blood on his hands. This is the kind of thing that gets her excited. So there's something archetypal in the Venus-ruled signs of Taurus and Libra, but especially in Taurus, which is rather primitive and turned on by blood and guts and sensuality. What I'm saying is that Venus is not the overdressed lady lying on a shaded lawn eating bonbons—which is the astrological image many of us have of her. She's not really like that at all. She's devious, she's tricky, she's sensuous, and she's not loyal.

The Moon is the essential, perpetual child within all of us. Unfortunately, if our inner child has certain qualities that we don't approve of or like, we tend to brutalize it, and we usually call in

Saturn to do the job. The Moon is the archetypal child, whereas Saturn is the archetypal parent. Saturn is the part of us that says, "Grow up, stop whining, quit complaining and get to work." Saturn is the part of us that says, "Take charge of yourself and keep that troublesome child under control." However, beating the child or locking it in a closet, or forcing it to stop being so infantile and grow up are not the right ways to deal with and handle our inner child. These attempts to tow the child into line don't really work in the end. Playing what I call "the Moon-Saturn game," which involves denying or repressing the child in us, only serves to make the child angrier and more vicious.

I believe the Moon is one of the key planets underlying addiction problems (Venus is as well, which we'll discuss later). The Moon becomes addictive because it feels unfulfilled emotionally. Problems with addiction can stem from our inner child—as shown by our Moon—crying out for the kind of nurturing and care and emotional fulfillment we needed so crucially in the past, but didn't receive. Like the Feiffer cartoon I told you about, our frustrated Moon and inner child is saying, "If you had really loved me, you would have found me. But since you didn't find me, it must mean you don't love me, which means I've been abandoned and left alone, and need to find some kind of solace to feel fulfilled and to feel good about myself." This is how the Moon can be a root cause of the addictive personality. How many of you think you have addictions? Quite a few. I thought so. You might ask what I mean by addiction. An addiction, as I see it, is something that we need to do or take into ourselves in order to make us feel better. We feel better in ourselves for having done it.

Audience: Can you say more about what you mean by "the Moon-Saturn game"?

Richard: Yes, the Moon-Saturn game is when you deny, repress, lock away, or project your Moon. This, of course, tends to be much truer for men than for women, for reasons I'll shortly be discussing. What happens is that Saturn, the superego and the archetypal cynic, comes in and starts beating up on the Moon: "You shouldn't be so weak, you shouldn't be so sad, you shouldn't be so helpless, you shouldn't be so needy, you shouldn't have feelings (especially if you're a man), you shouldn't be such a baby (especially if you're a mother yourself)" and so on. When Saturn beats up on the Moon, the Moon responds much in the same way a wounded child would respond, and it eventually starts acting things out. The child may appear passive and obedient, but as soon as Saturn has relaxed its hold on the child or is busy with something else, the Moon takes over again and all hell breaks loose. For example, let's take the dieting game, which is one of Moon-Saturn's favorite rackets. The Moon says, "Oh, I feel deprived and lonely, I'm having such a bad time, I really need a piece of chocolate cake." Saturn is quick to respond, "Listen, you fat creep, you know that you're prediabetic because it runs in the family, and you know that your blood pressure is high, and you know that you're already overweight and that none of your clothes fit you, which is why you can't stand yourself, and why your wife says she's going to leave you if you don't shed those pounds. So you better not have a piece of chocolate cake, you undisciplined moron. As a matter of fact, you should be going on a celery diet for 10 days." And maybe you listen to Saturn, and you go on a celery fast. You've been on it for nine days, and you just have one more day to go, but, by this time, the child in you, which has been locked in the closet and totally ignored, has turned into a raging tyrannosaurus, like the kind you see in horror movies. On the ninth day, the closet door flies open, and out comes your raging child, screaming and insisting, "I want cake!" By now, however, just a piece of cake won't do. Nine days ago, a small, slender slice of cake was all you craved, but you're far beyond that now. Now the child in you not only wants a huge piece of chocolate cake, but it also wants two hot-fudge sundaes, and at least one box of cookies. So you end up making yourself incredibly sick. Then what happens? Well, the chain starts up all over again, and Saturn re-emerges and comes down on your over-satiated pig of a little child like a ton of bricks, "I've got you now, you fat loser. You think I thought you were bad before. You don't know what bad is until I tell you how bad you are now."

People can go through their whole life doing this routine, instead of stopping and asking, "Hey, wait a minute, what is it that my inner child really needs right now? I feel lonely, so maybe that means it would be nice to call a friend on the phone and ask him to come over and keep me company. Or maybe it's a hug that my inner child really needs, or perhaps I'd feel better about myself if I could resolve that bad quarrel I had with a friend the other day. Or maybe I just need to be alone for a while, and take a leisurely stroll in the park." Do you see what I'm getting at? There may be quite concrete things you need to do to soothe your inner child, such as speaking up about something that's bothering you, or simply taking time to sit down and write a letter or read a book.

As a general rule, when you start to feel pulled toward addictive behavior, you ought to stop for a minute and ask yourself what your inner child really needs to feel nurtured. Of course, the two-year-old child in you might play a game with this: "I don't know what I need to feel nurtured. You're my mommy, you should know, you should tell me, you should make it all better." Carrying this game into adulthood will poison your adult relationships. What we really need to do is to take responsibility for our own inner child, although, I must admit, this is often easier said than done. We also should be careful about the language and vocabulary we use to describe our inner child. If we accuse it of being a bratty little boy or a bitchy little girl, we obviously aren't showing our inner child the right kind of love and understanding. How much better it would be if we could just appreciate the fact that our bratty or bitchy inner child has become that way because he or she has legitimate needs that have been denied, ignored or unfulfilled. If the nurturing mother in you can reach out with love and understanding toward your inner child, you may even discover that chocolate cake isn't really what you need or isn't really what you are hungry for.

Addictions are what I call "pain corks"—they cork up our pain, they are our way of blocking out our real pain. In other words, we become addictive as a way of avoiding pain. By the way, when I'm referring to addictions, I don't just mean the obvious ones such as food, booze, or drug addictions, or an addiction to coffee and cigarettes. What about being addicted to relationships, or being a workaholic, or a sleepaholic, or being addicted to going unconscious in front of the television set? Addictions are Taurean in the sense that they keep us firmly entrenched in our basic ground. Staying safely within our basic ground is one of the main reasons for addictive behavior. Take away the addiction, and watch how a raging monster comes out into the open. When you stop any form of addictive behavior, you are forced out of Eden and have to face your pain, you have to face the real you. This is why addictions are so hard to break. You could be addicted to one particular relationship: "God, this relationship is so bad for me, why can't I break free of it?" One reason we can't break free of a difficult relationship may have to do with the basic myth we carry around about ourselves. An addictive relationship is usually based on an unconscious contract we don't want to violate.

If we line up the seven inner planets in this way—Moon, Mercury, Venus, Sun, Mars, Jupiter and Saturn—then the Moon is the first planet and Saturn is the last planet, and these two form a pair. Mercury and Jupiter also form a pair, as do Venus and Mars, which then leaves the Sun in the middle. I consider the Sun to be the planet that can arbitrate the dilemmas posed by opposites. The Sun is consciousness, the flow or urge toward self-awareness and self-formation. Transactional Analysis believes that it is the adult in you (the Sun) that arbitrates between the parent in you (Saturn) and the child in you (the Moon). In this respect, TA is saying something similar to the Freudians, who believe that the superego (Saturn) is constantly trying to crush and control the id or the more primitive self (the Moon). Freudians also would say that the ego (the Sun) stands between the superego (Saturn) and the id (the Moon) and attempts to arbitrate between the two.

The first step in working with this situation is to try to get a clearer idea what your own Moon feels about your inner child. When doing this, don't forget there are also social myths about the Moon. We refer to it as a feminine planet and as a childlike planet, and since our society tends to devalue the feminine and the childlike, many of us will repress our Moon. Obviously, the Moon usually is more of a problem for men, because men in our society are not supposed to be "feminine"—that is, they are not meant to be passive or too emotionally receptive or to display their sensitive, nurturing side. It's also less acceptable for a man to act like a child than it is for a woman to do so. After all, right up until my grandmother's day, women were still considered to be perpetual children. You weren't supposed to mention bad words in front of women, just as you aren't supposed to say bad words in front of children. Nora, the heroine in Ibsen's A Doll's House,[2] was one of literature's first emancipated women, but she was still depicted as birdlike and childlike. Women are only now just beginning to

---

[2]Henrik Ibsen, A Doll's House and Other Plays (New York: Penguin, 1965).

break free of such stereotypes, but the way they have been portrayed in the past makes it easier for them to integrate the Moon than it is for men.

So how do you go about nurturing your Moon? How do you begin to be your own proper mother? These are important questions, because the failure to integrate your Moon increases the likelihood of projection in relationships, and also gives rise to more relationships of a symbiotic nature. (I'm not saying there's anything wrong in symbiosis—we are all symbiotic to some extent—but too much of it keeps us dependent and infantile.) One of the first major steps in integrating the Moon is to identify and name your inner child, and to find out what it needs to feel nurtured.

Let's go through the Moon by element and see what this tells us about identifying and naming your inner child. Remember, I'm going to be speaking in generalities, because you really should take the whole chart into consideration when referring to any of its parts. Generally speaking, however, the Moon in an earth sign says, "If you love me, you'll touch me, stroke me, feed me, and give me real and tangible things as a demonstration of your love for me." So an earthy Moon might see love as a pizza or as a diamond ring. Love is being touched, being held, being fed, and having good things done for you. This is very different from the Moon in a water sign, which says, "If you love me, merge with me, cry with me, be one with me. If you love me, feel what I'm feeling even before I feel it." Water signs are archetypally accustomed to pain because they're connected with transformation.

We tend to consider pain a dirty word, but there is nothing wrong with it. Interestingly enough, pain is erotic, whereas pleasure is static. Pleasure is Taurean, while pain is Scorpionic. When we speak of the Passion of Christ, we're not talking about the fact that he enjoyed or got off on his crucifixion. Jung himself said that we don't really change until we have suffered enough. Seen in this way, suffering and pain can lead to enlightenment, even though many of us in Western society don't wish to equate pain and suffering with anything positive. We have so much Taurus in our society, we're so comparatively wealthy and comfortable, that we think of pain as a dirty word, and we often equate it with death. We even think we can buy our way out of pain. If I can buy enough shoes, I'll live forever! But it doesn't work this way, does it? So we try to deny pain, even though it is our road to transformation.

When I connect the water signs with pain, I'm saying that pain is something good from which we learn and grow. Cancer is the awakening of the pain of mother love. The love of the mother for the child is painful. Not only is it physically painful to give birth (or so I'm told, as this is one thing I will never experience in this lifetime), but it's also painful weaning the child, seeing the child grow up and having to let go of the child. The whole process of breaking the umbilical cord is a painful one for both parent and child, and this is something which should be fully and openly acknowledged. Scorpio is the pain of the erotic—the pain of passionately desiring and caring for something or someone with whom we want to merge, but with whom we can never totally merge because two separate entities can never become one, in spite of any illusions that sex gives us. We may merge for a moment in blissful orgasm, but then we are suddenly separate again, left with what the French very beautifully refer to as *le petit mort*, the little death. Pisces also symbolizes pain: It is the pain of compassion, when our feelings and emotions are open to the entire collective, when we feel at one with everybody, and when our boundaries totally fall apart. Scorpio is connected with death and dying, but Pisces represents dissolution, which often can seem far more frightening than death. I think that most of us would choose death over madness.

I find the Moon in air a curious placement because it says, "If you love me, give me space and don't cramp me." Air is essentially objective, and says, "In order to get a clear picture on something, I have to stand back from it—I have to pull away from it. If you're crowding me or drowning me, how can I pull back and have space?" The Moon in air also says, "If you love me, communicate with me, talk to me and give me feedback. Tell me what's on your mind, but remember not to smother me, or devour me or eat me up." The Moon in fire says, "If you love me, play with me. Be positive. Encourage me to do things, and I'll encourage you to do things. I don't want to have to put up with negativity, so let's not be that way. My motto is onward and upward. Be brave, be daring, have courage, and go for it!"

Just by looking at this very basic and simplistic breakdown of the Moon by element, we already can see the kinds of problems conflicting Moons could generate in a relationship. What happens if my Moon is in air and I want distance and space, and your Moon is in water and you want emotional closeness, warmth and merging? If the relationship is going to work, we'll have to do some negotiating: "I'm clear about what my needs are, and I see what you need to be nurtured; however, I can't suddenly make myself a Moon in a water sign type of person just because that is what you need. But what I can do is to find ways to nurture you that satisfy you and yet which don't betray the basic principles of who I am." Or a woman with the Moon in water may have to accept that her Moon-in-air husband can't nurture her in the way she needs, and she therefore has to find a way of nurturing herself or she has to find other people who can fulfill the needs of her Moon in water. Having said this, I want to add that if people keep attracting mates, friends and partners who are fundamentally incapable of fulfilling their needs, then they are probably setting up this frustration as a result of the kind of basic myths they're hooked into. Obviously, this would harken back to the early relationship with the parents and what family myths were around at that time. You can see how problems would arise in childhood if a parent with the Moon in earth or water was trying to nurture a child with the Moon in air or fire. As I've said, we all tend to think that everybody is like we are, or ought to be like we are. However, the Moon by element has very different needs, and the key to nurturing others is to do it according to their Moon sign, not according to our own.

I'll give you a specific example. If a male child has his Moon in air, he needs space and distance to feel nurtured. But what if his mother has the Moon in a water sign, and her natural nurturing mode makes him feel devoured and swallowed up? Let's say her Moon is in Scorpio, and she's all over him most of the time. Mothers with the Moon in Scorpio can mix maternal feelings with erotic feelings (by erotic, I don't mean explicitly sexual, but that she has what might feel to others like an overpowering need for contact and connection). When there are problems between a parent and child, the child assumes it's his or her own fault, because children always view things very subjectively. So the child in this example will think that there must be something wrong in himself, because his mother keeps wanting closeness, and he keeps pushing her away. The mother also assumes there must be something wrong with the child, because unindividuated mothers think that their children should be the same as they are. The child will therefore conclude that there is something wrong with his airiness, and that he should be more like his mother with her Moon in Scorpio. When he grows up, he probably will end up marrying a woman with the Moon in Scorpio, or with a Moon-Pluto conjunction or something of that nature, and the whole system is constellated all over again, serving to reinforce his belief that there is something wrong with him because he can't make his relationships work. If you haven't severed the psychic umbilical cord with your parents, you are bound to reconstellate the unworked-out material between you and your parents in later relationships you have in your life. It's also likely that you'll re-create with your own children the same patterns you experienced with your parents, which is precisely how patterns are passed down from generation to generation. Any of you who have worked with the charts of different generations from one family lineage will know exactly what I mean. It's as if a family curse is passed down from parents to children *ad infinitum*, until one offspring finally comes along who manages to break free of the inherited pattern. I guarantee you that the unworked-through psychic material you still carry from your family and societal myths will be passed right down to the generations that come after you. The child who breaks free is the hero, because he or she cuts the umbilical connection, not only freeing the self from the family curse, but also liberating their own descendants from the unconscious repetition of family myths and family patterns.

Audience: Can you tell from someone's chart if he or she will be the hero, or do all people have a chance to become a hero?

Richard: All of you have the chance to be the hero or heroine in your own life, but the big question is, "Will you pick up the sword?" Whether or not you will do this isn't shown in the chart. Transits and progressions indicate when the opportunity is there to pick up the sword and act heroically by cutting the umbilical cord, but whether or not you take advantage of these opportunities is another story. The gods may be knocking at your door, but are you at home to answer it? People who conclude that they must have the wrong chart, or that astrology doesn't work because nothing important happened to them under this or that transit, probably have missed the chance to grow and change, most likely because they were asleep or simply unwilling to bite into the apple and embark on a journey of transformation. You can be the hero or heroine of your own life, but you must be willing to let transformation happen when the transits and progressions call for it. I should remind you again that amputating the child or beating up on the child or ordering your inner child to grow up is *not* the way to transform yourself. Everything you ever felt or learned is still alive and present inside you, and you can't just squash all this out of existence. But you also don't want this stuff to run and control your life, so you need to find a happy medium between exercising some control over your inner child and allowing it free rein. This is when you need to evoke your inner mother to help the child in you to grow by giving it the proper attention, nurturing and encouragement it needed but never received from your actual external mother. If you are still trying to turn your real life mommy or daddy into the ideal parent you needed but never had, you will never succeed in breaking free of your family patterns and myths. You have to find you own ideal *inner* mother and father and reparent yourself in this way, and then change is possible. Sometimes a disaster or painful experience is needed to turn you into the hero who can cut the psychic umbilical cord with your parents. This is what happened to Kore when she was abducted and raped by Pluto, and I call this kind of situation "becoming human by catastrophe." In particular, the transits of Uranus, Neptune, and Pluto can make us human by catastrophe, and in this sense, they bring us gifts from the gods. They shake us up, they tear us apart, in order to drag us out of the fixed, Saturnine, inner world of our basic ground.

I'd like to illustrate some of the things I've been discussing with extracts from the charts of a couple I've worked with in therapy. The man has the Moon in Capricorn, and the woman has the Moon in Libra, and they had been married for three or four years when they consulted me. Both of them complained of feeling unloved in their relationship, and they had already gone so far as to initiate divorce proceedings. Here is an example of the kind of dialogue that went on between them. She, with her Moon in Libra and its need for communication, would beseech him with, "How come you never tell me that you love me?" And he, with his Moon in Capricorn, would reply, "You know that I'm not the kind of person who goes around openly declaring his love." Then she'd say, "Well, I don't understand why you can't, because I do it all the time." And he said, "Yes, you do it so much it puts me off. Haven't I proved my love to you? Look at the beautiful home I bought for you to live in," which is a very clear statement about the way the Moon in Capricorn equates love with things that are solid and tangible. To which she replied, "Those kinds of material expressions of love don't mean a thing to me." Then he would come back with, "How can you say that to me? I worked and slaved to buy you a beautiful diamond ring and mink coat, and to take you on expensive vacations." And she would retort with, "I don't want those things. I feel smothered by all that stuff. I just want you to tell me that you love me." He then would complain about the fact that she never did any cooking, to which she replied, "I hate cooking, I don't like to get my hands dirty. I'm a terrible cook, and besides, we have a maid who cooks for us." Then he would say, "But I want *you* to cook for me. My mother cooked for me." To which she answered, "Well I'm not your mother. If you want your mother, go back home to her. I thought you liked our maid's cooking." Then he would say something like, "Yes, she's a good cook, but I still want you to cook for me."

In our counseling sessions together, I explained how they each interpreted being loved and showing love in different ways—he, according to his Moon in Capricorn, and she, according to her Libra Moon. In time, he began to send her Hallmark cards (if you can't say it, they'll say it for you). Whatever you might think of the quality of Hallmark cards, the cards he sent meant a great deal to her. Eventually he even started to cut out little poems from magazines which he then gave to her, or he would leave messages saying "I love you" under her pillow. Her Libra Moon was touched by these gestures. So he stopped giving her such expensive things, which she had felt was his way of trying to buy her, and he started to give her little things that had symbolic meaning for both of them—one red rose, one yellow rose, things like that. They began to nurture one another more in the way each one needed, although neither one of them could change completely into someone they were not. But the point I'm making is that they managed to find something in themselves to give to one another, which made each of them feel more cherished and appreciated.

Audience: Did she start to cook for him?

Richard: Yes, but badly, and certainly not every night! Even so, he didn't care—he still liked her meals better than the food prepared by the cook.

Let's take a water Moon with an air Moon as another example. The air person is likely to feel smothered and drowned by the water person. The more the air person retreats and pulls back, the more the water person will pursue the air person, or the water person might respond by being sulky and moody, and giving off vapors to indicate his or her dissatisfaction. Parents with the Moon in water often want to devour their children. Unless these watery kinds of parents can find some other way to satisfy their tremendous need for bonding and emotional closeness, they'll have terrible problems with a Moon-in-air child. There is no easy formula for resolving these kinds of dilemmas, but there are ways you can begin to work on them. I counseled a father with the Moon in fire who had a son with the Moon in water. The father's answer to everything was, "Let a smile be your umbrella," and he thought that his Pisces Moon son was terribly weak and whining, not a *real* man at all. When bullies at school beat up the boy, his father would say, "Tomorrow is another day. Go find some nicer kids to play with, and keep smiling!" Naturally, the son felt that his father was discrediting his feelings, so he disconnected from him emotionally, which just made his dad angrier and more frustrated. After I worked with the father for a while, he eventually learned to say, "Well, I can't identify with or share my son's feelings, but I can at least accept them without judging him. That much I can do."

Audience: Can you say more about the needs of people with the Moon in Libra as compared with the needs of people with the Moon in Scorpio?

Richard: Libra is the sign of marriage, and it tells us archetypally what marriage should be like. Libra says, "Two sides can balance each other, but they don't have to be each other. An equal partnership requires space and objectivity. The other person must be respected as an individual in his or her own right." So Libra doesn't think that two can ever become one. Scorpio, however, believes that two can become one. Scorpio follows Libra because the pain of the aloneness of an air sign must be followed by water's urge for emotional connection. Scorpio will continually attempt to bring two people together as one.

In the next chapter, we'll talk more about the Moon and its relevance to relationship.

THE PARENT-CHILD RELATIONSHIP: BREAKING THE PSYCHOLOGICAL UMBILICAL CORD

I want to continue with what we were working on during the last session and talk further about the relationship between parents and children, with a special emphasis on the Moon. One of the fundamental things to understand about any relationship is that you can only love another person to the extent that you can love yourself. Many people seem to want to turn that around: They think that if only somebody else would love them, then they would learn to love themselves enough to be able to love. But it just doesn't work that way. Our first experience of relationship begins with the relationship we have with our parents, and all later relationships will be influenced by it. Much of our ability to love stems from myths which are set up in the early family system. But how much love does a child need in order to feel all right about himself? This is something that no one has ever been able to determine. I don't think I've met a child who's been loved too much. I've met children who have been too *possessed*, but not too loved. Also, another thing you have to consider is the degree to which you can tolerate intimacy. Much of this hooks into the Moon in the chart. Intimacy is like food, we may have eyes for more than our stomach has room for. It's important to realize that each of has our own level of "intimacy tolerance." It also can be different at different times in your life, and it can vary from relationship to relationship. In other words, you can take more of some people than you can of others. Have you noticed that?

I believe that your early family dynamic influences your tolerance for intimacy. Certain families have rules about intimacy, rules about who you're allowed to be intimate with, and for how long and under what circumstances. For instance, you may find a mother who is very nurturing and caring to her baby when it is an infant, but that all this changes when the child gets a little older. When the baby begins to sever the psychological umbilical cord (which occurs roughly around the age of two—a phase sometimes referred to as "the terrible twos") and learns to walk and talk and starts running around saying no to everything, the once-loving mother may feel like rejecting the child. Or maybe mother or father is loving to a child until the point of adolescence, and then something happens. This may be the case when either the mother or daughter has a Moon-Venus aspect in her chart. When the daughter reaches puberty, the mother starts to see her as a rival. Suddenly the door closes and intimacy is cut off. You can get the same kind of rivalry between fathers and sons at this stage—I call it the "clashing of antlers" period. The father is a good and loving father until his son hits puberty and adolescence; then the boy is no longer just a boy, but an upcoming man, a rival who will one day supersede and replace the father. In many cases, the son enters the most vigorous phase of his manhood just as his father's potency and power is on the decline. So how does the father handle this?

Or the father is very loving, intimate, warm, and close with his daughter until she reaches puberty around the age of 13. Seemingly overnight, the whole family dynamic shifts and moves into a new space. Unfortunately, most families don't realize the kinds of issues and undercurrents that arise when a child reaches puberty, and even if they do, they are often reluctant to talk freely about what is happening. It's amazing the number of taboos that exist within a family system about openly discussing what is going on during a child's transition into adolescence and young adulthood.

I recently worked with a case where the mother had been a great beauty; she was what I would call an Aphrodite-type woman. But she had just reached 40, which is a very critical age for the Aphrodite-identified woman. Do you understand what I mean when I say a woman is identified with Aphrodite or Venus? She is beautiful and seductive, using her charm and physical attractiveness to get what she wants. This is how she finds her power. I think that, to some extent, most women are identified with Venus, but some women are very strongly influenced by this particular archetype. It's the curse of beauty. You never thought beauty was a curse, did you? Everybody works so hard for it, but it can be a curse, especially around the age of 40 when one is no longer so young and nubile. What happened in the case I was just talking about is that the mother turned 40 just as the daughter turned 14 and was blossoming into this stunning beauty, who actually looked very much like her mother when she was younger. Although the mother was unconscious of it, she began to see her daughter as a rival.

Picture the situation. The mother hits 40 and starts to feel old, and has to use more cosmetics and work extremely hard at the gym and health club to keep up her shape and looks, while there is this young natural beauty of a daughter who, of course, is beginning to be noticed by men. Even the girl's father (the mother's husband) comments on how sexy the daughter is becoming, and says something to the mother like, "That's how you used to look when you were young." So the daughter is caught in a double bind. She has always been close to her father, but now that he is beginning to feel attracted to her as a woman, things change. He also could be unconsciously picking up on the fact the mother turns very rigid when he kisses the daughter or when he bounces her on his lap as he has done since she was a little girl. The mother might make comments such as, "What's going on between you two?" or "Cut it out, that's disgusting."

In this particular case, it wasn't long before both the father and the daughter started getting messages that these things were no longer safe to do. Concurrently, the mother turned to the daughter and said something like, "You're so skinny, you're such a rail, why don't you eat more?" So the young girl started to eat more and grew heavier, and the more she ate, the closer her mother drew to her. But the more she would eat, the more her father would reject her. He would reprimand his daughter and say things like, "God, you've got such a lovely figure, why are you pigging out and letting yourself get so fat? Why don't you become more active, play a little tennis, and get rid of those love handles you're developing?" What happened was that the daughter very soon became bulimic. By the way, she has a T-cross between the Moon, Venus and Pluto, which is a classic significator for anorexia and bulimia. I'll come back to the astrology later, but you can see how the girl was caught between the mother and the father. If she did what her mother wanted and ate more, she lost her father's love. If she didn't overeat, she lost her mother's love. It's very hard for an adolescent to be caught in this trap, to have to choose between mother and father. So she was torn apart. What's more, if the family dynamic becomes stressful, if there is bad energy between the parents, or if a child feels rejected by a parent, the child will blame his or her own self. This negative self-image will be carried all the way into adulthood.

The Moon in your chart reflects the kinds of early experiences you met through the family, and it also inclines you to believe that you have created these circumstances. Children live in a very narcissistic world, an all-powerful world, and they do not view life the same way as adults. The child in you is still alive and kicking even when you reach adulthood, and doesn't see the world in the same way as the more mature and rational adult you. For example, if your parents divorce and you're left at home with mother after father moves out, you may deduce that daddy doesn't love you enough to stay with you, or you may believe that you caused your parents to separate. Interestingly enough, parents give power to this kind of myth when they say to their children, "Mommy and Daddy aren't getting along, and we'd like to split up, but we're going to stay together because we both love you children so much." Parents convince themselves that remaining together for the sake of the children is a very loving act. In reality, they are creating enormous harm, because a young child can't bear this kind of responsibility.

Or consider another example, the classic case of what happens when a parent dies. If a parent dies when you are still young, you often feel that, on some deep level, you have caused this to happen. Children think in a very primitive way. They often think things like, "I'm so mad at mommy, I wish she would die." Or if your mother took away your cookies before you had as many as you wanted, or if she scolded you a great deal, you may momentarily have felt like killing her. If then she should die for some reason, you may believe that it was your fault, that your negative wish has caused her death. You also might feel that if she had really loved you, she never would have gone away. This kind of situation can create the belief system that the person who loves you is going to abandon you one day. I've noticed that many children who had a parent die early on in life, or who come from a home where there was an early divorce, will constellate a mythic system whereby they later find somebody who will abandon them. In other words, they unconsciously set themselves up to be abandoned. Abandonment is the bottom line for them, and they will somehow create this situation in their later relationships. I'm not saying that every child who loses a parent will react exactly in this manner, but pushing people away is often the classic response. I'm sure many of you who have gone through this will know what I'm talking about. A variation of this scenario could be that you leave people before they leave you. You may find these kinds of early problems and disruptions when the Moon aspects Uranus, Neptune or Pluto. I'll be coming back to the theme of abandonment later today.

To name something gives you power over it. This is one way of interpreting the fairy tale about Rumpelstiltskin. He is a very angry dwarf, a symbol of the raging, primitive child within all of us. If the queen cannot guess his name, then she must give him possession of her first-born child. We may wish to relegate the angry and hurt infant inside us to the unconscious—to give it away—but the way to work with this part of our psyches is to name it, to recognize our inner child of the past rather than to deny or suppress its existence. If the queen can name Rumpelstiltskin, she will be able to keep her child. Likewise, the secret to dealing with our childhood complexes is to name them, to acknowledge and recognize what they are. What is the name of the myth you carry around from childhood? Is your myth Cinderella? Is it Peter Pan? Your myth may be a classic one, such as Oedipus or Electra or Hamlet, but it doesn't necessarily have to be linked up to stories such as these. Naming your family myth is absolutely critical. These are the kinds of questions I would like you to explore in this afternoon's workshop. Naming your myth is the first step in having power over it. Naming things is the basis of psychotherapy, which used to be referred to as "the talking therapy." This is why people who work as counselors must learn to listen carefully to what their clients say. Listening to a client's story is a way to find a name for his or her particular family myth. Herein lies the difference between the astrologer and the psychotherapist. The astrologer starts off by giving a reading, while the therapist will begin by asking a person why he or she has come for counseling. Asking clients to tell you their stories, to tell you what is going on with them, to describe how they see this thing called life or how they view the relationship or crisis they are in, is the first step in the process of defining their myth. I think that one of the main functions of the psychotherapist is just this – to help you define and refine the name of your myth. Once you know its name, then you know what kind of sword your need to use to deal with it and go after it. If it's a small, biting thing like a chipmunk, you don't need a huge machete to battle it. Maybe you just need a little bug spray. Do you see what I'm saying? You need to find the right weapon to fight something, and you can't find the right weapon until you know what you're up against. You could just close your eyes, aim in some general direction, and pull the trigger; but is this the way to hit the mark?

I believe that the Moon also has a lot to do with our preverbal experiences. By preverbal, I mean experiences and impressions that happened to us before we awakened to the cognitive phase of language development, before we had words to name things. Astrology has so much to offer psychotherapy, because by looking at the Moon in a chart you can detect early traumas that occurred in the preverbal stage. I'll give you an example of what I mean. I worked with a woman who had been in analysis for a great many years, and part of her presenting problem was frigidity. She also was very paranoid about rape, and used to have all kinds of rape fantasies. She was in her late thirties, married and divorced twice, and had a child by her first marriage. Unless she was very drunk (and she was already beginning to have an alcohol problem), she couldn't tolerate being touched by anyone, not even by her child. When her husband used to touch her, she would turn absolutely rigid with fear; but in spite of all the analysis she had undergone, the root causes of her frigidity remained unknown. I looked at her chart and saw a Moon-Pluto conjunction in her 4th house. The Moon indicates the kinds of circumstances we faced in infancy (both prenatal and postnatal) – things that happened in the very beginning of life that we carry around with us into adulthood. With her Moon conjunct Pluto in the 4th, I deduced that she had suffered a major trauma in her early, preverbal years. As I said before, the problem with probing into disturbances that occurred so early on in life is that they are often irretrievable on the conscious level because they represent events which happened before we had the necessary verbal skills to define or articulate them.

Early traumas may resurface in symbolic ways, such as in dreams, reveries or recurring fantasies. They may even reveal themselves through one's sensory perceptions. For example, I've always reacted very strongly to the smell of lilies of the valley. I never could figure out why this was so, but if I'm in a place where there are a lot of these flowers around, tears start to well up in my eyes. At first I thought it was just an allergy, but I couldn't help feeling that there was an emotional affect that went along with my watering eyes. We never had lilies of the valley growing in the garden of my childhood home, and my mother never wore that kind of perfume, so I really was stumped as to why I had this reaction to them. One day I finally asked my mother if lilies of the valley meant anything to her, and she replied that she had never been able to stand their smell. She then told me that as a small baby, I had a nurse named Ruby who used to soak herself in Lily of the Valley perfume. My mother had tried to get Ruby to stop wearing it, but to no avail. It turned out that this nurse stopped caring for me just around the time I was six months old. So you see how things from that far back can register on an emotional and sensory level and stay with you your whole life.

Anyway, let's get back to the case history I was discussing about the woman with Moon conjunct Pluto in the 4th house. The Moon was nine degrees behind Pluto, so by secondary progression, it would have conjuncted natal Pluto when she was eight or nine months old. In other words, what was promised natally came into precise conjunction at that time, and I thought that something traumatic must have happened around then. At first I suspected something to do with incest, because Moon-Pluto contacts can indicate problems of that nature. I'll be talking more about incest later, but as it turned out, that wasn't the case in this situation. I questioned her about her childhood. She said that she didn't know much about her early life, except that she was born in Rumania and that her father had died just before the war, and she and her mother had eventually fled from Europe to the United States. Her mother refused to discuss the past with her, so that was all she knew. To make a long story short, I started working with her primary therapist, who also was stuck with this case. Since he practiced hypnotism as well, I suggested that he regress her back to between eight and ten months old, to see how the progression of the Moon to Pluto might have manifested at that time. It took him more than a half a year to get her back to that phase of her life, but finally they succeeded. Regressed back to that period while in hypnotic trance, she began to sob very deeply and to cry hysterically, but she couldn't find the words to describe what was making her feel this way. At this stage, I spoke with the therapist and we decided it was necessary to bring in the mother and question her about what could have gone on back then. Eventually the mother told us the story. When my client was nine months old, the Nazis invaded the little Rumanian village in which they were living. It was then that the Germans killed her father. As a matter of fact, they actually shot a whole group of the men from this village in front of this little girl and her mother. Then, with the little girl watching, they raped the mother. She herself, only nine months old, was also manhandled by the invaders. The mother had never spoken of this horrific incident, and had hoped that her daughter had no recollection of it. But somewhere inside she did remember, and it was the source of her later frigidity and recurring rape fantasies. So you see how our early experiences (or our family myths) can affect us from a deeply unconscious level even though we don't consciously remember them? The woman in this case liked men and she liked the idea of being touched and having sex with them, but the little girl in her couldn't bear it. The little girl in her had never recovered from the pain and trauma of that experience. It was the Moon part of her that needed healing, not the Sun or her Saturn.

If the source of wounding is the Moon, the place that needs healing is the Moon. Now, you can't do this by just telling the Moon to grow up. The most healing thing for the Moon is a loving mother or a loving father. In psychotherapy, the therapist can play or model a loving, nurturing mother or father, and in this way eventually help clients to stand on their own. The therapist can enable the client to discover or build in an inner, loving mother or father.

Audience: Can you say briefly what other kinds of therapies besides hypnosis might work with preverbal experiences and traumas?

Richard: Yes, the therapies that focus in on emotions and also those that work with the body. Reichian therapy is one example. Rolfing could be useful, as well as other kinds of primal work. Things that happen early in life are remembered more in the soma than in the psyche. The body remembers and holds things; by working therapeutically with the body, you can get to and release what is stored in the psyche. The psyche also remembers things symbolically, which is why dream interpretation—practiced by most Freudians and Jungians—is another good way to access preverbal memories. Purely verbal or cognitive therapies are not as useful as bodywork or dreamwork in bringing up very early memories or traumas.

We must remember that the Moon is almost never an isolated thing in the chart. It might be aspecting Mars or Saturn or Uranus. Major hard aspects to the Moon give us clues as to the nature of preverbal experiences.

Audience: Would a planet forming a separating aspect to the Moon indicate events that took place prenatally?

Richard: Well, that's a thought, but I can't give you a definite answer because it's never been satisfactorily proven that a child *in utero* actually does pick up things from the outer world. I am, however, quite open to the possibility that this occurs. The developing embryo swims in the fluid of the mother's womb, so it is likely to be receptive to her psychic energy and to her needs as well as what she is going through in general during the pregnancy. The fetus certainly is sensitive to what the mother eats, drinks or puts into her body, so it must, to some extent, be picking up on the outer environment. But as I was saying, aspects to the Moon guide you to experiences and traumas in the preverbal phase of development.

We will be examining lunar aspects in more depth a little later, but before we do so, I want to stress that it makes a difference how early on in infancy a trauma or event occurred: the earlier the experience, the less accessible it is to the conscious mind and the more likely it is to form into a complex or a phobia. Deep-seated complexes and phobias will often reveal themselves through dreams, especially recurring ones or those with similar themes, and also through the kinds of dreams you have during periods of major conflict or stress. The other thing that needs to be considered is the degree of power or affect a preverbal experience has on an infant. This can be a little tricky to gauge, because an experience that an adult might not consider very powerful might seem extremely important to a child. For instance, I worked with a child who had just entered the verbal stage of development. The problem was that he would always cry and scream whenever he was picked up. It turned out that his grandmother used to say repeatedly to him something like, "You're so delicious I could eat you up." The child took her remarks quite literally, and grew to believe that anyone who loved him actually wanted to eat him, and therefore he would protest when loved ones tried to pick him up or hold him. The child even resorted to insisting that people eat cookies whenever they were around him, as if he were trying to make sure they would be filled up with food and therefore wouldn't be hungry enough to eat him. It sounds strange, but it's true. Finally the mother asked him why he kept making people eat cookies, and this is how she learned of the fears engendered by his grandmother's innocent expression of affection. As I have said, it can be difficult to gauge the power or influence an early experience can have on a child.

Let's say a mother accidently drops her baby, which may happen from time to time. Some children might not be so affected by this, while others might be traumatized as a result of being dropped too often. You have to learn to ask the right questions. In this case, you could ask the mother how frequently it happened, or inquire about how far up the baby was when it fell, and you might even need to ask what the baby landed on when it hit the floor or the ground. Also, you should find out what the mother's reaction was after dropping the baby, because this too will be programmed into the infant's memory bank. What if the baby had an alcoholic mother who was clumsy when she was drunk? A two-week-old infant who is handled by a drunk mother doesn't have the ability to equate being dropped with the fact that mother downed three bourbons for breakfast that morning. Nor can a child who isn't getting proper mothering reason that this is so because his mother was not well looked after when she was a child. Or if the mother seems ratty or unhappy, the tiny infant is not able to attribute this to the fact that she's going through a difficult patch with daddy.

These are not the kinds of things a child can think or register. What might form around the experience of being repeatedly dropped, however, could be the myth that the world "out there" is a dangerous place, and even those who love, stroke, and nourish you can do you harm. The potential for traumatic early experiences can be gleaned from the chart. So if you see an aspect or placement that suggests a childhood trauma, you should ask questions to determine the possible effects of the experience. You need to find out how early on in childhood it happened, because earlier experiences have the most impact. And you also need to establish how frequently something like dropping the baby occurred. A child who is only dropped once will not register this as much as a child who is repeatedly dropped. And, as I have already mentioned, you need to inquire about the way the mother or family reacted to the incident. If the mother became hysterical and started wailing, "Oh, my poor baby!" and immediately phoned the police or an ambulance, the whole experience will be empowered and become even more traumatic for the child. Chances are that an early crisis was dealt with in the same way that your family of origin deals with present crises — in other words, that crises are managed or handled in the same way now as they were then. Perhaps the family pattern for dealing with a crisis is to not cry and complain; or it might be to blame the event on someone else. These are just some of the typical patterns or typical games that families play.

Psychotherapy can be used in connection with astrology to foster the healing of early traumas and complexes. For example, take the case of a person who felt rejected, harmed and abandoned by his parents when he was a child, and who now unconsciously tries to set up this same dynamic with every therapist he goes to. It's as if his goal in therapy is to turn his therapist into someone bad or rejecting. If the therapist can handle this kind of transference, then the client's myth will start to lose some of its potency. This may seem like a good thing, but to the person with a deeply embedded complex, letting go of one's myth is almost like dying, because myths form the ground of one's being. Proving a myth wrong or taking it away is comparable to death or to having the ground under your feet removed. People will fight to their last breath to preserve their mythical systems. Nonetheless, through psychotherapy, it is possible for a therapist to model a loving parent whom you can trust, who is not going to drop you every time you are picked up and held. What happens is that the newly or recently formed image of a loving, nurturing parent (as seen in the therapist) begins to play against or offset the original early trauma. I believe that damage that has occurred during the preverbal phase of one's development will take the longest to heal; it is so deeply entrenched that it will take quite a time for new images or expectations to replace the old, existing ones. Speaking astrologically, I would translate this into saying that damage on a lunar level takes the longest time to heal: you'll probably need to open up and explore the early wound through nonverbal forms of therapy, and you'll also need a therapist who can act as a long-term substitute parent. A long-term transference must be made through which the therapist is seen as a loving mommy or daddy, or hopefully a combination of both. This diminishes the power of the earlier experience. So the powerfulness of the early experience needs to be offset against the powerfulness of the therapeutic experience. Hopefully there will be a configuration in the therapist's chart which indicates the willingness to take on the role of a good parent. The therapist who works long-term with a client should be the kind of person who can model a loving, nurturing parent. This may be shown by a strong, nurturing Moon in the therapist's chart, but it could manifest in other ways.

Audience: Recently I read about a study done in Russia. They put a cat in an upstairs room and her newborn kittens in a room down below. They wired electronic measuring gadgets onto the mother cat, and when they administered an electrical shock to her kittens in the other room, the mother cat simultaneously registered a response. This made me wonder. If a baby's mother dies when he's three days old, let's say, then he might register it somewhere in his psyche, although consciously he doesn't know that she has died.

Richard: It wouldn't surprise me at all if that were true. In fact, I strongly believe these kinds of things do happen. Most of us probably would agree that more goes on between people who are deeply connected than what appears to be happening on the surface.

Audience: I'm confused about something. Do you use the chart to deduce the kinds of early traumas a person experienced, or do you analyze the person's current problems and then try to trace these back to early traumas suggested by the chart?

Richard: You can do it both ways. You can go from the chart to the person and also from the person to the chart. Certain indicators in the chart will reveal childhood hurts and traumas, or they will at least help you to focus the direction of your inquiry. So I would look for natal indicators in the chart. But you can also glean information from clients; if you listen carefully to their stories, you'll gain an impression of what's going on with them on the deeper levels of the psyche. The problem with many astrologers is that they don't listen well enough, or they don't give enough time to a person to tell his or her story. The stories we get from clients should encourage us to ask certain questions that probe more deeply into their past and into their unconscious. Do you see what I'm getting at? There's an old Arab proverb that says since we are given two ears and one tongue, we should listen twice as much as we talk. Both therapists and astrologers should remember this. So the answer to your question is yes, you can work both ways. The counselor with an astrological background has an advantage over the counselor who doesn't know astrology, because the chart gives you fairly clear, visible clues as to what is going on in somebody's psyche.

Audience: I'm taking what you just said and connecting it with the case you told us about the woman who had been traumatized as a child in Rumania. It sounds like you went through the process you've just been explaining to us. You knew the woman had a history of frigidity, and this inclined you to examine the Moon and its early progressions in her chart. In other words, through her chart you homed in on some event that could have been the trigger for her problems, and then you went back into the therapeutic mode to work on that traumatic event. So you're going back and forth from the client to the chart.

Richard: Yes, that's exactly how I did work. I'm not trained in hypnotism, so I wasn't the person who actively intervened in her case, but at least we began to open things up by centering on the experience suggested by the early progressions of the Moon in her chart. There ought to be a kind of ping-pong game going back and forth between the astrology and the psychology of a situation. There needn't be set boundaries drawn between these two disciplines; they can feed and nurture one another. As I see it, astrology offers the most perfect model of the human condition that exists, much better and more thorough and complete than any model any psychologist has come up with. The astrological model subsumes and contains all psychological models within it. You can say things in the "lingo" of Freud, Jung, Gestalt, or Transactional Analysis that all can be translated back into basic astrology. That's why I call astrology the language of the least common denominator. Astrology, however, does not offer a practice or a method, it doesn't offer a therapeutic model—which is precisely what psychology has to offer to astrology. You can use the chart to identify a problem, but where do you go to from there?

I want to come back to what I was saying earlier, about setting off an early traumatic experience against a current positive transference onto a therapist. Against the frequency of the traumatic experience in childhood comes the frequency of the new, positive experience in adulthood. This is why, in the psychoanalytical model at least, it is suggested that a person who is working through some of these early life experiences has therapy two or three days a week, or maybe even daily if money and time allow. The more frequent the new experience, the more chance you have of re-creating new beliefs and values. To repeat, the powerfulness and intensity of the early childhood experience is offset against the power of the recent experience in the therapeutic situation. Plato quotes Socrates as saying that "Eros is the greatest teacher." What in the world does he mean by that? Surely he doesn't mean eros in the sense of going to bed with somebody. Eros is the greatest teacher, and eros is what happens when you have a healing therapeutic transference between therapist and client that serves to offset the frequency and power of childhood hurts and traumas. Any more questions at this point?

Audience: Wouldn't you say that the person who works both as an astrologer and psychotherapist with a client faces a certain dilemma? If you do the chart right away, you could end up telling clients things which they might not yet be fully open to hearing; in the process of therapy, however, the person sees things when he or she is ready to see them. You can tell somebody that the chart says this or that, but you know they're only hearing it with the head.

Richard: Yes, that's right. I hear you and agree that this could be a problem, because it gives rise to a tendency to label and define things too quickly, before the actual process can unfold itself.

Audience: It's for this reason that I prefer to do someone's chart after I've been working with that person for a while. At least then I know the client better and can judge more accurately what and how much to say.

Richard: This also applies to synastry readings. One of the things that can really interfere with a relationship is to do a chart comparison too early on. I used to do this. I would meet somebody at a party to whom I was attracted and I'd say something like, "Hello, my name's Richard, when's your birthday?" After obtaining the birth details, I would say "Don't go away, I just have to go to the other room and I'll report back to you in ten minutes." Of course, what I did was to check out the chart to see how it matched with mine. Does that sound familiar? Yes, you've done it too.

Now I'd like to spend some more time talking about the Moon. We have already looked at the Moon by element and touched on the general kinds of problems that arise when you have a mixed-Moon situation—such as mommy or daddy with the Moon in fire and air (yang, or positive, masculine signs) and a child with a *yin* Moon in water or earth (negative, feminine signs). It's likely that the child with a yin Moon will feel like a cluck, some kind of oddball within this family. For example, let's say that both parents have fire Moons and their son has the Moon in a water sign such as Scorpio. The family myth may be along the lines of, "Be up, be positive, look at the bright side of life, every cloud has a silver lining, don't be negative, tears are not allowed, have fun and let's all join together and praise the Lord." And along comes this little boy with the Moon in Scorpio! He looks at all this love and light and fun, and thinks to himself that something smells, that there's something hidden there. He sits there and examines these jovial, happy parents and he just doesn't buy the overt messages of positivity they are giving out. Very early in life, he probably did what most Plutonic and Scorpionic people do quite regularly and periodically; that is, he had an emotional catharsis, similar to a volcano erupting. At which point his mother went fleeing up into the stratosphere where she was safe from his outpourings, and the father went out and played a good game of baseball. They just couldn't deal with such a show of barefaced emotion. The child then thinks, "Aha, there must be something wrong with me." You see, he doesn't think that there is something wrong with the parents, instead he concludes that he is at fault, that there is something not right about who he is. This means that, in the name of winning his parent's approval and feeling all right about himself, he has to block or suppress a way of being which is quite natural to him— that is, he has to hide his darker, more negative moods and feelings.

I urge all of you to find out the Moon signs of your parents. Most of you will know your parents' birthdays, so you can look up their Moon signs. Of course, due to the relatively fast movement of the Moon, you may not be able to figure out its closest aspects if you don't have a pretty good idea of the birth time. So if your parents are still alive, you should try to ferret out their exact times of birth. If you can't, then you will have to use a solar chart or a noon chart to deduce the range of possible aspects to the Moon. Or you can experiment with different birth times to see what kinds of lunar aspects are made. You most likely know your parents pretty well, so through this kind of experimentation, you should be able to intuit what lunar aspects make the most sense—even if you can't pinpoint the exact position of the Moon by house.

You should also compare what I call the *orientation* of your Moon with the orientation of the Moon signs of your parents. Signs have *modality*, a form of motion such as cardinal, fixed or mutable. Signs have *functions*, which we categorize as fire, air, earth or water. And signs exhibit *polarity*—they can be yang or yin, masculine or feminine. However, I believe that signs also can be classified according to their *orientation*, by which I mean the way they are oriented in time and space. Aries is oriented very differently in time and space compared to Pisces. The orientation of Aries is something like, "me, here, now," while Piscean orientation is more like "not me, not here, not now" – or what some people might call "out to lunch." Or, to put it another way, you could say that Pisces orientation is "everybody, everywhere, all the time." Each sign orients itself differently in time and space, and I think it's important to understand these archetypal differences. Aries orients directly toward the self, while Libra orients directly toward the other. A sign's orientation is its grounding point.

The idea of orientation may be a new concept to some of you, so let me explain it further. The first four signs of the zodiac are archetypal personal signs, which means that, for them, nurturing is self-oriented. I also believe that the first four signs – Aries, Taurus, Gemini and Cancer – are premoral signs. By this, I don't mean that they have low or bad morals, but rather that they are archetypally primitive. I don't mean that they are unevolved; please don't hear that. When I describe them as primitive, I am saying that they are closer than the other signs to what I call the elemental forces of nature. There's such a thing as an instinctual level in human beings that certainly is connected with the first four signs, particularly with the first two, Aries and Taurus. The personal signs are fundamental signs that have a lot to do with survival. Their focus is on ego development: Who am I? What do I want? What do I like? They are oriented toward the pleasure principle. Aries is the pleasure of finding the self. Taurus is the pleasure of the senses. Gemini is the pleasure of experiencing and knowing, and it's a very childlike sign. Have you ever observed children when they first learn to talk? They love to hear and say things like "ibble, bibble, dibble, gobble, dobble, bobble" – words that don't even mean anything. Adult Geminis are often like this as well! Cancer is the pleasure of feeling, and curiously enough, the pleasure of hurting, the pleasure of pain. You may think, wait a minute, isn't it "sick" to find pleasure in pain? Not really, when you consider how many people love to sit and watch soap operas on television. Cancer is the pleasure of being open to feelings.

I call the second four signs, Leo, Virgo, Libra and Scorpio, the moral or social signs, not because their morals are good or exemplary, but because these signs are sensitive to other people as well as toward the self. Their orientation shifts to the not-self, or to others, which reaches its peak in the sign of Libra, the archetypal sign of the not-self. For this reason, the second four signs are interested in things like validation, interpersonal connection, social reactions, peer groups and so on.

As for the last four signs, I am constantly changing what I call them. We might label them universal signs, or the signs of the collective, or even call them transpersonal signs. Here the interest is no longer me and me, or me and you, but *me and everybody*. In fact, when you come to Aquarius or Pisces, the sense of me can disappear altogether. Sometimes I call the last four signs "post-moral signs," because these are the signs that believe in the importance of the greater whole, the signs that believe that humanity as a whole is much more important than those things that just affect one personally, or things that affect just you and one other person. The last four signs are more abstract than the other signs, more wide-ranging. Please understand that this doesn't necessarily mean that they are more evolved. Please don't hear it in that way.

Now, let's compare the Moon in these different categories and you'll see more clearly what I'm getting at. Let's say that Mama has the Moon in Aquarius, which probably means that she wants to nurture the whole collective in an abstract, detached way. She might be involved in charities, working selflessly to save the redwoods, or she might spearhead a group to foster neighborhood bee resuscitation, or perhaps she's an active member of the Daughters of the American Revolution. That kind of mother is fine for the child who has the Moon in Sagittarius or Capricorn, but it's not so easy for the little child with the Moon in Cancer. I worked with a mother-daughter situation just like this example. The mother had the Moon in Aquarius and the daughter had the Moon in Cancer, and the daughter kept accusing the mother of not loving her enough. The mother just didn't understand what the daughter was talking about, and would say things like, "Don't be silly, you are my dear daughter and I love you very much." The daughter would then reply, "Sure, and you love the postman just as much as me, and you love all the little doggies and pussy cats just as much as you love me." And the mother would answer back, "Well, yes, dear, because they are all part of the universe." Then the daughter would say, "But I want you to love me the best," which is, of course, the Moon in Cancer speaking. So you should check the orientation of the Moon. Someone with the Moon in a personal sign will always be oriented toward the self—the self comes first.

What about the mother with the Moon in a personal sign? She may not be objective enough to see the kind of nurturing her child needs. The personal signs are more likely to think that everybody ought to be like them, that whatever way they are is the way that everyone should be. It may be difficult for the mother or father with the Moon in a personal sign to actually see or understand a child who operates on a different level from them. Please don't take this as a hard and fast rule; I'm just presenting these examples as a possibility.

Audience: Have you found that parents with a personal Moon seem to want their children to nurture them, that they want their kids to take care of them?

Richard: Yes, that's a good point. It's as if parents with the Moon in a personal sign shift roles and try to get the child to satisfy and respond to their needs, rather than the other way around. Yes, I think that is often very true, and I've seen a number of cases that bear out this point.

Consider the Moon in a social sign—Leo through to Libra. The problem for people with the Moon in a social sign, and this often applies to the Moon in a universal sign as well, is that they often don't know what they need or want at a given moment. This is because the social signs are oriented toward you, or toward the not-self. I mean, how does Libra ever know what it wants? Libra says, "Tell me what you want and then I'll know what I want," or "I want what I want when you want it." With such an orientation, people with the Moon in social signs often have the problem of not really knowing what nurtures them or feels good to them until they're in a relationship with someone. You also might find that parents with the Moon in a social sign will extend their nurturing to their partner rather than to their child. Or those with the Moon in a social or universal sign may not really understand the "child-likeness" of a child. Not being in touch with their own childlikeness means that they have difficulty relating to their children. Consider the case of a mother with the Moon in Pisces who has a child with the Moon in Cancer. You might think that because these two signs are trine, the Moon in Pisces mother would naturally be able to foster and nurture the Moon in Cancer child, but this isn't necessarily the case. The hidden message of the Moon in Pisces is "Yes, it's fine to be sensitive and to grieve and have compassion, but we must do this in a larger Christian and universal sense; we must not indulge our own personal, selfish feelings." In other words, indulging one's personal needs is a no-no, which is precisely what the Moon in Cancer is most interested in.

A similar rationale applies when you consider the Moon in the different modalities, that is, when you compare the Moon in a cardinal sign with the Moon in a fixed or mutable sign. It's a fair bet that everyone thinks that everybody else is just like them or ought to be, so what happens when you have a parent with the Moon in a fixed sign and a child with the Moon in a mutable sign? Children with the Moon in mutable signs are usually quite labile and full of affect, and they tend to experience a wide variety of mood swings and emotional commitments — one way this day, another way the next day, one minute this way, the next minute another way. Now, if this child has a mother or father with the Moon in a fixed sign, such as Taurus, can you imagine what might happen? The parents will think that there is something the matter with their kid, that there is something wrong with the child. Interestingly enough, there is a great collusion between parents and children: if something is wrong in the relationship between a parent and a child, both the parent and the child agree that it's the child's fault. This is a very powerful collusion, and also a very powerful energy to put upon the child — especially a very young child who considers that the parents are next door to God. No matter how badly a child may be treated by a parent, in the child's mind the parent is always right. For this reason, if a child has a very different temperament from a parent, and if that parent is not a very differentiated person, the child gets labeled as "mad" or "bad," or is looked upon as a crazed delinquent. A parent will give the message, "If only you were more like me (or at least more like I wish I were), then you would be okay . . . but since you're not like me, I don't honor the different way you are." What do you think this does to the child? Probably, the child will then begin to deny or repress his or her own Moon sign. If the Moon is felt to be in some way unacceptable to a parent, children will deny their own Moon, and will end up living some kind of artificial Moon which they think will win the love of that parent. Repressing your own Moon and coming from a false place can give rise to psychosis or schizophrenia. If you feel that some part of you is totally unacceptable to the family or the culture you're born into, the only way you can deal with it is to disconnect from who you really are. And if you disconnect enough, you could end up disconnecting completely from reality.

Audience: Is there a particular modality or sign position of the Moon that lends itself to the kind of denial or splitting off that you're talking about?

Richard: No, it can happen with the Moon in any sign. What really matters is how much pressure parents put on a child to be different from how he or she actually is. Family pressure is the key factor. If a female child, let's say, has the Moon in a water sign and the rest of the family is low in water or are not living out their watery side, then she will become the scapegoat who must express the shadowy, watery part of the whole family. In other words, the family needs her to be emotionally overreactive so that they can blame her for being too feeling or overly sensitive. Every family has to have one! And should she not be like this anymore, or if she leaves the family constellation altogether, the rest of the family would then be faced with their own unintegrated water function.

Audience: Would it help if both the parent and the child had the Moon in the same element, such as two parents with a Scorpio Moon and a child with a Pisces Moon?

Richard: No, not necessarily. I've already given you the example of the Moon in Pisces mother with the Moon in Cancer daughter, where the Moon is in the same element, but one is mutable and the other cardinal. Not only is the modality different, but the orientation of these two Moons is also different. True, on one level, they both possess the feeling and nurturing qualities associated with the Moon in a water sign, and yet there can be problems because of their different orientations: Scorpio is interested in the erotic relationship, while Pisces is interested in the universal and empathetic, compassionate relationship. And should a problem arise because of this, it usually follows that the parents assume that what they're doing is right and what the child is doing is wrong.

Audience: What about the case where the child has an element predominant that isn't very strong or is missing in the rest of the family? I've noticed that the family may then put the child in a double bind. Subconsciously they want the energy of the missing element that the child could provide, but at the same time the child is made to feel that he or she doesn't really fit in or belong because of his or her differentness.

Richard: Yes, I agree. Only the exceptional family can easily or fully accept a child's differentness. It's more common that children are made to carry the shadow of the parents, that children will carry the unlived-out experience of the parents. For example, take the typical Mr. and Mrs. Libra who bring their son into counseling because he has been arrested for some kind of juvenile deliquency. They would probably say, "We don't understand how he could have behaved in this way. We are such a good family—we don't drink, we all go to church, we never raise our voices in anger, we don't talk about S-E-X. We just can't understand what happened to Junior." It's pretty obvious to me that something in Junior's chart picks up on and expresses the unlived-out parts of the charts of his parents. I call this the "odd man out" or the "odd woman out" phenomenon, where there is a collusion, often unconscious, to exclude one family member. By the way, it's not always the child who is made the odd person out, it might also be one of the parents who gets to live out the family shadow and who is made to feel that he or she doesn't really fit into the family. Modern family therapy is based on the premise that if you are going to treat somebody who is the odd person out or who is wounded in that way, then you have to treat and work with the whole family. The problem is in the family system, not just in the person who is singled out.

There are a few more important issues I'd like to explore with you. What happens if a parent and child have the Moon in the same sign? What in the world does that mean? I call this situation "Siamese Moons," and believe that it can be fraught with all kinds of potential perils. At first glance, it may seem like a wonderful thing for a parent and child to share the same Moon, but this isn't always the case. With the same Moon sign, it's possible that the parent and child could merge into one person so that umbilical cord separation is made very difficult. It's a classic Demeter-Kore situation, where the mother sees herself reflected in the daughter or the son. The child may then end up carrying too much of the mother's stuff. Problems arising from the same Moon sign can also occur between father and daughter, or between father and son. As I was saying, there is so much closeness that it becomes difficult for the parent to separate from the child and for the child to separate from the parent.

Another problem stemming from this situation is that of role-reversal between the parent—mother *or* father—and the child. Nobody's sure who is supposed to be the daddy or mommy and who's supposed to be the child. I happen to have the same Moon sign as my father, and he used to say things to me like, "Gee whiz, sometimes I think things got mixed up, and you're the daddy and I'm the little boy." And I used to reply, "Yes, I think that's true." It even got to the point that I used to read him bedtime stories to help him get to sleep when he had insomnia. Of course, he would also do that for me, too. But it was very confusing as to who was supposed to be in what role.

Audience: I have the same Moon sign as my mother, and it was as if I got my initial stroking by parenting my mother. It would be interesting to see how many people who shared the same Moon with a parent later grew up to become an astrologer or therapist.

Richard: Yes, that would be an interesting study to undertake. You do it.

Audience: What about two married people with the same Moon sign?

Richard: We're not getting into exploring marital relationships right now, but it is a specific problem we'll be discussing later. For the time being, suffice it to say that the same kind of difficulties can arise; that is, there can be confusion as to who is supposed to do what to whom. It may seem fortuitous for two partners to share the same Moon because each of them would understand what kind of nurturing the other one needed. Very often, however, it gives rise to a battle or conflict as to which partner gets to be the child and which one gets to play the parent. This is similar to the conflict that can arise when a child has the same Moon as his or her parent.

Do you remember the film, *Ordinary People*, with Donald Sutherland and Mary Tyler Moore? It was a very powerful film, and a perfect psychological profile of a certain kind of family. Mary Tyler Moore played a mother who had a strong identification with her recently drowned son—they probably had conjunct Moons, or maybe her Moon was conjunct his Sun or vice versa, something like that. In any case, there was a tremendous connection between this mother and her lost son. When her beloved son died, the mother projects her own negative animus onto the surviving son, and she starts driving him toward suicide. She indirectly communicates things like you are the one who should be dead, not the one with whom I identified. She almost succeeds in driving her son to do it. Of course, all of this is unconscious. You may ask whether these kinds of things really do go on in families of today. The answer is yes, from the days of Greek tragedies straight through to the present. What happens in the film is that the son goes into therapy, and the therapist becomes the deus ex machina, the god who descends in a machine from a great height and saves the day. Through therapy, the boy realizes just what is going on between him and his mother. And what happens? When he no longer is willing to take on the role of his mother's scapegoat, the mother leaves the family. She leaves rather than staying and having to face her own anger, rage and inability to love. Those of you who saw the film will have noticed how the mother sent out double messages about her son going into therapy—one part of her encouraging him to do so, but another part attempting to put him off it. Unconsciously she knew that if he sorted himself out, she would eventually have to look at what was going on inside her. In mythology and in classical literature, the tragic hero is very often the child who must act out and complete the family's unfinished business. In other words, the hero is the person who cleans up the family curse. Orestes, Electra, Oedipus and Ariadne are examples of individuals who carry the burden of having to sort out the family curse, the nasty entangled family business that one person is left to bear. Hamlet is a perfect example in Shakespeare. You can find

another example in what I consider to be the best American tragedy ever written, Eugene O'Neill's *Long Day's Journey into Night*,[1]
which is, of course, autobiographical. The young boy, Edmund
Tyrone, is really O'Neill, and he is describing his own family. By
the way, the play was first staged posthumously; it was so painful
and personal to him that he couldn't bear to have it done while he
was still alive. It was dedicated to what he referred to as his
beloved ghosts—his father, his mother and his brother. Writing the
play was O'Neill's way of purging himself of the family burden he
carried. How many of you have seen the film or the play *Amadeus*?
It's really a dramatization of Mozart carrying out his family curse of
genius. And look what happened to him.

This all leads me into something else—that for some poor
souls, the only way to break the umbilical cord is to die. You can
see this in certain people's addictive, self-destructive behavior. The
umbilical connection to the parents is so strong that they cannot
separate themselves except through the extreme measure of killing
themselves. I suspect that many of the teenage suicides one reads
about in the news these days are related to what I call an "impacted
umbilical cord," a situation in which the parents can't let go of their
child. Very often you find this in upwardly mobile "yuppie" families who have great expectations about what their children should
be like and what they should achieve. The kids may feel that it is
impossible to live up to these expectations, which leads them to
think that in order to be true to themselves, they must give up the
parents. But they may not be ready to give up their parents and
individuate on their own, which leaves only one way out—to
destroy themselves. In the next lecture, I'll be discussing lunar
aspects in terms of what it is we need to feel nurtured.

---

[1]Eugene O'Neill, *Long Day's Journey into Night* (New Haven, CT: Yale University
Press, 1989).

LUNAR ASPECTS:
WHAT YOU NEED TO FEEL NURTURED

I want to deal with specific Moon placements. Rather than going through the tedium of moving one by one through each of the signs, I'd rather examine the Moon in aspect to the other planets, which will accomplish the same thing in the end. We'll begin with the Moon in aspect to Mercury. The Moon in aspect to Mercury is similar to the Moon in an air sign because what is important here is dialogue and communication. I've found that the critical thing for people with Moon-Mercury aspects is that there is some kind of articulation of feelings within the nurturing situation. It doesn't make any difference what the nature of the aspect is, square, trine, opposition, quincunx, or whatever. I don't even believe in good or bad aspects, and I don't even like using the words *easy* or *hard* aspects either. I prefer to call them aspects of *acceptance* or aspects of *resistance*. I consider the square and the opposition to be aspects of resistance, that is, the dialogue between the two planets is worked out through resistance. The trine and the sextile are aspects of acceptance: they find the line of least resistance for communication. There's no good or bad about any of them. The quincunx is a special case which I refer to as an aspect of paradox, and I'll be going into the quincunx in more detail later.

As I was saying, it is critical for Moon-Mercury people to articulate and verbalize their feelings, to be able to talk about their feelings and what is going on inside them. If a child with a strong Moon-Mercury connection is born into a family in which the myth is that you don't talk about how you feel, then the child will be in trouble. Another danger for Moon-Mercury is a tendency to detach from the feelings and intellectualize them. As a planet, Mercury represents the desire to label things. Mercury wants to give everything a name because that seems to make things feel safer; naming something brings it out of the dark night, out of the dark world into light. Accordingly, I believe that certain kinds of psychotherapies, particularly the talking therapies, are advantageous for people born with Moon-Mercury contacts because it satisfies their need to verbalize. I myself have a strong Moon-Mercury contact in my chart, and I often comment that I don't know what I'm feeling until I hear what I'm saying, until I put it into words. So Moon-Mercury is saying, "If you love me, listen to me. If you love me, talk to me. Tell me what is going on with you. Tell me what you feel." Obviously, when we refer to specific aspects, we are talking about bits of a chart and not really getting the whole picture. It's for this reason that I can't give you an exact formula for Moon-Mercury aspects, because the Moon could also be in aspect to other planets besides Mercury, and the house or houses involved will vary from chart to chart. I can get you started, but you'll have to put the pieces together and do the synthesizing yourself. That's going to be your homework, and part of the work you'll be doing in your smaller group workshops.

Let's move on to Moon-Venus contacts. At first glance, you might think that the combination of the Moon with Venus would be an exceptionally nice aspect, bringing together two archetypal feminine significators and linking the Moon with beneficent Venus. Don't be fooled. The Moon in aspect to Venus can mean big problems in many cases. It can be especially dire in the chart of a woman precisely because it brings two different aspects of the feminine into conflict with one another—the woman as mother (the Moon) and the woman as lover (Venus). In other words, any Moon-Venus aspect can create confusion in a woman's mind between being a motherly, maternal type or a seductive, flirtatious Venus type. I've noticed that women with the Moon in aspect to Venus often receive double messages from the mother as to the role of women in general. Is a woman a nurturing, maternal creature or is she the perpetual Aphrodite? With the Moon and Venus in hard angle, such as the square, the opposition or a difficultly placed conjunction—aspects of *resistance*—or in quincunx, semisquare or sesquiquadrate—aspects of *paradox*—you'll very often see that the relationship between mother and daughter turns sour when the daughter hits adolescence. I've also observed that women with Moon-Venus aspects in their charts often have weight problems. Check this out for yourself, and you'll see that it's true. The weight problems can usually be traced back to the double messages the mother sent out to her daughter regarding the role a woman should play in life. Let me explain this more fully.

You can look at Moon-Venus aspects as a kind of Snow White and Wicked Queen gambit. "Mirror, mirror on the wall," goes the Wicked Queen, "who is the fairest of them all?" For years the mirror says that the Queen is the fairest of them all—that is, until the time when little Snow White reaches adolescence and starts to blossom, at which point the mirror no longer says what the Queen wants to hear. Snow White becomes the fairest of them all, and the Queen then turns into Hecate. The Queen changes into the monster-mother whose position as the fairest of them all is being challenged and replaced by the daughter in the bloom of youth. So much for the notion that Moon-Venus is a benign or harmless aspect! When the daughter reaches adolescence, mother may start giving her the message that she will reject, destroy or create trouble for her if she blossoms into a beautiful young woman and replaces her mother as the most attractive in the land. Very often the daughter will react to this by developing addictive behavior, particularly eating disorders. If the daughter's Moon-Venus aspect is contaminated by aspects and issues from Mars, Uranus or Pluto, she might even turn schizophrenic at this point.

A Moon-Venus aspect can be a problem in a man's chart as well, causing confusion about whether his mother is his mother or his lover. Later, he may be confused as to whether he is marrying a lover or his mother, or he marries his lover and then turns her into his mother. It's as if the male anima is uncertain about whether he wants a woman to be his mother or his lover. Very often he has received mixed messages from his mother, especially if his Moon-Venus aspect is linked in some way with an aspect from a planet like Uranus or Pluto. In his mind, mothering and nurturing (the Moon) get mixed up with sensuality and eroticism (Venus). In other words, the lunar principle is linked to Aphrodite, a Venusian goddess. Aphrodite is a very sensual goddess, in love with her own body. In some of the myths, she is portrayed as highly sexual and self-indulgent, lovingly masturbating herself. This is not a model of the feminine which has found much favor within the Christian Church. In a sense, the goddess Venus has been lost or banished from our culture, although the women's movement is hopefully bringing some of her back. If you have a Moon-Venus aspect, you are nurtured through things that are sensual and aesthetic, things that feel good to your body. I also believe that along with the Moon, Venus is another planet of addiction. The Moon is addictive because of emotional denial; Venus turns addictive when there is a lack of physical contact or a lack of touch. People with a strong Moon-Venus connection in their charts need to indulge themselves physically and do things like getting massaged or having a roll in the grass, or they need to let themselves enjoy masturbation. If you don't know how to pleasure yourself, how can you expect somebody else to pleasure you? One of the great myths around womanhood is that a woman is supposed to be a kind of Immaculata who knows nothing about her own body until a man comes along to awaken her. You see this theme over and over again in best-selling women's romance books and magazines. A common myth today is that a woman is not meant to be responsible for her own body. And just as women are not supposed to be responsible for their sexuality, men are not meant to be responsible for sensuality. When a man is touching someone, the implication is that it has got to be sexual, which is why men are not allowed to touch each other. I think that these kinds of myths are really unfortunate, because they get in the way of an awful lot of good things that could happen otherwise. Women are much freer to touch each other than men are.

Moon-Venus requires touching. The Venusian child—the child of Aphrodite—needs to be held and loved a lot. You cannot wear a child out with too much touch. Indeed, in Polynesia and Malaysia it's common practice for a mother to masturbate a crying child in order to calm him or her down. There is a great myth—which I have more to say about later—that children are not sexual. However, as Freud pointed out very early on, children are not just *sensual* creatures but also *sexual* creatures. The real problems come in when the natural, unformed sexuality of the child is taken advantage of by an adult. If you have a Moon-Venus aspect, you need to become your own nurturing mother. It's important for you to surround yourself with things you find aesthetically pleasing; sensual, artistic things that make you feel good. Are you arranging to take care of the fact that your body needs to be touched on a regular basis? If you're not in a relationship, perhaps you should visit a masseur or a masseuse. Do you get your hands into the earth? Do you work with flowers? Do you make things with your hands? All of these activities are very satisfying to Moon-Venus. Also, do you look beautiful, do you dress beautifully? I think it's important for Moon-Venus people to make themselves into the most attractive package possible. If I look at a chart with a prominent Venus, and the person has not done very much to enhance his or her looks or attractiveness, I wonder what the problem or blockage is in this respect. If a woman has a Moon-Venus aspect and has not done what she can to make herself beautiful, I suspect she has fallen prey to what I call "the poison apple game" that mothers and daughters often play. By this I mean that there are some daughters who end up biting into the poison apple. The daughter fears that if she becomes too beautiful, the mother will cut her off or the mother will destroy her. I've seen grown-up daughters whose mothers are far advanced in years, but the mother is still offering the daughter poison apples, and the daughter is still eating them. "God, you're so fat, your hair is so stringy. Why don't you lose some weight? Why don't you gain some weight? Why do you wear pink when it looks so awful on you? No man is ever going to look at you. You're not like your sister Jane, who is the pretty one. At least you're the one with the nice personality in the family, maybe someone will fall for you eventually." With Moon-Venus aspects, these are the kinds of messages that come down from the mother to the daughter. It's a very hard one to break.

Let's move on to Moon-Sun contacts, which can produce some pretty problematical situations as well. I've been practicing and teaching astrology for 20 years now, and all this time I've been looking for the Moon sextile or trine the Sun to mean something wonderful, but it usually fails to turn out that way. Why should this be? One major drawback with these aspects is that consciousness may have difficulty differentiating from the unconscious. In other words, the developing ego as symbolized by the Sun gets consumed in the lunar/umbilical contact. Funnily enough, this situation occurs more frequently with the sextile or trine aspect than it does with the square or opposition. So in terms of Moon-Sun aspects, the square or opposition can be easier to handle than the sextile or trine. The reason for this is that the trine is an aspect of acceptance. Therefore, a person with Moon trine Sun is likely to delay or even permanently postpone the individuation process because the umbilical connection with mother feels so good. It feels so good to be connected to one's roots or to one's family myths that there is nothing to push or coerce the person into differentiation. I remember working with a woman who had a Sun-Moon trine and she considered her parents the most idyllic, wonderful people she had ever met. Nobody could be as loving or as nurturing as her mother; nobody could be as dynamic and as powerful as her daddy. One consequence of this idealization of her parents was that she felt secondary and inadequate when compared with them; she felt that she could never be as great or as wonderful as her mother and father. Another problem arising out of this was that no later relationship could ever equal the wonderfulness of her relationship with her parents. So you can see how a great deal of her development was arrested on account of the Sun-Moon trine. It's much easier to break the umbilical cord with parents who archetypally fall into the role of monsters than with the ones who are experienced as saints and angels. How could I ever hurt or leave a creature as magnificent, loving and perfect as *my* Mom? This is a very, very dangerous trap.

What nurtures someone with a Moon-Sun contact? To begin with, the solar energy says "notice me," which means that nurturing comes from being the center of attention. The Sun is a symbol of active creativity—the act of self-expression and self-replication through some kind of creative medium or some kind of life purpose. So people with Moon-Sun contacts feel nurtured when they are seen as a star, when they can say "Hey, look, I am the greatest!" whether that be the greatest cook, the best tap dancer, flower arranger or whatever. To put it bluntly, performing something and being praised for it is the key to a Moon-Sun contact. A quincunx between the Sun and Moon can be a very difficult aspect. In this case, you often get a double message from the parents—they want you to perform and be marvelous, but when you do perform they criticize you and end up making you feel as if you could never live up to their ideals and expectations. One example that comes to mind is the daughter who is encouraged to take up the piano, and then everyone laughs at her when she makes mistakes in her playing. I worked with a man who had a Sun-Moon quincunx. The family joke was that as a little boy he was quite a bit more developed than little boys normally are. The family game was that his mother used to yank his pants down and display him to all her lady friends, and this was a big joke—the whole family would laugh about it. Do you know what he grew up to become? Any guesses? No, not a porno star, but you're close. He actually grew up to become a flasher. So it was okay to do it if mother does it, and it's okay to do it when you're little and you get praise and attention for doing it, but doing it when you're older is a definite no-no. I'm pleased to report that the man in question has resolved these difficulties through many years of therapy, but you can see how this is a graphic example of the kinds of double messages parents often transmit to children.

Let's consider Moon-Mars aspects, which can be summed up in the phrase "If you love me, fight with me." Moon-Mars can be a big problem because we have social and family myths that tell us that we should never raise our voices in anger to those we love. Because of these taboos, people with Moon-Mars contacts often end up suppressing their Moon altogether; they end up repressing the whole Moon business because they can't handle the Mars aspect to it. I have a strong Moon-Mars connection in my own chart, and before I can really feel safe in an intimate relationship, I first have to pick a fight. So if I unleash my Moon-Mars energy on partners with Moon-Venus or Moon-Saturn aspects, they may feel viciously attacked or feel that I'm trying to threaten their control over things. What provides safety and security for me may not be what provides safety and security for you. Moon-Mars says, "Let me assert myself, let me express my anger or my rage, let me express the competitive part inside me, and I hope you can receive these kinds of things." Children who have Moon-Mars contacts in their charts often have a hard time, because children usually are not loved for expressing anger or rage. If such a thing existed, I would be a charter member of the Children's Liberation Movement. I agree with the fact that women have been discriminated against for ages, but I actually think that children face even more discrimination. It's not fair that children are not allowed to get angry. Unless you come from an exceptional family, the message you receive very early on is that anger is not allowed, or that anger is something permitted to adults but not to children. So children never get the chance to practice expressing anger in a way that is safe and acceptable. And they usually don't even have good role models for dealing with anger, because most parents don't know how to express and deal with the rage and anger in their own natures.

Moon-Mars aspects also heighten sexuality because Mars represents a very libidinal energy, the desire for penetration. I classify Moon-Mars as a "proto-incestuous" combination, something which I'll speak more about a little later. Children with these aspects are actually nurtured (the Moon) by sexual assertion (Mars). Do you follow what I'm saying? Society has not made it easy for Moon-Mars children to deal with their yang energy, by which I mean their naturally assertive sexual drive and craving for contact through penetration. I don't necessarily mean outright sexual penetration, but an inherent libidinal need to give expression to the self through assertion and power over others.

Audience: So someone with Moon-Mars can express his or her need for penetration by trying to get to know someone really well, by penetrating into the being of another person.

Richard: Yes, I agree, but there are different ways of going about this. Mars wants to provoke. Mars wants something to push up against. Mars is saying "If I express myself assertively or angrily, please don't fall apart into a puddle of Jell-O. Don't run away from me, don't push me away or refuse to communicate with me. Please just receive what I'm putting out to you, because that's what love means to me. What I need is to have the Mars part of me accepted."

I see a lot of puzzled looks in the audience, which says to me that some of you are having a hard time connecting anger with intimacy and nurturing. To nurture a Moon that is connected to Mars may involve getting into something that is highly competitive. If you have this aspect, one way your *inner mother* can nurture your *inner child* is to be a winner at something. You could take up fencing or polo. In particular, getting into some form of martial art is a way of dealing with Moon-Mars aspects, because one of the most fundamental faces of Mars is that of the archetypal warrior. I think you can't get to him in any better or clearer way than through taking up kung fu or karate, or if that is a little too yang for you, you could take up aikido or tai chi. I mean there aren't too many ladies who are going to take up boxing, although I personally don't see why they shouldn't if they are so inclined. Mars can be a very big problem for women. But why shouldn't they honor their Mars? I've noticed that Mars is not particularly interested in team sports — it usually prefers individual, one-to-one contact. There's no reason why you can't get into a fierce game of tennis or golf or hair-pulling or whatever your particular sport happens to be. And if you are not the kind of person who actually likes physical sport, you could give expression to your Mars through playing a very competitive game of bridge, where you are determined to annihilate your opponents. The rule should be that you have to really want to win, and then your Mars is being used. The Mars urge is annihilation, total annihilation. If you refer back to the god Ares in Greek mythology, you'll see that joy for him meant causing death, destruction and annihilation to his opponents. Of course, this is an area in us that we're afraid of, a part of ourselves we don't like, a part that's been civilized out of us, which means that it is relegated to the unconscious where it comes out in very, very destructive ways. If you don't deal wisely with a Moon-Mars configuration, you could constellate the destructive side of Hera or Hecate in relationship.

Audience: I think this is a chicken-before-the-egg type of question. If you have a Moon-Mars contact, then that ought to signify a parent who is aggressive, who yells and screams, which would mean that you learn yelling and screaming from that parent. So my question is, who is it that starts the ball rolling? Is the child provoking or eliciting that kind of behavior from a parent or does the child learn it from the parent?

Richard: The answer to your question is yes. It is a chicken-and-egg thing and we've talked about this kind of situation many times. Does the child have something innate in its nature that provokes a particular constellation of responses from the parents? I feel the answer is yes. There is something innate in the natal horoscope that not only describes how I basically am, but also implies what kind of responses I'll trigger in my parents. I recently worked with a family who were a good example of this. The son, who had Moon in Capricorn, was complaining that his mother never nurtured him as a child. We finally brought the mother into the session, and the son continued to dump on her, saying how cold, detached, unloving and forbidding she was. After hearing all this, the mother told him that when he was a baby, he would always scream, cry, kick and fight whenever she tried to pick him up. "On the other hand," she continued, "when your dad picked you up, you would quiet down right away. Naturally, I felt rejected and that's why I reacted the way I did to you." I see you have many questions and comments on this issue, but we'll have to save these until later in order to get through the rest of the planets. Write them down for now. So to conclude, nurturing yourself with Moon-Mars means asserting yourself; it means finding ways of channeling the competitive, destructive side of Ares, the Greek god of war. A safe way to do this could be through a game of bridge or a game of tennis, or a chess match or something like that.

Moon-Jupiter is similar to Moon-Saturn in certain ways because they share something that I call "Great Expectations." People with these aspects share a feeling that there is something very special about themselves and therefore they deserve more in life. The difference is that for Moon-Jupiter the glass is always half full, but for Moon-Saturn, the glass is always half empty. Moon-Jupiter says, "I should have everything I need and then more, because I'm a very special child." Moon-Jupiter believes that there is a kind of wonderfulness about oneself. From early life, the message for Moon-Jupiter people is that they are the apple of their parents' eye. There's something very special about you that entitles you to the lion's share. It's a kind of magical fairy godmother effect. You not only feel entitled to the best, but you also feel entitled to everything, to all of it. Moon-Saturn is also demanding, but in a slightly different way. Moon-Saturn says, "I have been so deprived in my early life that it's up to you out there in the world to make up for it." Moon-Saturn carries around a huge deprivation complex. There's never going to be enough. Moon-Saturn is an enormously hungry position—I call it the itch that cannot be scratched.

When I first started studying astrology, I was interested in the detriments, falls, dignities and exaltations of the various planets—how a planet is meant to be so good in its own sign, and so bad in the sign opposite, and so on. I decided to investigate these claims. I went through about 4,000 to 6,000 charts of celebrated people just to see if they had a large proportion of planets in dignity or exaltation. What I discovered was that the most common Moon sign for these people was Capricorn, the so-called sign of the Moon's detriment. So why is that? Saturn, the ruler of Capricorn, represents the desire for perfection on the material plane. Anything less than perfect means that there is something terribly wrong. People with Moon-Saturn or the Moon in Capricorn have a tendency to sublimate and compensate for their lack of emotional closeness and connectedness. What is enough loving for a person with a Moon-Saturn contact? The answer is that there is never enough. They feel that whatever they get is not going to be enough, so the myth these people are carrying around with them is that they are, and have been, profoundly deprived in some area. They take this feeling of deprivation and turn to other people to make it up for them. This is what I mean by Moon-Saturn being perpetually hungry. Out of this hunger comes a lot of sublimation and compensation—the feeling that if I can't get complete and perfect satisfaction or fulfillment on the emotional level, then at least I can be the one who builds a better mousetrap or paints the perfect painting.

Another thing I've noticed about Moon-Saturn or the Moon in Capricorn is that there is often confusion in the roles between mother and child, or parent and child. People with these placements are constantly saying that they were cheated out of their childhood, because they had to be a parent to their parents. This is probably so because the child with the Moon linked to Saturn or Capricorn is born with natural parenting instincts and actually may turn out to be a better parent than the parent. The child then feels that he or she has had a difficult childhood or has been cheated or deprived of a happy, loving childhood. There may be many different reasons for this—perhaps the family was very poor, or it could be that there simply wasn't enough love and nurturing available to the Moon-Saturn child. It is in the nature of Saturn to weigh and judge, and children with Moon in aspect to Saturn or with the Moon in Capricorn often weigh things up and come to the conclusion that their little sister or brother got more love than they did. In other words, their state of uroboric bliss or oneness with a parent was shattered when a new child came along. As I said earlier, it is this sense of deprivation that makes Moon-Saturn so hungry.

Moon-Saturn people might also have weight problems, because they use food and eating as a way of compensating for their feelings of lack and deprivation, for the feeling that there is never enough around for them. I've also noticed that Moon-Saturn people often end up playing the role of the helper. Since many of them assumed a parental role in their childhood, they continue to play the parent figure later in life as a counselor, astrologer or psychotherapist. In other words, their inner child is not comfortable being a child, so it tries to be a parent. They desperately want a relationship in which they can let out the child in them, but they never allow this to happen. How can they be a child when they are so uncomfortable exposing their vulnerability to anyone? Being strong and being in charge is what makes them feel safe.

Now, let's move on to some of the things that are nurturing for people with Moon-Jupiter aspects. I've found that Moon-Jupiter is nurtured by ritual and group experience, which is a facet of Jupiter about which I have more to say later. Jupiter is an integrative planet which connects us with the collective community. Moon-Jupiter is nurtured by things which are expansive, playful, jovial—things that connect us to something greater than ourselves, to something outside of ourselves. Moon-Jupiter is drawn to things like traveling, exploring, teaching, learning, higher education and anything that feeds the mind. I have a strong Moon-Jupiter aspect in my chart, and teaching nurtures me; it is fundamental to me, and something that I need to do to feel okay. I don't know whether this makes me a better teacher or not, but it's part of what makes me feel good.

By contrast, Moon-Saturn is nurtured by being alone, and the same could be said for Moon-Neptune. People with a strong Moon-Saturn or Moon-Neptune need time alone to recharge; they need space and distance, and therefore may come across as cold or aloof. Saturn is the planet of boundaries, and it's very important for the person with Moon-Saturn to establish his or her own boundaries. Many people with strong Moon-Saturn connections really cannot live with a lover, husband or wife. They get along much better if they live in separate quarters. Of course, this flies in the face of the myth that when you love somebody and want to form a relationship with that person, you have to live together, entwined like a strangling fig in the same bed forever. It's nice when that happens, but it isn't so easy to do forever. Right? Moon-Saturn needs some place where it can be the boss, where it is in charge, where it is being the parent. Moon-Jupiter needs some place where it can be the instructor, the teacher, the wise old man or wise old woman. The difference is that Moon-Jupiter naturally believes that it is wonderful and deserving of respect, while Moon-Saturn feels that it must earn its honors and accolades by working extremely hard for them, by struggling to achieve the respect and position it so desperately strives for. Moon-Saturn people are often nurtured by being workaholics, constantly doing, constantly busy at something, constantly being productive. You try to tell these people to relax and be easier on themselves, but they still feel they must constantly slave away at some work or some project. Slaving away is what makes Moon-Saturn feel good; it is their idea of a good time. Moon-Saturn veers toward being obsessive and compulsive. If you want to nurture Moon-Saturn people or to do them a favor, then you should assign them a really rough task to do. Give them a deadline! Moon-Saturn carries an awful lot of guilt, and therefore they also carry a great deal of blame. They blame themselves for things that aren't right or they blame other people for things that are wrong. With Saturn there is always the feeling that something is wrong, something is missing or lacking, and that this is either my fault and I should feel guilty about it, or it is the fault of other people and they should be blamed for it. Getting out of that guilt/blame game is one of the hardest things for Moon-Saturn. But it can be done. It may take twenty-five years of therapy to free themselves from that trap, but it can be done.

Another thing that nurtures Moon-Saturn is a nice bout of depression. We tend to see depression as something awful or terrible that ought to be avoided at all costs. I don't agree. I think that depression is one of Saturn's ways of teaching you. James Hillman once said that if depression were an animal, it would be a pig, and pigs love to wallow. There's nothing wrong with having a good wallow when you need it. If you have a Moon-Saturn aspect, you'll probably find that you have these periodic depressions—what people around you may call moods—but what Abraham Lincoln, who had the Moon in Capricorn, used to call an attack of the "black awfuls." So Moon-Saturn may feel nurtured by temporary periods of depression, by allowing depression its own time and space. "Oh great, my next depression cycle is coming up!" When I go through a depressive phase, I dress up in black and I don't go out during the day, only at night, when I hunt the streets like a vampire. I play very sad music, feel very sorry for myself, do a lot of writing in my journal about how unjust the world has been to me. And believe it or not, all that feels nurturing to me when I allow myself to go through it. Or sometimes I just want to stay in bed with the blankets up over my head. Whatever works for you. People have a tendency to deny Saturn and say that such periods of depression are negative and bad and that one shouldn't have such cold or distant feelings. Many of us think that we should never feel depressed; instead we believe that we should always be Jupiterian or Venusian. So Saturn is locked in the closet, which is the same place you put your Moon when it brings up feelings you don't think you should have.

My brother has a very strong Moon-Saturn aspect in his chart. He used to disappear into his room, and my mother would say that he was having one of his "sulks." She would knock at his door and ask what he was doing in there, and then she would tell him to come out and have fun, and to stop feeling so sorry for himself. The message is that it's not good to make room for depression in your life. But if you've got a powerful Moon-Saturn aspect, please allow yourself these kinds of periodic withdrawals and these dark phases of turning inward which Saturn wants you to have. Maybe then depression doesn't need to be such a fearsome thing. Don't get me wrong, however—I'm not saying that there aren't times when depression can become pathological or too intense and entrenched, and you may need professional help to get out of it.

Audience Let me get this right. You're saying that if we can accept the Saturnian need to be alone and go through depressions from time to time, then it can actually be a nurturing thing—that depression can be eased by our accepting it as part of life, by realizing that it's a phase which will pass and change into another mood.

Richard: Yes, by acknowledging that it's a regular part of your life, and by accepting it. In other words, we can recognize that depression is cyclic and that it won't last forever. One of the worst things that can happen to a child or adolescent is when they get into a depression and think that it's going to last forever, and that they'll never get out of it.

Let's take some time to discuss the Moon in aspect to the three outer planets. With the Moon linked to Uranus, Neptune or Pluto, something that's primarily and fundamentally personal (the Moon) is connected to the transpersonal or archetypal realm (the outer planets). These aspects create the expectation of something magical, mythical or larger than life from the parents. Mother may be seen as the archetypal ogress, the beautiful princess or the Queen of the Night; Father becomes Sir Galahad or the ravenous Minotaur who's going to devour the child or tear the child to pieces. So what I'm saying is that people with the Moon in aspect to the outer planets – or people with the Moon in Aquarius, Pisces or Scorpio – usually don't see the mother or the nurturing parent as a real person. That's why children with these aspects have such a hard time breaking the umbilical connection, because they are dealing with the parents as mythical figures and not as real people. The way out of this is to try to name or pinpoint the exact nature of the archetypal projection that has been put onto the mother or the father. Remember Rumpelstiltskin, and the need to give a name to something. One woman with the Moon conjunct Neptune had a paraplegic father and she felt that her mother didn't really love him. She believed that if she could give her father enough love, she could somehow heal him – that was the myth she carried around in herself. She felt that there was this magical person hidden in the father's wounded body, and that if she loved him enough and never abandoned him, she would make the father healthy and whole again. Among other things, she read the Electra myth and also the story "Beauty and the Beast." She had this idea that her feminine love could save or transform the wounded man.

One specific problem for Moon-Uranus is the fear of abandonment. If you have this aspect, you probably have a tendency to constellate situations in which abandonment happens. By the way, I've noticed that many astrologers have Moon-Uranus contacts in their charts. How many of you have this kind of aspect? You see, that's a very high proportion. The Moon wants something very personal and intimate, while Uranus is the planet that wants *agape*, the Greek word describing a kind of love which is more wide-ranging and universal – the Aquarian or Uranian feeling that everybody is my brother or sister, the need to love the entire world. The myths that these children bring into adult relationships often have to do with experiences of abandonment. This doesn't necessarily mean that Moon-Uranus in the chart describes a broken marriage between the parents, although it very often does turn out that way. More broadly, children with these aspects are left with the feeling that the rug was suddenly pulled out from under them, and, as a result, they can never again fully trust other people.

Another game that happens with Moon-Uranus is, "I will abandon you before you abandon me." Or people with these aspects find partners who will not be there for them—somebody who is already married, someone who is inaccessible or who lives in another part of the globe. Or if I am a man, I fall in love with a woman who is lesbian, and I'm going to try to reform her. Or a woman falls in love with a gay man. Or there is an enormous age difference between the person with this aspect and his or her partner. Whatever the particular scenario, what happens is that the myth gets validated that something is going to suddenly break or end. I call it the Humpty-Dumpty effect. Many people with Moon-Uranus aspects feel like an egg teetering on the wall when it comes to receiving nurturing in relationships. Maybe it's better to give the egg a push off the wall and break it, rather than to sit there with all that tension wondering when the egg is finally going to drop.

Moon-Neptune, as I was saying, has a tendency toward the magical, but here the projection is along the victim-savior axis. This can work two ways. I am the nurturing savior for the mother, or I create myself as a victim so that I invoke the savior quality in another person. I have met many people with strong Moon-Neptune contacts in their charts. Very often the mother has taught them that they have to fall apart in order to receive nurturing from her. The mother communicates something like, "I need to see you vulnerable," or, "Seeing you wounded and hurt is what will evoke the nurturing mother within me." So the child is trained to be in a perpetual state of falling apart in order to get mother's nurturing. Sometimes the reverse is the case and the game is played the other way round. The impression is that mother is this poor wounded, divine, ideal creature that needs succour and protection. People with strong Moon-Neptune contacts are like Moon-Saturn in this way, exhibiting the need to parent a parent. These are the people that end up in adulthood playing the rescuer or savior in one of the helping professions.

Time is running short, and we still have to cover the Moon in aspect to Pluto. I promise I'll get to it. Meanwhile, do you have any questions on the material we've covered so far?

Audience: We've established that many people in this room have Moon-Uranus contacts. I am one of them, and I offer my story up for consideration. I have a tendency to feel emotionally abandoned and not recognized, and one day I asked my mother if she could think of any reason why I ended up this way. She told me that when I was born she had to have a Caesarean and that she didn't see me for 20 hours after my birth. Then she said that when they brought me to her, she thought to herself "Who is this stranger?" and that she felt absolutely nothing at all toward me. My brother doesn't have a Moon-Uranus aspect. He was born six years after me without recourse to a Caesarean, and my mother immediately bonded to him.

Richard: This is exactly the kind of thing you could be getting into when you break up into your smaller workshops. I'd like to see one of you put a message on the notice-board announcing that all Moon-Uranus people are invited to a meeting to work out these kinds of issues. This is the way I hope you will use the workshops. Please think about this.

Audience: Does a Moon-Mars connection automatically suggest an anger problem with the mother or women in general, or would you need an outer planet aspecting the Moon-Mars contact to make it manifest in that way? I'm specifically thinking about this in a man's chart.

Richard: Yes, you raise a good question. Moon-Mars can signify a mother who is angry or who has a problem dealing with anger. A man with this aspect may project this onto certain women in his life and attempt to work it through in his relationships with them. Does that answer your question?

Audience: But doesn't it take an outer planet playing into the Moon-Mars configuration to bring it out in this way?

Richard: No, not necessarily. But it is true that an outer planet will complicate the issue because it constellates archetypal and transpersonal images that magnify everything into mythic proportions.

Audience: Aside from attending astrology conferences, how can Moon-Uranus find nurturing?

Richard: Well, maybe one thing is to accept that the kind of intimacy and nurturing that society upholds as normal and right isn't what Moon-Uranus types really need. Maybe Moon-Uranus people are the kind of people who need multiple relationships, a man or woman in every port. Or maybe Moon-Uranus needs to be able to say that although I love you very much today, I can't promise about tomorrow. The combination of Moon with Uranus is a difficult mixture to satisfy. I have a name for people who have a strong connection between the personal and the transpersonal planets—I call them "Number Thirteens." They're divisible by nothing. They are the square pegs who can't fit into round holes, the people who have to find their own path. The normal kinds of family and social pigeonholes that most people fit into never seem to work for them. That's why I stress that in order to individuate, Moon-Uranus types need to say, "I know who I am and I am willing to go my own way, even if it means breaking the umbilical with both my family and with my society." This is not an easy thing to do, and none of us ever succeed in doing it totally. But, certainly, what is nurturing is the investigation of the transpersonal. For Moon-Uranus people, this could be through exploring symbol systems such as astrology. For Moon-Neptune people it could mean exploring the transpersonal through art, music, poetry or something creative. Neptune particularly loves getting into a trancelike or egoless state, either through communion with music or through yoga or meditation.

Audience: When you described Moon-Saturn, it sounded as if it was as prone to addiction as Moon-Neptune.

Richard: Yes, Moon-Saturn can be very addictive. Different astrological configurations suggest the different reasons for addiction. Moon-Neptune addictions stem from a deep inner sense of ungroundedness, a feeling that there is nothing to hang onto. Therefore people with these aspects are desperately looking for an anchor to root them in life. Moon-Saturn is the feeling of loss, the feeling that there is never enough for the self, so people with these aspects keep searching for something that will make them feel more full, whole or complete. Of course, Moon-Saturn will never find any one thing that will make them finally feel full and satisfied. That's the thing they have to accept, that they will never be totally and completely fulfilled. But you can see how that urge to feel fulfilled will spur them on to be classic sublimaters and achievers.

Now let's look at Moon-Pluto contacts. But, before I begin with Moon-Pluto, are there any questions still puzzling you?

Audience: We've been talking mostly about the major aspects to the Moon, such as the square or opposition, but can you talk more about the significance of some of the minor aspects to the Moon?

Richard: Yes, but first let me say something about the conjunction aspect. A conjunction is like two horses harnessed together pulling the same chariot, and it's very difficult to disconnect one part from the other. The planets in conjunction are welded together for life, like Siamese twins. For example, if you have the Moon conjunct Neptune, you will find it extremely hard to disassociate anything lunar from anything Neptunian. Planets in conjunction are forever intertwined in their energies, they're constantly reacting with each other. So a person who has Mars conjunct Saturn in the natal chart can never experience what Mars is like in a pure archetypal sense, because it's always contaminated with Saturn. In other words, they have a Saturnian Mars or a Martian Saturn to deal with. In actual fact, this is true for two planets in any aspect to one another, not just in the case of the conjunction. The energies represented by two planets in aspect to one another will be intertwined and interconnected, whatever the exact nature of the aspect.

The semisquare (45-degree angle) and the sesquiquadrate (135-degree angle) are two minor aspects I consider to be very important. Orbs are a matter of preference and your own choice, but I normally use quite a small orb for minor aspects, no more than one or two degrees. The semisquare seems to be an aspect of stimulation without completion. It's half a square. I feel that the square aspect represents an irresistible force coming up against an immovable object, and, as far as I'm concerned, the square is the single most dynamic aspect you can find. The square is my favorite aspect. As you know, squares usually bring together planets of the same modality but of different polarities. So a square can be between planets in two of the cardinal signs, two of the fixed signs or two mutable signs, but one of those signs will be a yang sign, and the other will be a yin sign. In a Jungian sense, a square represents an inner battle, the movement or stress that constantly goes on between what's conscious and what's unconscious. And it is this struggle or battle between conscious and unconscious forces that generates and fuels the individuation process. This is why I value my squares and would rather give up anything else in my chart. I don't want to put down the trine, but, in terms of psychological growth and evolution, trines are not necessarily so wonderful. I'm saddened by the fact that a long time ago some astrologer came along and decided that squares were an affliction, because if you see them that way, you'll turn them into something bad. Be grateful for your squares.

As I was saying, a semisquare is half a square. To use a sexual metaphor, semisquares are like foreplay without consummation—they stimulate you but don't always bring completion or follow-through. A semisquare has a nervous quality about it. It is an aspect of irritation, setting up expectations without bringing matters to completion. I wouldn't label it as either good or bad, because a semisquare can feel both stimulating and aggravating. It's an aspect that can make you feel wired. It's also anticipatory, giving a sense of constant readiness, as if one of your shoes has fallen off and you are waiting for the other shoe to follow. The semisquare can be a very creative kind of aspect, especially when it's connected with other aspects in the chart.

The sesquiquadrate—a 135-degree angle—can be understood as a square (90 degrees) plus half of a square (45 degrees). It's as if you have made a completion (the square) but the completion has led to new stimulation (the semisquare). I really like sesquiquad-

rates because they indicate that you have consummated something, but instead of relaxing after consummation as you would do
in the case of the square aspect, the sesquiquadrate signifies that
the consummation has served to stimulate you again in a new way.
It's as if each completion sets up a new incomplete. The sesquiquadrate is an aspect of constant dissatisfaction. Because it suggests a completion that creates new stimulation, the sesquiquadrate has a kind of constant hunger about it. It can't rest easily, it
must keep searching for further completion or fulfillment, and for
this reason I consider it a brilliantly creative aspect. It's also marvelously neurotic because there's no sense of ever alighting and feeling calm or settled. In comparison to both the semisquare and the
sesquiquadrate, the square is a more relaxed aspect.

If the Moon is involved in a semisquare or sesquiquadrate,
there is a constant kind of emotional hunger giving rise to a lot of
feeling and affect. I sometimes refer to this as free-floating affect
looking for a place to land and alight. A semisquare to the Moon
makes it hard to complete or to resolve feelings. With Moon sesqui-
quadrates, it's as if you have completed a feeling, but that completion serves to give you appetite for more feeling.

Audience: Can you say anything more about Moon-Neptune
aspects in general?

Richard: I believe that Moon-Neptune and Moon-Pluto contacts
present the most difficult problems in terms of the process of
breaking the umbilical cord, even more troublesome than Moon-
Uranus. Uranus is very yang, and that makes it hard to hide its
effects. Neptune and Pluto, however, are transpersonal yin planets, and by nature rather devious, hidden, murky and submerged.
Moon-Neptune often produces the fear of annihilation or the fear
of loss of boundaries, the fear that you are going to disappear into
another person, that you will be swallowed alive by someone else.
Very often, the mother or the nurturing parent has relayed many,
many double messages. Your ground is never solid or clear. I can
give you an example of the type of double message Moon-Neptune
people often get from a parent. I worked with a woman with this
aspect whose mother was a born-again Christian. When the
woman in question was a child and innocently touched herself in

"bad" places, her mother would put her hands into boiling water in order to purge the devil from her. The mother would say, "I'm doing this because I love you and want to save your soul." In other words, the mother was implying that the soul is more important than the body, and hurting her child in this way was done in the name of love. Another thing you can get with Moon-Neptune is a parent who is elusive, the parent who is never quite there. Nurturing is there one day, but not the next day. One day it's sit down and eat all your food because your mother has prepared a wonderful meal for you, and the next day she doesn't bother to cook at all. This is what I mean when I say that Moon-Neptune aspects can indicate that the ground beneath you is very shaky. Moon-Neptune will contaminate the Moon with victim-savior issues, with issues around helping, saving and rescuing. As I said before, Moon-Neptune children end up believing that they can only get nurturing if they are wounded, hurt or suffering in some way. They associate being in pain with gaining love.

I knew a little girl with the Moon conjunct Neptune in Sagittarius whose mother was a very airy person with no planets in water. The mother was frightened of feeling, and was always trying to reason with her daughter, to make her daughter be more detached and objective about things. The little girl resorted to going into a corner and digging big gouges in her arm in order to show her mother how badly she had hurt herself. It was only then that she would receive the kind of emotional sympathy and concern she needed from her mother. It had to be that extreme to get the effect she wanted. So I think there can be a definite tendency toward self-destructive behavior with Moon-Neptune, because nurturing is associated with being wounded or hurt. A mother may model Moon-Neptune to a child. She does this by being wounded in some way, or she is an alcoholic or someone who just can't cope with life. Mother may play the victim, and yet she somehow manages to manipulate everyone because she appears so hurt and vulnerable. Moon-Neptune people also have the tendency to search for the divine in everyday life, looking for the Fairy Princess in another person, or looking for another person to be Prince Charming. This can also happen with Venus-Neptune aspects. Moon-Neptune and Venus-Neptune people often find it hard to form satisfying relationships, because they keep pricing themselves out of the market. What they want is so illusory, numinous or ideal, nothing living in the physical body can ever meet their expectations. If this need for the divine is projected onto a parent, then the child is looking for a Christ-like father or Madonna-like mother figure. If you project such transpersonal archetypes onto a parent, you will be reluctant to sever the umbilical bond with that parent. It's much easier to separate from a parent who is seen as a tyrant or ogre, who is experienced as a wicked queen or harsh king, or as a devouring monster.

I've also noticed that Moon-Neptune people may have difficulty making emotional contact with other people, and even with themselves. They say, "Oh, I don't know what it is that I really need," or what they need is constantly shifting from one moment to the next. They think that loved ones should automatically be able to intuit their needs—"If you truly loved me, you would know what I need, and give it to me without my having to say anything about it; and if my needs change from moment to moment, you ought to be able to shift gears and follow me." Parents may find it hard to nurture a child born with the Moon in aspect to Neptune or with the Moon in Pisces, because the child may never really be clear about what he or she needs from them. If you sense that Moon-Neptune children are in pain and you ask them what is wrong or what they need from you, they often don't know themselves. This is probably because Neptune is one of the channels through which we tune into the collective unconscious, picking up all sorts of feelings out of the air, such as feelings of psychic pain, angst and fear—emotional states that we can't quite label or which come from God knows where. Moon-Neptune people, especially in the case of women with these aspects, often are identified with being the great savior Mother, who cuts off from her own needy child and instead gathers hurt and wounded beings around her who need nurturing or rescuing. They seem to surround themselves with wounded people as a way of avoiding having to acknowledge, face and come to terms with the hurt or wounded child within themselves. I refer to these kinds of people as "collectors of poor souls." By the way, how many of you have a Moon-Neptune aspect or the Moon in Pisces or the 12th house? Yes, many of you do. I've noticed that these kinds of placements frequently show up in the charts of astrologers. The same is probably true for Moon-Pluto.

Audience: What does one do to nurture a Moon-Neptune combination?

Richard: I thought we'd already covered that, but I'll go over it again. First of all, it helps to realize that you're never going to find someone out there in the world who is going to be able to make it all right for you. It's also important to let go of and forgive parents who have disappointed you by not fulfilling your need for a magical, transpersonal, all-encompassing wise person to nurture and care for you. Of course, letting go of that need or that projection is easier said than done. You should also realize that much of your emotional satisfaction ultimately has to come from the transpersonal realm. This could be through meditation, through yoga, music, dance—anything where you can lose yourself or surrender yourself to the great collective in some way that is not damaging to yourself or to other people. Do you see what I'm getting at? I think that anyone with strong Moon, Venus, or solar contacts to Neptune must have some form of creative self-expression through which they can tune into and channel the collective unconscious—whatever that might mean for you. For some people, this may mean a religious experience; for others, it may require long periods of solitude or turning inward. An elderly lady came to me for a consultation who had Moon conjunct Neptune and Pluto in Gemini in the 12th house. She challenged me to guess how she nurtured herself. It turns out that she has an attic room which is locked and to which she has the only key. For years and years she has been using that room to write pornography under a pseudonym. Actually, she started first by writing detective stories, and then realizing that this was not really her genre, she had a go at pornography and discovered that she loved writing it and had a real forte for it. Nobody in her family knows that she does this because her attic room is off-limits to everyone else and, as I said, she writes under a pseudonym. That's her way of earning a little pin money.

All right, let's move on to Moon-Pluto, which is a heavy-duty combination. Pluto symbolizes eros, sexuality, power, death and transformation, and when linked to the Moon, it brings these qualities into the relationship with mother or the nurturing parent. In early life, Moon-Pluto children get the message that their feelings are unacceptable and taboo. They believe that nobody is ever going to understand their deepest needs and feelings. Even worse, they fear being killed, exiled or turned into anathema should the parents find out what is really going on inside them. Accordingly, they learn to hide their feelings, or, to put it another way, they mythologize that their innermost thoughts are not acceptable and must be kept dark and hidden. I've also noticed that Moon-Pluto often indicates that the whole issue of nurturing is contaminated with eroticism, which may manifest in an incestuous relationship between the person and the nurturing parent. Please understand me, when I say incestuous, I don't necessarily mean anything explicitly sexual, just that the so-called nurturing relationship is mixed up with erotic feelings.

Power struggles can be another hallmark of Moon-Pluto. Very often the mother is seen as an ogress, a witch, a devouring negative force, someone who wants to eat them up, to suck the life force from them. The mother is seen as someone very powerful or dangerous, such as Lady Macbeth, Clytemnestra or Medea. A Moon-Pluto child usually will have a strong umbilical connection to the nurturing parent, which manifests in an intense relationship between them. Remember, the Moon is not always literally the mother; it is the parent who has been cast in the role of caretaker, and this could mean the father in some cases. In fact, for female children, daddy is the one who often carries the nurturing. Daddy carries the *mythos* of the one who is the nurturing, loving breast. Whether mother or father, the nurturing parent is seen as a source of power, and to disconnect from that power seems to carry the risk of death and dying. Staying close to mother—or the caretaking parent—feels like being swallowed or eaten up, but not being with her makes them feel frightened and bereft. You can see what I'm saying, that the relationship with mother tends to be very, very tense and troubled.

Audience: Does an 8th house Moon have the same feeling as the Moon in aspect to Pluto?

Richard: Houses describe the setting in which the dynamics of a sign or planet are carried out, and the Moon in the 8th will bring out some of the same issues as the Moon in Scorpio or in aspect to Pluto. However, the most potent manifestation of what I've been talking about will come more through the Moon in Pluto's sign or in aspect to it, rather than the Moon just being in the 8th.

There actually may be a genuine hatred between the mother/nurturing figure and the child with Moon in aspect to Pluto. Hate is a taboo thing, something that's not supposed to occur between parents and children. Now, there is bound to be trouble if a strong feeling such as hate is not acknowledged. In the Greek myth, Pluto leaps up from the underworld, grabs the maiden and takes her down below. The feeling of being devoured, consumed and ripped away is a very Plutonic kind of situation. Demeter and Kore have a Moon-Pluto type relationship, and this is why Pluto—Hades himself—is summoned to break the bond. Do any of you remember who it is that summons Pluto up from the depths to do this? In some versions of the myth it is Gaia, the goddess of the earth who calls Pluto forth; in other versions, it is Aphrodite or Venus who gets Pluto to abduct Kore. Aphrodite is another incarnation of the earth mother, so it doesn't really matter which version you consider. Aphrodite doesn't feel good about the manless mother-daughter bond existing between Demeter and Kore, so she evokes the dark god from the underworld to sever the attachment between them. Demeter then goes into deep grieving and mourning; she becomes the evil witch who casts the whole world into darkness and does not permit any more life to grow on earth.

Audience: I thought it was Zeus who summoned Pluto.

Richard: In some versions it is Zeus, but in the older tales, it's definitely an earth goddess who does the summoning. When the goddess-ruled society changed into a god-ruled society, the people who made all the big decisions got switched from goddesses to gods. So in the oldest versions of the myth, it's Gaia or Aphrodite.

In the play or film of *Amadeus*, you can see a Plutonic, devouring parent-child relationship between Mozart and his father. What normally happens in this kind of situation is that the nurturing parent never approves of the spouse chosen by the Moon-Pluto child, and wants to interfere with and intrude into the relationship. This is when Moon-Pluto children have to break the cord with the parent. There's a marvelous play by Sidney Howard called *The Silver Cord*, where you also can see a classic Moon-Pluto parent-child relationship. If you've never read it, you really should. And if you have a Moon-Pluto aspect in your chart, you should read it immediately.

I've also noticed a tendency for Moon-Pluto types to become loners. One reason for this is that, on some level, they're deeply afraid of consuming intensity and passion of their own emotional needs. They often project these feelings onto other people, and fear they'll be eaten alive by another person. In other words, they take their own desire to eat up other people or their own fears about their emotions being all-consuming, and project these onto partners or the world in general. An astrologer friend of mine who was an ex-Mother Superior of a convent did a random study of the Sun/Moon/Ascendant signs of over 200 nuns. She expected to find Virgo strong in these charts, but what she discovered was that Scorpio was the most prominent sign. Her findings didn't surprise me at all, because Scorpio often wants to transmute eros into something else. It's as if eros is too hot to handle, and they've got to put it somewhere. Maybe it's better to have a divine passion for Jesus to whom you can give your all, rather than to get too closely involved with an actual living human being. The theme of possession is familiar to Moon-Pluto. A person can literally be possessed by his or her mother or father. Some Moon-Pluto types sublimate possessiveness by actually becoming possessed by some form of art or creative expression, in which case you often see some very rich and creative activity happening. The Greeks would say that a person like this is possessed by a creative *daimon*. You are also possessed by a daimon when you fall madly in love. Those of you with Venus in aspect to Pluto will know what I'm talking about. For you, falling in love can feel like being taken over or possessed by something or someone.

Death is often an issue with Moon-Pluto. Moon-Pluto children might start asking questions about death at a very early age. If they come from a family where death is a taboo subject, they're usually not told that someone has died, but rather that the person has passed on or gone to the arms of the Great Redeemer or some euphemism like that. So Moon-Pluto children may be blocked in their desire to understand and learn about death. What happens then is that issues around death are relegated to the unconscious where they manifest in the form of dreams or in other indirect ways. How many of the Moon-Pluto people here today had heavy nightmares when you were small? Yes, you can relate to that. For Moon-Pluto children, the process of breaking the umbilical cord connection can feel very much like dying. Also, if Moon-Pluto people go into therapy, they often make a very strong transference onto the therapist, and this bond can be another one that is extremely difficult to break. Letting go is one of the hardest things for the Moon-Pluto person.

So how can Moon-Pluto types deal with all of this? It's a tough one, but the first step would be for them to acknowledge the depth and intensity of their feelings. They need to find some place in life where they can feel the powerful influences inside them, where they can touch and give expression to their daimon. Many of them go into therapy. Some even become therapists or counselors themselves, perhaps as a way of fulfilling their need to look at what is dark or hidden in life. Most people I know who work as therapists have had to go through therapy themselves as part of their training or as part of their individuation process. I would say that, in particular, Moon-Neptune and Moon-Pluto aspects bring up the kinds of issues that invite some time spent in psychotherapy. Because their issues are so deep, so painful and often so buried, they need a guide to help them through the labyrinth of the psyche. Of course, not everyone needs to take this path, and there are several other avenues to follow which could lead to further growth and individuation. Some take a mystical or religious path, while others may develop their creativity as a way of constructively harnessing their obsessive drives and working through the more difficult stuff they carry around inside. A-not-so-useful way to deal with Moon-Pluto is to embark on a never-ending search to find another person to play the part of the godlike or ogrelike nurturing parent. It saddens me to see people who are perpetually hunting for friends and partners to cast into these models. Some Moon-Pluto types attempt to do this through guru worshipping. The guru of the moment is not just a teacher, or a leader, or a mother or father figure, but is someone who is seen as divine and much bigger than life. I'm not saying that doing this is always a bad thing; it's an experience and one way that Moon-Neptune or Moon-Pluto people find to satisfy their inner urges and drives.

There are a number of clues or signals to look for in a chart that point to problems to do with breaking the umbilical cord connection. One of them is when the Moon is in the 12th house. I understand the 12th house to be an area where we collect matter that is not acceptable on the conscious level. I call the 12th house the closet, because it is where we put those things which we prefer to keep out of sight. Placements in the 12th often symbolize drives, urges, complexes and feelings that we keep locked away in our psychic closet. Of course, the 12th house has other representations besides this one. It is also an avenue or channel that leads to the collective unconscious; dreamers, prophets and creative people usually have something strong affecting the 12th house. But for now I wish to dwell on the 12th house as the place where we store unacknowledged pain left over from early nurturing problems. This is especially true if the ruler of the 4th or 10th house happens to be placed in the 12th; if this is the case, you can be pretty sure that mommy and daddy issues have been repressed into the unconscious because they are too painful to recognize. Another way you might see repressed material from early bonding is if you find Cancer on the cusp of the 12th. This could also apply to Leo on the 12th, although Leo there suggests that stuff around father is an important concern. Capricorn on the 12th suggests problems with the parent who represents the authority figure, rather than the nurturing one. The Sun or Saturn in the 12th are other indicators of stuff around the parents locked away in the closet.

Parental issues are also important if the Sun, Moon or Saturn are in the 7th house. As you know, the 7th is wide open for projection, because it designates "the other"—those qualities and traits that we feel belong to other people and not to ourselves. The 7th is where we project parts of our own nature onto the outer world; it's where we feel we have no control over what happens to us, and describes what we expect to meet through the outer world. When considering the chart in terms of parental stuff, you should also examine the 4th and 10th houses, especially if you find Uranus, Neptune or Pluto—the transpersonal planets—in either of these houses, or if one of the signs they rule—Aquarius, Pisces or

Scorpio—falls on either cusp. I hope that as astrologers you would not make a judgment based solely on one placement. You need to accumulate lots of clues and get affirmations from many places in the chart before you label something an issue or a serious situation.

Umbilical cord connection problems and other bonding difficulties can be seen if the Moon is involved in a tricky major configuration such as a T-cross, grand cross, or yod formation, particularly if the Moon is the focal point of these complex planetary patterns. For instance, if you have Mars opposite Venus, and the Moon is the planet that receives the square from both sides, or if the Moon is the focal point or apex of a yod—that is, the planet that quincunxes the other two in sextile. The focal planet in these types of configurations—which I call "out-of-balance major configurations"—is the planet that receives the most stress. If the Moon is the focal point of a T-cross, regardless of what house it is in, it means that the person with this in his or her chart has borne the brunt of any tension or conflict between the parents described by the two opposing planets that square the Moon. If the Moon is the focal point of a yod, then it may indicate that the parents colluded with one another to make the child the odd one out, to turn the child into the one in the family who is labeled as sick, weird, neurotic or disturbed. If the Moon is an important part of a major difficult configuration, you can safely deduce that there was a lot of drama or conflict generated by parental issues. As soon as you see a focal-point Moon, you would be right to start wondering about what heavy family demons this person is carting around. If a woman with this kind of configuration insists very strongly that she does not wish to be a mother, you can be pretty certain that this decision has been influenced by early bonding problems. As a general rule, if a woman's Moon is caught up in a stressful, major configuration, it almost invariably makes a big issues out of whether or not to have children. A man with a difficultly configurated Moon is likely to project his mother issues onto other people. If he has not completed his umbilical work, he will still be looking for a divine mother somewhere out there in the world. A problematic Moon in a man's chart suggests an enormous maternal-type anima waiting to find a target to which it can attach itself. No

matter how he comes across in relationship, what he's really looking for is mama.

You should also look to see if the Moon is a singleton in the
chart. By singleton, I mean that it is the only one of its kind in a
category—for instance, if it is the only planet in an earth sign or in a
fire sign, or the only planet in a mutable sign, or the only planet in
a personal sign, or the only yin or yang planet in the chart, or the
only planet in a hemisphere. Any singleton planet represents an
exaggerated need. Ten puppies go for a bowl of milk, and the
singleton planet is the one that gets there first, elbows out the
other puppies and drinks all the milk. Singleton planets tend to
suck up and control lots of psychic energy. Breaking of the umbilical connection with the mother will be a big issue if a singleton
Moon appears in someone's chart.

Audience: Have you found a correlation between food issues and
Moon-Pluto aspects?

Richard: Yes, because Moon-Pluto gives a deep hunger which can
lead into addictive forms of behavior. People with Moon-Pluto
aspects need to live a deeply erotic life, and since most of us are not
programmed to live this way, they look for some other means to
deaden their hunger or ease their pain. That's what addictions do;
they're an attempt to deaden hunger and pain.

I think we have mooned ourselves out for the time being, so
let's shift psychic gears now. We will spend the rest of the afternoon "workshopping," and I'll give you guidelines for doing this.
First of all, you should form yourselves into groups of five or six
people. You can be with whomever you want, but it would be
better not to be in a group with someone you're very intimate with.
In other words, if you're here with a spouse, a lover, a parent or a
child, you should split up and join different groups. You can be in
a group with a friend or a buddy, but it's better not to be with
someone with whom you have big emotional agendas.

The issues I think you might want to explore are some of the
things we have talked about up till now. For instance, what are
your family myths in terms of nurturing? Have you worked
through these myths? This is just a suggestion—you can go in any
direction you want. You can begin with the chart and go to your

own experience, or you can start from experience and go to your chart. But don't do whole chart interpretations, just stick to lunar issues—the 4th and 10th houses, the Moon and her aspects.

People in the groups are meant to act as mirrors. You're not to play counselor, you're not to play astrologer, you're not to read or interpret anyone else's chart. Instead, the idea is that you are an active, interested listener. You might ask questions like "How do you think the Moon-Uranus square in your chart is operating?" or "How do you experience your 12th house Moon?" or "I hear you talking about the fact that you felt emotionally disconnected from your mother, and I was wondering if you have worked through that?" I warn you once more: This is not an opportunity to play counselor or chart interpreter. There are a lot of skilled astrologers and counselors in this group, and I'm inviting you not to work in that way. I'm inviting you to be the neutral mirror and simply reflect things back to other people. This will give them a safe space in which to explore themselves in their own way, so that they won't feel driven or pushed in any direction. Try exploring those issues we've discussed that have triggered you off. While lecturing, I've been seeing lightbulbs popping on all over the room. What things have touched or triggered you the most? These may be the issues you want to share and receive feedback on. You might say to the members of your group, "Gee, I have Moon square Neptune and I don't think anything Richard said fits with my relationship with my mother." Then a group member may ask, "Did your mother give you double messages?" or "Might it have been your father who picked up on your Moon-Neptune more than your mother?" Then you might answer, "Oh no, it was my grandmother. She was the nurturing figure in my life." The aim is to ground your experiences, to ground those things that we have talked about in a very heady or intellectual way. Any questions?

Audience: I'm not clear. Do you want us to look at the chart of the person who is speaking or not?

Richard: If the person speaking wishes to share his or her chart, then look at it by all means. But see if you can look at it without commenting on it. I know that's awfully hard. Let me put it this way—comment on it without judging it. Please don't scream out,

"Oh my God, look at that afflicted Moon, you poor thing!" That's not what I want you to do. You can, however, comment on a person's Moon by saying, "I notice that your Moon is a singleton in your chart, that it's the only planet in water. How do you think you experience that?" Or you may notice a close Moon-Mars square in a chart, and you might want to ask the person if anger is an issue in relationship or in other situations involving nurturing. The person could reply, "What do you mean, I never get angry! You're not my therapist, don't push it." And then you might respond back with "Well, a connection like this shows in your chart, so I think it might be something you'll want to think more about."

PART TWO

REALIZING THE SELF

EROS AND PROJECTION
IN ADULT RELATIONSHIPS

Now that we've established the basics – solved all our family problems, and cut our umbilical cords – we're ready to embark on the subject of so-called adult-adult relationships. Questions we'll be posing are ones like, "What is eros and what does it have to do with relationships?" and also "What is this thing called love?" What is love and what do we mean by it in terms of relationships between adults? Should love necessarily lead to marriage? How do we choose our partners? We'll be passing the ball back and forth about all this. Let's start with some of your questions.

Audience: Can you describe the dynamics of projection in a little more detail?

Richard: Jung felt that projections were quite natural to us, and that we tend to do more projecting in the morning of our lives, but as we move toward the afternoon and evening, hopefully we have individuated enough so that we can at least begin to see the projections we put onto other people. For me, a very simplified definition of projection is that we look outside of ourselves for material or qualities that for some reason are unawakened, unintegrated or unacceptable within ourselves. We disown parts of ourselves and then see these parts in other people. We can project both negative and positive stuff. Positive qualities in ourselves that we have not yet developed may be the same qualities we admire in other people; negative things we don't like in ourselves will also be projected onto other people and put out there onto the world. I believe that the relationships we make in our life aren't haphazard or random – they just don't happen by accident. Projection has a lot to do with whom we draw to us.

Bear in mind that there are certain sensitive areas in the chart that are more likely to be projected than other bits of our charts. For instance, in our society, women are not supposed to have a Mars. So what do they do with Mars? Well, they are meant to marry him. They're supposed to marry Mr. Mars and live happily ever after. For all of you women who don't want to do martial arts, you can honor Mars by marrying a boxer. No, I jest. But I do believe that there are certain areas socially and certain areas within each family that are very open to projection. It's not unusual for men to project their Moon and probably their Venus as well. Women are more likely to project the Sun and Mars. The whole issue of projection is further complicated by the fact that we live in a linear, monotheistic society. In other words, God is One, God is perfect. We are made in the image of God, and therefore the implication is that we should be one and perfect (and by implication, that we should be male). But when we look at the astrological chart, we see that it is polytheistic, or at least it's polymorphic. It's made up of parts. Each of the gods and goddesses has his or her own little niche within the chart, so how do we deal with the fact that we are really one person made up of different parts? One way that we deal with this is to project parts of ourselves out onto others. Rather than acknowledging the existence of a whole cast of characters within us, and instead of owning the fact that all the dramatis personae are contained within one's own self, we look for other people to enact parts of ourselves.

Audience: Don't you think that some people are too hard on themselves?

Richard: Yes, people often dump on themselves for not living up to some kind of perfect idealized picture of themselves. They think that there must be something terribly wrong with them if they haven't found their ideal other, or if they haven't made a relationship or marriage work in the way they dreamed it would. Not only should we be easier on ourselves, but we should be easier on our relationships as well. We need to be more forgiving, especially of our parents. When you integrate your inner mother, you are better able to forgive yourself and your loved ones for being less than perfect.

Audience: I've noticed that there can be certain archetypal dilemmas in a chart that play right into the phenomenon of projection. For instance, my chart is very fiery, but I also have a few planets in earth. I often find myself owning and acting out my fiery side, and attracting other people to carry earth for me – they might help me get better organized or they are willing to look after my mundane and everyday needs.

Richard: There is also the air and water dilemma. Is there any way of resolving within yourself the fact that air needs distance and objectivity in order to find itself, while water seeks closeness and merging? What in the world do we do with this inner tension? Let's say this dilemma is in a man's chart and shows up in squares between planets in air signs and planets in water signs, or by something like a Moon-Uranus conjunction. In our society, it's likely that he would identify with his yang or masculine energy and project the watery, feminine part onto women in his life.

Audience: I've also noticed that people project their missing elements, that is, they import or attract people into their lives who bring in the nature of an element that might be missing or weak in their own charts.

Richard: Missing elements in the chart are absolutely crucial to look at because, as you say, they represent areas that are very likely to be projected. Since we can't get hold of that element in ourselves, we look for it out in the world, or, in some cases, we are compulsively driven to develop that element in ourselves. Michelangelo had no planets in earth, and he is a perfect example of what I'm saying because he constantly was seeking to give shape to the ideal form in his creative work. When he was asked to define the meaning of his work, he replied that his task was to realize God, and to find the form hidden within the stone. You'll find many brilliant writers with no planets in air, such as Tolstoy and Sir Walter Scott. Thomas Jefferson was probably the most intellectual of the American presidents, and he had no air in his chart. You'll find an enormous number of philosophers with nothing in air. Joan of Arc had no fire in her chart, and yet she displayed enormous daring and courage. Some people may end up being more creative with their missing element than the person who has that element strong in the natal chart. Beethoven had no water in his chart, and yet his music surged with feeling. When one critic described his work as cold, Beethoven replied by saying something like, "Whoever has the ears to hear my music, which God in his mercy has forbidden me to hear, will know that every note has been written in blood and tears." Some people display true genius in the sphere associated with their missing element. Seen in this way, a missing element is like a gift from the gods. It seems like a paradox, because there can be something so wonderful coming out of what appears to be nothing. And yet, there is often a great deal of pain and suffering involved in trying to give expression to a missing element. It comes from such a deep part inside of us that it takes real effort and struggle to bring it to the surface.

Audience: I've noticed a correlation with missing earth and weight problems.

Richard: Yes, maybe it's because people with no earth don't know when they're full. Some people with a lack of planets in earth often have problems around sexuality. It's as if they don't know what turns them on, and they don't know when they're really satisfied. So there's a tendency to either do too much or too little in terms of your missing element. I sometimes compare this to a switch or faucet that can only go all the way on or all the way off, and the person seems to have very little control over the situation. There's none of the little gradations you normally get when there are a number of planets in an element. When something is not properly integrated, it often surges out of the unconscious in a way that can feel overwhelming, as if there's no vessel to put that energy into. If you have no water in your chart, you may be disconnected from your feelings, but when these do come out, they explode in a very extreme way, perhaps even giving rise to a nervous breakdown. I have the image of water building up behind an earthen dam, and eventually enough water pressure builds up to cause the dam to break. I have a friend who is a psychotherapist, and he has a dominant air function and no water in his chart. He doesn't know about astrology or that his chart shows no water, but he says that his feeling function is entirely undeveloped. He told me that he didn't think he ever had a feeling in his entire life. And yet, he is marvelous at evoking feelings in his clients. Interestingly enough, he has had two nervous breakdowns in his life, and he describes these as times when the feeling function came up and overwhelmed him.

Audience: Missing elements must play an important part in terms of the kinds of relationships we seek.

Richard: Yes, this is true in spite of what traditional astrology has to say about compatability. Classical astrology would say that if you had a load of planets in Libra, you would be attracted to Geminis or Aquarians, but I haven't found this to be the case. The thing that eroticizes relationships is when somebody comes along who seems to manifest the qualities that are weak or missing in your own chart. Of course, living with this situation is a whole other thing. The most erotic relationships occur when unlike seeks unlike, not when like seeks like. The ancient Greek god Eros was depicted as a prime creative force in the universe because he created the universe by bringing together chaos and matter, two very different things. The 7th house is traditionally called the house of the notself as well as the house of marriage. It's as if we want to marry what isn't in us. In relationships based on this kind of projection, we feel attracted to the person, but we also may feel anger and repulsion at our mate because of the way he or she differs from us. This is one reason why the house of marriage is also known as the house of open enemies.

The other day I was explaining my theory about personal, social and universal houses and signs, and what we've been saying about missing elements can also be applied here. If you have no planets in social signs—Leo through to Scorpio for instance—you might find yourself attracted to someone with many planets in social signs. Queen Victoria had no planets in the social signs, and she married Prince Albert whose dominant orientation was the social realm. He helped her to perform the social function, and in this sense, their relationship was symbiotic. When he was alive, Victoria seemed like a normal, social, outgoing person. But when he died, she retreated into her packed 12th house, from which she never really emerged again. Howard Hughes also had a weak social function. In his youth, he was a great womanizer who went out with very glamorous and public-type women. But when the relationship would fall apart, he turned back into being a recluse. You may be able to live comfortably in a symbiotic relationship for quite a long time, but the crunch comes when something happens that destroys that relationship. You are then left on your own without the person who carried your projections, and you may have no tools of your own with which to replace what has been taken away.

Audience: What if you have no planets in water signs in your chart, but you have many planets in water houses? Do the planets in water houses make up for the lack of water signs?

Richard: No, I don't think a busy water house makes up for a lack of planets in water. To borrow from the language of the theater, I compare houses to arenas or stage settings: each house is a set in which certain actions take place. If you have no planets in an element—even if you have planets in houses associated with that element—there is nobody around to play the role of that element. Besides, I don't believe that anything can really replace anything else. Consider the human body, for example. If one part ceases to function, the other parts tend to gang up to try to compensate for the malfunction, but it's still not the same thing. If you lose an eye, your depth perception will be completely cockeyed in the beginning, but eventually your remaining eye will adjust to do the work of two eyes. And yet, it's not the same as having two eyes.

Audience: What if the Ascendant is the only thing you have in a particular element?

Richard: If your Ascendant is the only placement you have in a particular element, you may feel fated or called upon to play a role that you inherently don't feel suited to play.

Audience: I'm confused about something. According to Jungian typology, fire (intuition) is the opposite of earth (sensation), and air (thinking) is the opposite of water (feeling), and yet in astrology, fire and air form opposites, and water and earth form opposites.

Richard: I think it's a mistake to try to force a marriage between psychological terminology and astrological terminology. There are many amazing parallels, but you'll run into trouble if you rigidly try to translate Jungian typology into astrological elements. There's time for one more quick question.

Audience: How do you feel about retrograde planets?

Richard: I do think that you might feel more introverted by nature if you have a good number of retrograde planets, but I don't think anything is lessened by being retrograde, and I would not put a value judgment on a retrograde planet. Frankly, I'm not so interested in retrogradation, but what does interest me is the relative speed at which a planet is moving. I've noticed that a stationary planet in the birth chart has a very powerful effect on the psyche, and I have more to say about this in a later lecture.

What is This Thing Called Love?

I now want to address the question "What is this thing called love?" We'll be putting love under the microscope, and comparing our society's present-day concept of love with the way the ancient Greeks understood it. Just look at how nervous the majority of you get when I say the word "love," as if it were a dirty word. All I have to do is to announce that we're going to look deeply into love, and immediately papers start rattling, feet start shuffling, and a lot of shaking hands reach out to pour glasses of water. This all goes to show that love is a loaded word; we're even afraid to say it in our society. I'd like to start our exploration of love by reviewing how the ancient Greeks looked at it. It's my belief that they had a better intuitive understanding of the fact that love wears many different faces than we do in our society. Today we associate love mostly with the idea of *romantic love*, and we generally believe that everyone should experience it, and also that being in love should lead to marriage. We have grown up believing in romantic love and marriage, perhaps never realizing that, historically speaking, modern Western men and women are almost unique in perpetuating the myth that a man and a woman should fall in love, get married, live happily ever after, and that the romantic, erotic intensity that was there when they first started courting is something that ought to continue on forever and ever. It's a kind of fairy tale, like "Cinderella." We've been fed on Gothic romances, beginning all the way back with courtly romance and the tradition of the troubadours and the minstrels, through to the Brontë sisters and *Jane Eyre* and *Wuthering Heights*, through to Thomas Hardy and *Tess of the d'Urbervilles*, through to Scarlett and Rhett in *Gone with the Wind*, right up to the kinds of things that you see today on soap operas or you read in the pulp magazines and books that come under the heading of women's romance stories. Our society's concept of love obviously appeals to something very basic in us, but I want to emphasize that this is something really quite unique to our own time and place. It is not universal. It's true that every society has its ideas about romance and what that means, but very few societies actually expect you to marry the object of your romantic longings.

I imagine that some of you have read *The Road Less Traveled*[1] by M. Scott Peck. It's a good book and you should take a look at it. One point he clearly makes is that in order to learn to love somebody, you first have to fall out of love with that person. This notion may seem paradoxical to those of us who carry around the ideal that romantic love means falling in love with someone and consummating it in marriage, after which it's supposed to be this pink cloud of bliss for the rest of our natural lives. This simply is not the case. Recently I saw an ad for a movie that really turned my stomach. The ad showed a picture of the two stars of the film in a kind of romantic beckoning pose toward one another. The caption underneath read something like, "Only once in your life will you meet that one person who changes you forever." It seems to me that our society's idea of romantic love and marriage has been mixed up with or contaminated by the Christian concept of salvation. The caption in the movie advertisement could just as well be referring to Jesus from the point of view of a charismatic Christian. In short, I believe we have confused *personal* love with *interpersonal* love and with *transpersonal* love. There is a love that is quite personal, a love that is interpersonal, and a love that is transpersonal. The trouble starts when we mix these up into a kind of potpourri, a stew in which we expect all levels of love to happen simultaneously in one relationship.

Let's examine how the ancient Greeks understood love. Of course, they didn't have the word love as we know it. They referred to love in various ways, and one word they used for it was *epithemia*. In colloquial American English, the closest word to epithemia is the word "horniness." To the Greeks, epithemia represented what man had in common with the animals: an instinctual urge toward touching, caressing, that expressed itself as an inner tension in the body that needed to be relieved. There was nothing romantic or even very erotic about it. Epithemia was

---

[1]M. Scott Peck, *The Road Less Traveled* (New York: Simon and Schuster, 1988).

accepted as natural and never judged, and there was hardly any morality associated with it. The Greeks were really saying that the body has its own drives, its own needs and desires that should be honored. Archetypally speaking, I connect epithemia with the sign of Taurus, which I believe is the fundamental sign of sex (not Scorpio as many of you might think). Taurus is the fleshly sign, the sign of indiscriminate sensuality, as I would call it. Taurus is very primitive (remember, I'm speaking in terms of archetypes, so you Taureans out there don't have to identify personally with all this, unless you want to or you think it fits). Freud had four planets including his Sun in the sign of Taurus and he was obsessed with sex. He said that we are all born polymorphous perverse, which means we are all born with the potential to be turned on by anything. The association of love and sex with polymorphous perversity is not only indicative of Freud's own Taurean qualities, but also encapsulates the views of the society in which he lived. Freud was a middle-class Jewish man living in Vienna in the 19th century, and his choice of the phrase polymorphous perverse says a lot about the typical Victorian attitude toward sex and epithemia. In any case, it was a problem for Freud, and a good thing, too, because it led him to establish some very basic building blocks of psychological thinking. Labeling epithemia as perverse also reveals the attitude of Judeo-Christianity toward Aphrodite, the goddess who personified lust and who is most closely associated with the sign of Taurus. In actual fact, the Greek gods and goddesses never really fell in love. They were not capable of doing so. Aphrodite, for instance, had many sexual encounters with both gods and mortals, but you couldn't call it love in the same sense as we use the word. In most cases, Aphrodite, Zeus, Ares, Apollo, and other Greek deities were motivated by epithemia, by an innate drive that says, "I want, I desire, and my desire is a natural thing that should be fulfilled." If you look into earlier incarnations of the Greek Aphrodite—such as Inanna, Ishtar, Astarte and other Middle Eastern love goddesses— you'll find that she is even more primitive and demanding of her right to explore her body through sex and masturbation.

So Taurus, the first earth sign, is indiscriminate. In fact, all the first four signs (the personal signs) are indiscriminate, and relate to a kind of primeval childlike state that is actually quite naive. I connect both Aries and Taurus with survival, and Taurus specifically with survival through the awareness of the senses. Children can have everything they need in the world, but they'll still die if they're never handled, caressed or touched. Experiments were done with war orphans in Nazi Germany, in which some of these children were picked up and handled on a regular daily basis, while others were never touched. Almost all of those who were never handled died. You can see this same need for touch in animals, but in the case of animals, we call it grooming. It isn't just sex. If you watch animals, you'll see that they constantly lick and fondle each other. Just observe a group of monkey for a while. It's even more interesting to watch a group of humans watching a group of monkeys, and you'll see how the whole epithimial, Taurean part of our nature has been relegated to the shadow. Judeo-Christianity seems to want no part of this area of life. Aphrodite is a banished goddess, there is no room for her. Judeo-Christianity believes that even in the form of Mary Magdalene, womenkind carry sin and tempt men into evil. The Garden of Eden story, which reflects the fall of man, points the blame at Eve, labeling her as the carrier of epithemia. Even today, in many fundamentalist Moslem societies, women must keep their hair and body covered. Now, if women excite men, why shouldn't men be made to walk around covering up their eyes? Oh, no, it's the woman who is seen as the culprit, as the one who incites a man to lust.

Modern Western society (and I include Islam in this as well) has a very distorted view of the whole function of epithemia, and therefore of the whole Taurean function. Christianity doesn't know what to do with this aspect of love at all, except to urge us all to sublimate it. I touched on this the other day when I was speaking about addictions. The Venusian type of addiction is related to the fact that we are hungry to be touched, to be held and caressed. Look around the room we're in, and you'll see how everybody is spaced a safe distance from each other. If we were an African tribal group sitting here or a bunch of lemurs (from whom we are not so far away descended), most of the room would be empty and everybody would be piled in a heap in the corner. In the late 60's and the 70's, there was something called group grope therapy, where people rediscovered their bodies and their need to touch and be touched. Because our attitude toward epithemia (the basic, archetypal Taurean force) is so distorted, the three other forms of love about which the Greeks spoke—*philia, eros,* and *agape*—are also open to distortion. Our pleasure-seeking, consumerist society is rife with sublimation. If you're feeling anxious or alone, television and magazine commercials tell you that you would feel much more satisfied and complete if you were to purchase a certain make of car or if you would only change your brand of cigarettes. Have you noticed how many cigarette ads use sensuality (Taurus) to sell their product, or show people smoking in a very beautiful outdoor setting? These ads summon up Aphrodite or Gaia, the earth goddess herself, and are almost saying that if you're lonely, lost and looking for some kind of contact, you can make up for it by smoking a cigarette. America is the archetypal consumer society, with the ideology that the way to be safe and comfortable is to acquire more and more. According to Freud, our earliest sense of pleasure comes through the mouth. Isn't it interesting how many addictions – such as food, alcohol and drugs – are connected with the mouth? What we would really like to be doing is kissing, sucking, biting or nibbling, but we're often cut off from these things because they aren't considered the acceptable thing to do. So we find substitute gratifications that can lead on to addiction. Have you ever watched animals getting acquainted? They get right down to basics, don't they? Compare this with the dance that humans do when they first meet one another.

Audience: I wanted to point out that when we touch people, we often say excuse me.

Richard: Yes, it's as if you've done a bad thing. Have you ever watched people in a crowded elevator? It's absolutely amazing, everybody standing there rigid, nobody looking at anything. Instead of going, "Wow, look at all the energy in here!" everyone is thinking, "When is this going to end?"

Audience: The rules of body language are very different in the Middle East, where they'll cram as many people as possible into an elevator and even leave a bit of clothing outside the door as it shuts.

Richard: Yes, every society has its own particular variations on the rules. In the Middle East or Egypt, for example, men can touch each other in public, women can touch each other in public, but men and women — even if they are married — don't touch each other in public. It's wonderful in Greece to watch the Greek sailors walking down the road holding hands or with their arms around each other. And you can see the Greek girls, lines of them with their arms intertwined. We have our own taboos in our society. Women are allowed to touch each other, and men can touch women, but men can't touch men. Jung once said that we tend to feel that everybody is either like we are or should be. I love to watch how shocked many Americans are when visiting the Middle East and seeing, for the first time, men walking down the street holding hands, kissing and dancing with one another. Of course, it's also fun to watch people from India or the Middle East who come to America or Western Europe, and go into shock when they see men and women handling each other in public. In Russia, the men kiss each other on the mouth. My family are Russian Jews, and I remember my father and brother seeing me off at the airport with all this hugging and kissing, and all the white, Anglo-Saxon Protestants wondering what in the hell was going on. Once I was at Frankfurt airport, and some sheiks in their white robes were being met by two German businessmen. The sheiks swept along the concourse and met these two very neat and proper Germans with a whole lot of hugging, kissing, patting and pinching. The two Germans were in total shock, as if their lives would never be the same again.

The ancient Greeks believed that the urges of the body were a good thing, not something evil. Notice how the beautiful story of the Garden of Eden has been twisted into the fall of man. And the fall of man is associated with the awakening of epithemia.

Audience: And it was all Eve's fault.

Richard: Yes, and it was all Eve's fault. Women have been living with that burden in Christian society for 2,000 years, so I can understand why they might feel schizoid. On the one hand, women hear that if you want to nab a man and live the great romantic dream, you need to be slender, beautiful, alluring and tempting; on the other hand, women who act that way are considered to be whores. According to Christianity, women are the daughters of Eve, full of sin and evil. Of course, when I speak of Christianity, I'm not referring to the teachings of Christ, which were very, very different. I'm talking about the teaching of the Christian fathers coming down from Paul, who obviously had a bad problem and should have been in intensive psychotherapy. St. Augustine and Thomas Aquinas should have joined him, because, in my opinion, they were all sick men who, in the name of Christianity, labeled natural bodily needs as evil. In terms of their way of thinking, Aphrodite is a consort of the devil. But I believe that we all pay dearly for the loss of the goddess—especially women, who live in a schizophrenic-making society, where no matter what they do, they are accused of getting it wrong with men. Judeo-Christianity has us believe that the archetypal feminine consists of two kinds of women, the madonna and the whore. I can't tell you the number of men I've talked to in this day and age who told me that they didn't marry their girlfriends because they had slept with them. In other words, the kind of woman who allows you to seduce her is not the kind of woman you should marry.

Another belief about epithemia is that it's something childish which we should outgrow. Freud concedes that polymorphous perversity is natural in a certain stage of primitive infancy, but that we are meant to develop beyond and grow out of this stage. It's not long ago that doctors and psychologists were saying that masturbation causes insanity. You see it over and over again, this idea that the pleasuring of the body equals sin. The Greeks had some stories that dealt with epithemia. I want to tell you the one about Apollo and Daphne. Apollo was the Sun god and Daphne was a very beautiful river nymph, a virgin lusted after by many of the male gods. (In fact most of the male gods lusted after anything that would stand still long enough to be lusted after!) Apollo chased Daphne, and although she ran very quickly, he was the god of light and air and was fast enough to catch her. Apollo pleaded with her to turn around to see who was chasing her, but she wouldn't. Just as he was about to reach out and grab her, Daphne called upon her father Peneius for help. At that moment, Peneius changed her into a laurel tree. You can see a beautiful sculpture of this by Bernini in Rome, which depicts Apollo just reaching out and touching Daphne as her hair is turning into laurel leaves and her toes are turning into roots and her arms changing into branches. From then on, Apollo was always seen wearing a laurel wreath. And later, when the Olympic games were held in honor of Apollo, the winners were crowned with laurel wreaths. The myth of Daphne and Apollo conveyed a number of messages to the Greeks. One of these was that if you denied epithemia (which is what Daphne did by running from being touched), you were denying the power of nature and you would then be turned into something that was not human anymore. Daphne never turned around to see that it was the god of light who was chasing her, which conveys the Greek belief that if you deny epithemia—your basic, instinctual bodily needs—you are denying the awakening of consciousness that the god of light would bring to you. Another thing this tale points out is that the undifferentiated daughter tied umbilically to her father cannot become fully human. In other words, because Daphne turned to her father for help rather than looking around to see who was chasing her, she never had the chance to separate from her father and become a person in her own right. Instead, she ends up as a tree, something less than human.

A similar theme is touched upon in the story of Odysseus and Circe. On his way back to Ithaca, Odysseus encountered Circe, a marvelous representation of the devouring, negative, frightening anima that men carry around inside themselves. Circe was a sorceress who used her sexuality to enchant Odysseus's crew of sailors and turn them into pigs. Like the myth about Daphne, this story also suggests that unintegrated epithemia reduces us to something less than human. Later, the Puritans would deal with all this by saying that you shouldn't feel lust at all. My definition of a Puritan, by the way, is someone who is afraid that somebody else out there might be having a good time. The United States carries a huge Puritan shadow, which keeps raising itself again and again out of the collective unconscious of this country. You can see this in the "born-again" movement, and in people like Jerry Falwell. We learned in our history storybooks that the Puritans had to leave England because they were severely persecuted there. This is wrong, this is not what really happened. In actual fact, the Puritans had to leave England because they were trying to turn all of England around to their way of thinking. They were insisting that everyone must have the same values as they had, so naturally things got rather hot for them and it's then that they had to flee

England to establish the way of life they wanted in a new land, to create a *new* England in America.

What I am talking about then is the distortion of epithemia, a distortion of the natural urge of Taurus and Aphrodite, a distortion of Venus's natural urge for touching, sensuality and closeness. The fundamental drive of Venus is to reach out to the "not-self." Venus is the desire to connect with that which is not the self. On the level of epithemia, Venus is very much like Aphrodite. Venus craves pleasure and touch, and that means smelling, tasting, feeling and hearing all of those things that make you feel good, including finding pleasure in your own body. Animals are naturally sexual, and they know it. Children are also naturally sexual, but parents and society do a pretty good job educating them into distorting sexuality. As children, we learn to repress, deny or sublimate sexuality. When we deny the needs of our body, we sublimate these needs into drinking too much, smoking too much, eating too much, rather than allowing ourselves the kind of comfort and healing that can happen when we touch the body of another person, or when we are lovingly touched. We make our bodies sick by literally disconnecting the body from some of its most basic needs. Sickness and ill-health, in many cases, can be understood as Gaia's and Aphrodite's revenge on us for not listening to what our bodies need. Another thing we do is to confuse passion with romance by trying to meld them both together. Before I go on, do you have any questions or comments about what we've covered so far?

Audience: Are you saying that one of the things Venus represents is the desire to merge with something other than the self?

Richard: Yes, Venus is the awakening to the idea that we are separate and out of this comes the desire to heal our separateness by merging with another. On a very primitive level, the Taurean side of Venus is the desire of the body to be merged with the mother in the womb. The Libran side of Venus, however, is the desire to connect with the aesthetic or idealized other, which is closer to the Greek idea of *philia*. Philia is a concept that I associate primarily with the sign of Leo. You'll recall that I consider Leo to be the first of the social signs, and it represents the excited awakening to the existence of other people in the world. Aries awakens us to our own self, and Sagittarius awakens us to the universal self, but Leo awakens us to our social self.

I'll explain this another way. Aries is the fiery enthusiasm that comes when we discover that we exist. Leo has the same kind of excited awakening, but in the case of Leo, it is the excitement that comes when we discover that there are other people in the world. The awakening associated with Leo depends, however, on our going through the Cancerian process of cutting the umbilical cord. If we haven't broken the umbilical bond, then we can't get to philia. On an archetypal level, Leo is the joy, enthusiasm and excitement of discovering the existence of an "other." Just as epithemia is a Taurean or Venus-Aphrodite kind of love, philia is an Apollo kind of love. Philia is solar love, a love based on consciousness. It's no accident that we connect Leo with the Sun, and that we connect the Sun with consciousness and ego-awareness. "Who I am," says the Sun, "is someone distinct from other people." This is the true beginning of the process of individuation. It's interesting that the sign before Leo is Moon-ruled Cancer, which represents the mother and the umbilical cord that we must sever in order to get to Leo. I'm not sure how many of us ever completely cut the cord, or to what degree we succeed in cutting it. Hanging on to the umbilical connection means that we continue to hang on to mommy and daddy, and keep carrying the burden of the family myth. People who don't cut the cord don't want to give up their umbilical connection or their basic ground, and yet they still want to have love and romance as well. So they fantasize about love, they watch the soap operas, and think that if they were bigger, shorter, smarter, stronger, blonder or darker, then this wonderful thing called love would happen to them. Remember Daphne, she couldn't get beyond the umbilical issues with her father and therefore became less than what she was.

Philia basically means friendship. In my mind Leo has more to do with friendship than Aquarius, the sign we normally associate with it. Leo has to do with philia, because Leo-love involves finding someone special, finding that person who fills your heart with love. The Greeks divided the idea of love into two parts, the lover and the beloved. The lover was called the *eratos*, and the beloved was the *eromenos*. The lover and the beloved had two separate roles, and it was the role of the eratos to be the ideal toward which the eromenos aspired. In other words, the lover served as a source of inspiration to the beloved. Beatrice inspired Dante to write his great work, even though he only met her twice in his life. The Greeks would have recognized this as the classic connection between an eratos and an eromenos. It doesn't matter that Dante and Beatrice never had a relationship with one another—she is still able to light the fire in the other. Leonine, philial love is a fiery love just as epithemia is an earthly love. Even today, writers, poets and musicians often dedicate their work to someone they love, as if that love is the inspiration that frees their creativity and enables them to blossom fully into themselves. The beloved's sense of self-worth is enhanced by the fact that he or she is worthy of being loved by someone who is felt to be so wonderful. In this way, the beloved can grow and improve as a person. If you look closely at it, one of the things that accompanies falling in love is the feeling that I love who I am when I'm with you, and I love who I think I may be when I'm with you. I don't believe that you can separate epithemia from philia, or to put it another way, philia isn't possible without epithemia. Many people would like to skip epithemia and move right on to philia, but it isn't possible to get there in that way. If we are disconnected from our bodies, we won't be able to experience love on the level of philia. Friendship doesn't have to include sex, but it does need to allow for the possibility of touching, holding or hugging the other person.

Traditionally, philia starts to develop strongly around the time of adolescence. It may come in the form of hero-worship and it can be the kind of love a male feels for another male, or a female feels for another female. During adolescence, young boys idealize male role models, such as sports heroes, and girls fall in love with whoever represents the female ideal at that moment. I'm not inferring a homosexual relationship or bisexuality in all this, although we'll be covering these subjects later. What I'm emphasizing now is the idea of finding out who you are by modeling yourself on an ideal. To find the hero or heroine within you, you may have to fall in love with the hero or heroine outside of you. Think about it, who did you want to be friends with in your school days? Was it the beautiful majorette with all that blond, curly hair? Was it the Tarzan-like guy who captained the football team? Because they represented heroic ideals, these were often the kinds of people we wanted for friends during adolescence. You felt better about yourself if their light shined on you. The next stage after this would be to internalize this light, to experience it as stemming from inside yourself. When you have incorporated this light into yourself, you can then move from the role of the eromenos into the role of the eratos, the one who provides a source of love and light for others.

Philia, like the sign of Leo, is the impulse toward creativity. It is the feeling that love and light are inside you, the feeling that your cup runneth over, the feeling that the world is wonderful and that you are wonderful, and from this comes the desire to share all that love and light with another person. This is the world of the eratos. The eromenos is the one who is there ready to receive your love and light. Philia is different from epithemia in that philial love sees another person as different from the self. Epithemia is willing to use another person for the purpose of satisfying the need to touch and be touched, but epithemia does not see that person as someone separate and distinct from the self. With philia, there is an awareness of separation, and this marks the beginning of the whole idea of wooing and courtship. Wooing and courtship are fundamental parts of philia, and to a large extent, these things have been lost in our society. We don't woo and court each other. How many of you have had a love poem written to you lately? Or have any of you here had someone play the mandolin under your window late at night? The Greek gods were more or less limited to epithemia, and never really experienced philia. The ability to love is directly related to an awareness of one's separateness and one's mortality, and since the Greek gods were considered immortal, they didn't have the capacity for philia. The only exception was the god Eros, who fell in love by accidentally piercing himself with one of his arrows. As far as we know, human beings are the only animals who know they will die. This is why animals, as far as we can guess, do not experience philia. Many philosophers have defined human beings as the only animal that is aware of its own dying. It is the awareness of our mortality that gives us the urge to close the gap of separateness we feel between ourselves and others.

I associate the awakening of consciousness with Leo and the Sun. The Sun gives us the ability to recognize ourselves as a separate individual. The symbol for the Sun—a dot bounded by a circle—is a symbol for individuality, a symbol that says that I am a separate entity with my own intentionality and with my own future. And it is the process of cutting the umbilical cord and defining ourselves as a separate person that gives us the awareness of death. By the way, some of us don't realize this awareness until our parents die, which often occurs pretty late in life. When your parents are gone, you realize that you are an orphan, that the umbilical cord, at least physically, is broken forever. But it's sad that we often have to wait so late in life before we can sever the umbilical connection and open the way for relationships based on philia. One of the archetypes of Leo is the hero, the person searching for truth or having adventures out of which comes self-discovery. Part of the hero's journey is finding out who you are. Leo follows Cancer, so you can't find out who you are as a person in your own right until you have broken the umbilical cord. This is the theme of many heroic tales. Parsifal is a good example; he has a clinging mother who tries to hold him back from following the hero's path. Parsifal's mother doesn't want him to go out into the world and face his destiny. She doesn't want him to break the umbilical cord, because when that is done, he would have to face the inevitability of death. In a sense, his mother is saying, "Play it safe, stay with me and you will be immortal." On another level, Leo represents the awakening of the heart chakra. The creative urge arises from the heart, so the awakening of the heart center is necessary to inspire us toward creativity. The search for the good, the true, and the beautiful is also related to the Apollonian or Leonine instinct in us.

I'm also reminded of a play turned into an opera called *The Makropoulos Secret*, written by Karel Čapek, a Czech playwright. In it, a woman sells her soul to the devil. The bargain is that she would be granted eternal life so long as she never fell in love. She could have everything else—power, success, fame, beauty, talent—but she was not allowed to fall in love. The story opens just at the turn of the last century. The woman in question is a beautiful, wealthy and famous opera singer admired by the world, but she feels dead inside because she cannot feel love. The only way she can have love is to break the contract with the devil, which means, of course, that she would have to face death. In other words, she cannot feel love until she accepts the fact that she will die. She then finds a young woman who is willing to carry the devil's curse for her, and this allows the famous opera singer to fall in love and die. In order to love, she has to accept the inevitability of death.

Philia is not equal love. In philia, there is a difference between the lover and the beloved. For instance, a natural part of the Greek culture was love between men. In this kind of love, which was common among upper-class Greeks, it was expected that a young man who was identified as an eromenos would take a lover who was an older man. The older lover would become the eratos. Both Plato and Socrates believed that eros was the greatest teacher, and they meant this quite literally. Of course, the Victorian schoolmasters in England bowdlerized the translations of the Greek works and altered erotic love into platonic love—a kind of idealized, sexless love. The Victorian Christian mind just couldn't cope with the idea of eros between men. Besides, they were teaching all these school boys, and they feared the consequences of perpetuating eros between members of the same sex. In ancient Greece, however, it was the father of the young boy who often took it upon himself to pick the eratos, the older male lover who would educate the boy to take his place in the state's political system. This was considered a natural part of growing up. As the eromenos himself grew older, he would then become an eratos, an awakening figure, for someone younger than himself. For the Greeks, this kind of initiation into society was normally limited to male-male relationships, but sometimes it could happen between men and women. As a matter of fact, the archetype we are talking about can easily exist between a male and female as well. This is what happened in the medieval romantic epics where male-female love was meant to be an inspiring and awakening force. In philia, we gradually begin to internalize or reclaim our exteriorized projection of the ideal hero and heroine, and in doing so, we move toward the process of individuation or self-awakening. The self-awakening associated with philia naturally leads on to eros, the next category of love.

Eros occurs when two or more separate entities combine in such a way that they are totally transformed by the experience. Isn't it terrible what we've done to the wonderful word *erotic*? We think erotic means sexual, but it is much more than that. I associate eros with Scorpio and Pluto, with the watery quality of love, a love which involves suffering. Eros is the desire to merge your soul with the soul of another person. Archetypally, Taurean epithemia love is interested specifically in the merging of bodies. Scorpionic eros love, however, wants to merge souls and psyches, and this is why it can be very painful. Sometimes we confuse eros with epithemia. Eros can arise between a teacher and a student, or between a therapist and a client, and since we don't know the difference between eros and epithemia, we think we're lusting for the other person. We think we want to have sex with them. Many of us are deprived of epithemia, deprived of touching. Because we are in a state of horniness or lust, we meet someone who turns us on and we think we're in love with them. We say "God, I'm so passionately in love with you," but what we are really saying is "Hey, I like your body and it would feel good to touch you and hold you." How many of you who are in relationships sometimes just want holding, touching or caressing rather than all-out sex? This is as true for men as it is for women. The myth is that men are perpetually horny and women are perpetually sensual. This is absolutely false. Men also crave holding, touching and caressing, and want to be able to enjoy these things without necessarily having to perform a sexual act. Of course, men buy into the myth that they're supposed to be highly sexual, while women buy into the myth that they are meant to be sensual rather than sexual. According to our societal myths, women are not supposed to be sexual and lusting. They are not meant to think, never mind the foreplay, kid, let's get on to the main course!

Eros implies that love involves pain. There's a suffering quality in eros, because that moment of ecstasy, that moment of psychic joining together cannot last forever. This is why the French call the orgasm *le petit mort*, the little death. We also have the concept of postcoital depression, which comes when separateness rears it head again after we've had an intense kind of closeness. We would love to find some kind of way to live in the perpetual ecstasy of union with another person. Eros is the kind of love that implies biting into the apple, just as Eve bit into the apple and things were never the same again in Eden. The story of Persephone conveys something similar. Because Persephone had bitten into a pomegranate in the underworld, she was not allowed to return permanently to the upper world. There is a definite connection between the apple in the Garden of Eden and the pomegranate. Indeed, apples didn't even grow in that part of the world from where the Eden story originated, so the fruit Eve bit into was most likely a pomegranate. The pomegranate is a very interesting fruit, because when you open it, it bleeds. The opening or breaking of the pomegranate is representative of the breaking of the maidenhead. The breaking of Persephone's maidenhead symbolizes the breaking of her bond with her mother Demeter, and in this way, it's akin to the severing of the umbilical cord. When Eve eats the apple, she is disobeying God and following the advice of the serpent, one of the faces of Lucifer. Eating the apple is like cutting the umbilical cord with her father and entering into a marriage with Adam. She is no longer just God's child; she is now the wife of Adam. After the apple episode, Adam and Eve must leave Eden just as when a man and woman are joined together in marriage, they leave their parental homes to make a new home of their own.

What happened in the myth of Demeter and Persephone is similar to the Garden of Eden story, and I'd like to go into it in more detail right now. Demeter was one of those goddesses who wasn't particularly interested in men. According to most of the myths about her, she only had one relationship with a man—some say it was with Zeus, others say it was with Poseidon. Whoever the father was, Demeter gave birth to Kore, which in Greek means maiden. Demeter and Kore lived together in this primeval Eden-like world. Demeter (known as Ceres in Roman mythology) was an earth goddess, a primeval earth mother, in charge of the crops and all things that grow on the earth. One day Kore is out in a field picking flowers. Do you remember what particular flower she picked? No, not daisies, but a narcissus. Kore was living in this narcissistic state of oneness with her mother, but when she picked the narcissus, her uroboric world was destroyed. By the way, it was Aphrodite who had planted the very narcissus that Kore picked. This is significant, because Aphrodite or Pluto will take their revenge if a parent-child bond interferes with a child's growing into a person in his or her own right who is capable of forming a union with someone other than the parent. According to Aphrodite and Pluto, the prolonged closeness of Demeter and Kore was unnatural and unhealthy. After Kore picked the narcissus, the earth opened up and Pluto abducted her, dragging the screaming and protesting maiden down into the underworld where he raped her.

Demeter then went into this tremendous period of depression and mourning, which is exactly what happens to the umbilical-binding mother when she has to let go of her child. As a way of trying to get Kore back again, Demeter resorted to blackmail. If her daughter weren't returned to her, she threatened to starve the world by not allowing any crops to grow on earth. The gods were extremely upset about this. It wasn't that they loved mankind so much that they hated to see people suffer; the gods were upset because if there was no food, then there would be no mortals left to worship them. They went clamoring to Zeus, the father of the gods, and asked him to do something about this dire situation. Zeus intervened and forced Pluto to return Kore, now renamed Persephone—which translates into the "lover of darkness" or "she who destroys the light"—back to her mother. However, because she had eaten six seeds of the pomegranate while in the under-world, she was considered officially wed to Pluto, and therefore not allowed to leave the underworld for good. A compromise was struck between Pluto and Demeter, in which Persephone lived as queen of the underworld with Pluto for six months of each year, and was allowed to return to her mother Demeter for the remaining six months. During the time that Persephone was reunited with her mother—during spring and summer—the crops would flourish; but when Persephone returned to the underworld, Demeter would go back into mourning and the crops weren't allowed to grow—the autumn and winter months. It's a lovely story, describing not only a phenomenon in nature, but also an archetypal process of growth, evolution and the development of self-awareness. So the implication is that the breaking open of the pomegranate is the breaking of the maidenhead. Indeed, in many tribal and medieval marriages, the bed is inspected for blood after the marriage night as an indication that the marriage has been consummated. It's not the putting on of the rings and the "I do's" that make a man and a woman one, but the breaking of the maid-enhead that binds them together.

In Japan there is an operation to replace broken maidenheads—it's called a hymen transplant. Even to this day, in a well-bred Japanese marriage, the bride is gynecologically examined by the groom's female relatives. If there is no maidenhead there, the wedding is called off. Believe me or not, I imagine that there are a lot of

Western women going to Japan to be rehymened. I was going to say hymenized, but that sounded too much like being simonized. I wonder who the donor is? I also read a terrible story in the news not long ago that took place in Greece. It was about a Greek woman who turned quite crazy because she had been chained in a cellar for 25 years. At the age of 17 she had taken a man as a lover, and this was such a disgrace to the honor of the family that they imprisoned her in the cellar. The whole village knew what her family was doing to her, but it was still allowed to happen. Here we are thinking that we live in such modern, enlightened times. It just isn't so.

Eros is accompanied by an ecstatic kind of feeling, almost a religious kind of ecstasy. The Greek Eleusian mysteries have a Scorpionic or Plutonic flavor to them that has a lot to do with eros. Christian mystery and ritual also recall eros—the joining together with the beloved. There is a symbolic devouring quality that is associated with eros, Scorpio and Pluto. Pluto is fundamentally the rapist or the seducer, the one who yanks us out of Eden (uroboric wholeness with a parent) to which we can never return again. Eros is an initiation: the experience of eros takes us out of childhood into adulthood. The rites and rituals associated with eros are mainly based on pain. This could involve a heroic task such as slaying a lion, or it could entail the scarification[2] of a young maiden before she is given away in marriage. Or a man is ready to be seen as an adult or ready to be married, and he is then circumcised without anesthetics. I've heard that the Jewish wedding ritual of the groom breaking the glass with his foot was originally intended to be done barefoot. The breaking of the umbilical cord and the initiation into eros is associated with things that are painful. An ecstatic, erotic relationship inevitably implies pain. So what I'm saying is that the erotic experience belongs to the realm of the religious, the mystical and the creative. It is a tremendously powerful feeling that can be quite overwhelming. Society needs safe ways of channeling all this, and the creation of a priest caste is one way of doing so. In other words, priests are the people to whom we have given erotic power. It is the priest who announces what

---

[2]Scarification, meaning to scar or make an incision, would here refer to the ritual of breaking the hymen of a virgin as preparation for her marriage.

kind of sexuality is permitted, and it is the priest who deals with issues to do with death and with rebirth and initiation ceremonies, and with times of generation and regeneration. Of course, we're happy to give this power to them, because it is too much for us to deal with by ourselves.

Western civilization is as anti-erotic as it is anti-epithemial. I do feel that the Taurus-Scorpio axis is probably the most psychologically potent, dangerous and usually the least integrated area of a chart. This also goes for Venus, the ruler of Taurus, and for Pluto, Scorpio's ruler. Most of us have been taught to deny, repress or reject Venus and Pluto, or to compensate for these energies in some indirect way. Consider your own chart in this light by looking at the houses that have Taurus and Scorpio on the cusps, by locating planets posited in these signs, and by examining the position of Venus and Pluto by sign, house and aspect. I believe that Pluto is the fundamental planet representing eros. If you don't open your soul to the ecstatic energy symbolized by Pluto—an ecstatic relationship in which merging is akin to dying—then Pluto will operate unconsciously and invisibly. If repressed, it will find some way of dragging you and any planet it aspects down into the underworld. This is why a lot of people go about living life like zombies. Have you noticed that some people can have really lively, interesting charts, and yet they still walk around like mummies? Having cut off from eros, they are lifeless, nothing seems to be going on in them. You ask them what is happening in their lives, and they just say that everything is fine. You ask them about their relationships, and they mumble back that these go along okay. You ask them what their relationship with their parents was like, and they say very nice, just fine. You ask them what they want out of life and they say they don't really know. The way I see these kinds of people is that Pluto has grabbed their soul and relegated it to the underworld. It is only through deep pain that the soul can be reclaimed, which is why Jung remarked that we don't change until we have suffered enough.

Eros is telling us to honor the fact that love involves pain, that love entails letting go of the self and dying as an "I" through merging one's soul with something other than the self. It is only then that we are reborn, and Jung referred to people who have gone through this process as "the twice-born." He also said that there are extremely few "twice-born" people around, and I agree with him. Religious rituals and initiation rites, past and present, were designed to help people go through the death-rebirth process associated with eros. It's as if society is saying that there is a time for you to make this passage and here are rituals and rites to help you through it. The Irish wake is a good example of this kind of thing, as were the Saturnalia and the Bacchanal. We have some remains of it in the Brazilian carnival festival. Did you know that in certain renditions of myth, Dionysus (Bacchus) was believed to be the offspring of the marriage of Pluto and Persephone? Dionysus was a Christ-like figure or a kind of proto-Christ, the one who goes down into the depths and is reborn again in order to save mankind. Interestingly, the sacrifice and dying of Jesus on the cross (where God gives away his only begotten son to suffer and die for the sake of mankind) is not called the epithemia of Christ or the philia of Christ, but is referred to as the Passion of Christ. In other words, the death and resurrection of Jesus is a symbolic act of eros, depicting God breaking the umbilical cord with his son by offering him to the world. So the communion ritual is basically erotic in this sense. After all, what is involved in the act of communion? It is when you symbolically eat the body and drink the blood of Christ, and thereby partake of his passion, death and redemption. Christ died for our sins, and through communion we die by becoming one with Christ, by partaking of his flesh and blood. More primitive societies omit this intervening step of eating the wafer and tasting the wine; instead, they literally do eat bodies and drink blood. I heard a story about this. Some tribe in Ghana or Guinea or somewhere got together and sent the brightest young man of their tribe to be educated at Oxford University. He did very well there, achieving a postdoctoral degree in law. When he returned to his native land, the tribespeople put him in a pot, cooked him, and everybody ate a little bit of him. By doing this, the entire tribe had a chance to share in this sacrificial victim's education.

•   •   •

During the break a lot of people came to me with very interesting questions. All I can say is that I wish I could talk on the topic of love for 12 hours a day, because there is so much to say, and no matter how long we have, I always feel that there is so much left unsaid. My spirit is willing, but I'm afraid that my body just couldn't handle it. What do they say?—the spirit is willing but the flesh is weak. One question that did come up was about the difference between Taurean love and Scorpionic love. Archetypally for Taurus, the other person doesn't exist at all, or the other person is an object who equals pleasure. The reason for this is that Taurus is a personal sign and has not yet come to the point of differentiating the self from the not-self. Taurus seeks pleasure for itself, and other people are there to help this along. This is a very different perspective from that of Scorpio. Scorpio has achieved a differentiation between self and others, and therefore can see another being as a person in his or her own right. For Scorpio, pleasure is not just self-pleasuring. The erotic connection for Scorpio involves finding ways to give another person pleasure. Scorpio is inspired and stimulated by arousing and awakening someone other than the self. We can also look at all this in a nonsexual way. For instance, the drama between a therapist and a client is erotic in a Scorpionic sense because there is a dance going on between the healer and the healed, not totally unlike the dance that goes on between the lover and the beloved. If therapy is working properly, eros is happening from both sides. It's not meant to be a hierarchical relationship in which the therapist functions solely as the power source and the client functions solely as the receiver. The same applies to the relationship between teacher and student. I want to be a receiver too, which is why I've brought my antennae here, or whatever you wish to call it. By the way, I am not judging Taurus when I say that it uses the other person as an object. Fundamentally, this is just the way that Taurus is, and it shouldn't be judged as good or bad for it.

Another question that came up during the break concerned the Persephone story. Somebody asked me why she ended up going back to her mother at all, even if only for six months. There are two ways of looking at this. First of all, we can say that breaking the umbilical cord doesn't mean leaving your parents forever and never being able to return to them. What it suggests is that in order to relate to your parents as equals—in order to have an adult-adult relationship with them—you must first be empowered through the process of leaving the parental home and forming a relationship outside the scope of the family. This is part and parcel of the hero's journey or the hero's quest. It's only after breaking the umbilical bond that you can then go back to your parents and have a relationship of equality with them. The other way of looking at the link between Demeter and Persephone is to remember that originally they were at one with one another. In a sense, Demeter and Persephone are really two phases of the same thing. Originally they are one, then they separate, and only after that does the cycle come back full circle when they once again reunite as one. They started off bonded together as one, but then Kore undertakes her heroic journey into the underworld and becomes Persephone, a woman in her own right, no longer a maiden wed to her mother. The journey into the underworld empowers Persephone, and enables her to rejoin the mother, but in a different way than before.

Primitive societies dealt with the urge toward eros through religious and tribal rituals that are no longer practiced very widely. These rituals were based on the Plutonic urge toward regeneration through death and rebirth. Or to put it another way, these rituals involved catharsis, a cleansing act that is still part of Christianity and very close to what Pluto is all about. Indeed, in its own way, sex can be a cathartic, cleansing ritual. Theater and drama also started out as religious rituals based on the rites of Dionysus, another figure who was reborn after a journey into the underworld. Aristotle wrote that the function of drama is to provide catharsis and cleansing. He observed that catharsis works through the experience of shared pity and terror, and that this applies to both tragedy and comedy. The only difference is that tragedy ends unhappily, while comedy has a happy ending. When someone slips on a banana peel, we share pity and terror with that person. Because it's a comedy, we know that the person who slips isn't going to break his or her back or die as a result, so we are able to laugh at the mishap. The function of catharsis is to cleanse, and it forms a basic part of religious and group ritual. I believe that much of Pluto's work ought to be done on the group level, which is why we have set up the small-group workshops. Cleansing and catharsis do not usually happen on the level of the intellect alone. You could rightly wonder why the Greeks went to the theater as much as they did, since they already were familiar with all the plays and stories. They already knew all about the fate of Clytemnestra, Agamennon, Orestes or Oedipus, and yet they never tired of watching these stories over and over again. Greek audiences identified with the archetypal core of these dramas, and therefore, as a group, they were able to participate in the cleansing and purging process generated by the enactment of the plays.

This leads us to something very important about our society and what it's done to drama: We've forgotten about the pity part and have started to emphasize the terror part instead. We have forgotten the element of compassion and dwell more on the element of horror, which probably has a great deal to do with the way we see our world—a world in which we're sitting on the edge of nuclear disaster, a world where there are wars and revolutions going on all over the place. The powers that be in Hollywood seem to think that escalating terror to a very high degree is the only way to arouse a cathartic reaction in audiences, and pity doesn't come into this very much. It's almost as if we've forgotten how to pity. Many years ago, I saw Irene Pappas perform in *The Trojan Women* at the Circle in the Square Theater off Broadway. It was an amazing performance to watch. A great many of your New York theater-going audience tend to be subscription-ticket buyers, people—often businessmen and their wives—who come in from Westchester County and Long Island because they want to support the theater. *The Trojan Women* is a classic Greek story. Having conquered Troy, the Greeks have slain almost all of the Trojan males, leaving the females behind to survive on their own. The only male still living is the grandson of Hecuba, the Queen of Troy. Because the Greeks want no one to survive from the royal lineage, they rip the baby from his mother's arms and throw him off the walls of Troy. So the only people who are left are abandoned women, abandoned widows and mothers. This is a very archetypal situation. Just think about what happens in war. It's usually the case that the women are left behind to grieve and mourn for the loss of their men and male children. I was very moved by the chorus in *The Trojan Women*. The chorus in Greek drama stands for you—the audience—and acts out the Plutonian role of grief or elation which you feel while watching the play. The chorus goes "Aieeee" and the hair on everybody's head in the audience stands on end. The chorus talks directly to the audience, invoking you to participate in the terrible tale of these women who have survived the death of their men. And all these sophisticated New York theater-goers were sitting there sobbing and crying throughout the play. The interesting thing is that by the end of the play, you actually come out feeling cleansed by what you have seen and experienced. In spite of it being a horrible story, it leaves you with a feeling of how significant and wonderful it is to be human. You feel renewed and cleansed by the play, because the archetypal principles of pity and terror have been evoked. This is eros working at its best.

Aristotle pointed out another function of eros related to the sharing of pity and terror. He believed that it bound the community together into a unit through its members sharing and participating in the same tragedy or the same ritual. In a sense, this is what's behind the Christian ritual of communion, the name itself suggesting the joining together of the community. Now I don't know for sure how many people involved in Christian communion actually succeed in feeling the pity and terror this ritual is meant to evoke, but I'm certain this was the original intent behind it. I also don't know how much of contemporary theater succeeds in evoking the pity and terror that it originally meant to arouse. Without pity and terror, there is no communion on the group level. Because our so-called civilized world no longer has access to these rituals in which the erotic is performed on the group level, as it was in the Roman Saturnalia or the Greek Bacchanals and other rituals such as these, we are mostly cut off from eros. You can still see some of it in the Irish wake or in Jewish funerals, where you rend your garments and anoint your head with ashes and all those kinds of things, and yet, in general, our society is cut off from eros. What happens, as a result, is that eros gets blocked or constipated, and we start looking for it in our personal one-to-one relationships because we are not getting it anywhere else in our lives. So we end up combining pity, terror and catharsis with our love affairs. Eros gets all dammed up, channeled into the narrow space of personal relationship. We look for eros in the orgasmic, erotic union between ourselves and a lover, and no relationship can bear such pressure. This displacement of eros explains why we carry around such huge expectations of what it is to fall in love and have an exciting relationship. You should meet somebody and the earth should tremble. Right? I mean, just read the torrid and dramatic stuff in romantic novels or magazines—"the Earl of Oxford walks into the room and the heroine's heart flutters like a bird trapped in her breast and the earth shook under her feet as she gazed upon his firm, hard, passionate, manly eyes." It's this kind of thing that sells.

Audience: You seem to be saying that because we don't have the right kind of group rituals to evoke eros, we look for it in personal relationships. But are you also implying it's impossible to sustain eros in a one-to-one love relationship?

Richard: Yes, I think people do try to find eros in personal, intimate relationships, but it's very hard to sustain it in that way. What happens is that it wears off in a passionate one-to-one relationship, so we go out searching for another relationship, for a better lover who can renew the experience of eros for us. We associate eros too much with falling in love—you know, little Eros with his bow and arrow goes twang and you go "Oh, gazong, there she is, my anima, the woman of my dreams." After that, however, we usually revert back to the static vertical relationship of mommy, daddy and child. A man might think he is marrying his lover when in actual fact he is marrying his mother. There is a lot of talk about how to keep romance alive in marriage. Some people say that a married woman should still try to look sexy and seductive in order to keep her man lively and interested. Others might think that reading the *Kama Sutra* and following the positions it suggests (such as "Let's try position 17b today"), is the way to keep eros alive in your marriage. Or you imagine that if only your wife was thinner or your husband more tender, or if only you could more readily verbalize your needs during sex, then you would live in a perpetual state of erotic ecstasy. If these attempts fail, your relationship fails, and you need to go looking for another lover who will be able to invoke the mystery of eros within you. You might even succeed in finding someone else who can do this for a short time, but unfortunately, it's a fact of life that familiarity is the very thing that kills off eros. It's true that when you do fall in love with someone erotically, the earth might shake and quake for you, and it could feel terrifying. And there is your beloved with trembling looks and lips, shaking and falling apart, not able to eat, and that will arouse pity in you for that person. But this is not sustainable in a longer-term love relationship, because eros thrives on mystery. Eros thrives on the unknown. Eros is the god of the underworld who dwells in the invisible realm. It's only through darkness and mystery, through plummeting into the unknown, that the erotic can happen. You can try to keep a little mystery in your marriage, but this is easier said than done. In days gone by, you never thought of your marriage partner as your best friend. But now, what is meant to happen is that your partner not only must carry epithemia, but he or she is also supposed to be your best friend, the beloved in the sense of philia. And on top of all that, your marriage partner also is meant to be the one who perpetually arouses your romantic interest, who perpetually makes you quake and shake, and by doing so keeps eros alive for you. How can you keep mystery alive with someone who is your best friend? It's very hard to do.

Finally, besides sharing epithemia, philia and eros, you and your partner are also supposed to share *agape*, which is a loving, godlike, detached kind of love that I'll be speaking more about later. When applied to marriage, agape asks something really difficult: it asks that you have an open marriage, that your partner must love you enough to let you go out and have relationships with other people and somehow not feel jealous about it. But if I'm not meant to get jealous, how can I get erotic? Do you see what I'm saying? We really are asking too much of one relationship. Including agape—the desire to connect with the divine through a partner—we've imposed four different kinds of love onto the marriage situation. I don't believe there is any marriage that can carry such a load.

There is also something basically tragic about Plutonic or eros-type relationships, for the simple reason that you cannot live in a perpetual state of ecstasy. This is why Romeo and Juliet had to die young. Can you imagine Romeo and Juliet an old married couple with twelve *bambini*? Juliet has gotten a little wide in the hips, and Romeo's chasing after younger women, and she greets him at the door with "Hey, whatsa' matter with you?" just before she throws a frying pan at him. What I'm saying is that eros always implies death, and that pain is inherent to an erotic relationship.

A similar interaction exists between therapist and client. The therapist invites the client to step beyond his or her basic ground. The therapist offers to help the client take this step, but taking such a step is like biting into the apple—once you take it, you'll find it very difficult to go back again to the way you were, you'll find it very hard to go home again. This kind of thing can happen only when there's an erotic bond between the therapist and client. And in this case, by erotic, I don't mean something explicitly sexual. The therapist must summon up the power of Pluto to enable you to break the bonds of resistance that bind you to your family myths and to your past, thereby allowing you to move onward. The therapist is like Virgil, who guided Dante down to the ninth pit of hell. And if you remember that story, the guide found it as painful to go through hell as did the person he was guiding. The therapist who has not, or will not, partake of that journey is afraid to invoke eros, and consequently is cut off from his or her own self. Only those who have been wounded and damaged themselves can guide another person down into the depths—which gets us back to the idea of the wounded healer. Dante chose Virgil as his guide because Virgil was known as the poet of the broken heart.

If you wish to lead another into dark places, you must first have had your own heart broken. This is what eros is all about, this is what eros teaches us. What is the symbol of the valentine? It's the broken heart, the heart that has been pierced through and broken into by the arrows of Eros. When I was in South Africa, I heard an interesting little story pertaining to this, a story about the courting rituals of the Bushmen living in the Kalahari Desert. When he sees a woman he wants to court, he shoots her in the rump with a tiny bow and arrow. If she leaves the arrow in, it means that she has accepted him. If she pulls the arrow out and throws it on the ground, it means that she is rejecting him. So here we have love and courtship quite literally symbolized by the pain and piercing of an arrow. Eros pierces the heart. We can also see this symbolism in Christianity where Jesus and sometimes Mary are portrayed as having a bleeding heart. Christianity has picked up on these ancient structures, although it has distorted them in certain ways. Time flies! I still have so much to say, but are there any questions right now?

Audience: Do you think that the image of the bleeding heart is a kind of cultural projection?

Richard: Yes, it could be seen as a Neptunian projection. Jesus is very Neptunian, espousing compassion and turning the other cheek. Perhaps the bleeding heart is a way of toughening us up, a way of balancing out being too soft, mushy or compassionate.

Audience: We all have to go through periods of death and rebirth, so aren't we courting eros a lot of the time?

Richard: Yes, it's true that we go through periods of dying as we are to be reborn anew, but it's also true that most of us don't relish the idea of death in any form. Most of us are terrified of death; most of us want to have things basic and easy. We want to have our cake and eat it too. We live in a society that doesn't provide enough outlets for eros. Just as Christianity has turned Aphrodite into a sinful whore, Pluto has been turned into Satan. The Greeks would never have seen the god of the underworld as a satanic figure. In the Judeo-Christian model, however, both Aphrodite and Pluto have become outcasts. This is why I refer to the Taurus-Scorpio axis as "the dark axis." It is very difficult for us to integrate this axis into our lives in a positive way. What I'm emphasizing now are the difficulties and hazards that occur when we try to find all the different types and levels of love in one relationship. Some people marry because they have a very strong need to touch and be touched by another person; in other words, marriage has to bear the power of epithemia. This reminds me of something. I have a cousin who is around my age. When we were both 21, he said that he was going to go out and find himself a wife. When I asked him why, he told me that he needed a wife because he was so horny all the time. He was tired of having to go out every Saturday night to the singles' bars looking for a woman to sleep with. He was lonely and he liked sleeping with someone, so he figured it was time to get married. Within a week, he found a woman who was similarly inclined. They courted for a year (as one did in those ancient days) and eventually they were married and have stayed together ever since. I'm not judging whether marriage is good or bad, but I am saying that a lot of people get married for the same reasons as my cousin did, for the sake of assuaging loneliness and finding someone to touch, hold, caress and sleep with at night.

Just as we might marry for the sake of epithemia, we also might marry in pursuit of eros. Since our so-called civilized society provides very few channels to satisfy eros, we look to a marriage partner to satisfy our needs for it. And we also look to a marriage partner to be a friend, as well as some kind of divine other who will redeem us. So you see, marriage is really loaded. We hope to experience all these different kinds of love through marriage, but, in actual fact, it's impossible for one other person to live up to or meet such a range of demands. Which is why so many of us end up disappointed. We either break the relationship in order to look for someone better to fulfill our needs and fantasies, or we're constantly trying to get our partner to change – to get taller or thinner, to become more heroic or less clinging, to become more passionate or less demanding, to touch us more or to touch us less, and so on. We believe that if our partners could magically transform themselves, they would be better able to satisfy more of our urges.

Audience: What you're saying is that the Greeks had outlets for people to experience eros, such as the catharsis shared by a group or audience sitting together and watching a drama unfold. And then you're saying that we don't have such outlets in our society, so we seek eros in a one-to-one relationship, or we try to grab all that energy from one person. I'm still not sure why eros is best dealt with through a group experience.

Richard: Eros, the chthonic energy of the underworld, is so potent that it can make you blow a fuse quite easily. Such powerful energy is very hard to contain within a one-to-one love relationship. This shouldn't come as a surprise to anyone who has ever been involved in a really erotic partnership. It's so intense that it can burn out your sockets. The energy of eros is best grounded by experiencing it within a group or around a number of other people. Things like music, dance, chanting and ritual also help to ground and disperse its intense power. All I can say is that the energy of eros is too much for a one-to-one relationship. It even poses grave dangers within the therapeutic situation, which is why the therapeutic relationship tends to be very structured. You need this structure. The therapist needs to be extra aware of the kinds of transferences and countertransferences evoked through the erotic healing process of therapy or analysis.

Audience: Could a good football game serve as a channel and focus for eros?

Richard: Well, yes, there's certainly some amount of purging going on in those who share the experience of watching an exciting game. But, in actual fact, I would classify this more as a vicarious Mars exercise or experience, because it doesn't involve enough of the pity and terror associated with Pluto. I think that a Spanish bullfight comes closer to dealing with Pluto. Remember that the modern-day bullfight originated from old Cretan bull dancing, which was symbolic of death and transformation. In this respect, a bullfight is much more realistic and satisfying than a football game. I believe that the reason for all this soccer-match violence could stem from sheer frustration: the crowds go looking for a Plutonic kind of catharsis, but, because there is no terror and pity involved, they only end up with Mars.

Audience: But, Richard, there must be some very good, long-lasting marriages in which pity and terror are also experienced.

Richard: Really, do you know of one?

Audience: I'm thinking of marriages where both people are allowed to change and grow. In this kind of relationship, you'd have a great deal of anxiety and fear about whether it can successfully survive such changes, or whether you'll change and not want your partner anymore, or your partner will change and not want you any longer. It seems to me that a long-term partnership or marriage actually includes all four of these different kinds of love but they are experienced at different stages or phases of the relationship— you know an intense epithemial period, an intense philial period, an erotic period and so on. Maybe these kinds of changes are what keep up the mystery and interest?

Richard: Yes, I guess that can happen, but your response reminds me of the adage that hope dies hard. Sorry. Most of us are still carrying around the baggage that there is that one special person out there who will be everything we need. You know, once in your life, or maybe twice, if it doesn't work the first time, you'll meet that person who changes you forever; and it will have a fairy-tale ending where you will live happily ever after, or, at least, live together ever after. Okay, it could happen. But what I mean to imply is that it's very difficult. It takes two very individuated people who are in touch on one level or another with all of the different forms of love that we've been discussing. It would take two people who are living as adults; two people who have to some extent broken the umbilical cord or who are channeling some of the intensity of eros into their work or into something creative. Or they have friends outside of the marriage who carry philia for them, and they would also need to be in touch with epithemia enough to handle it wisely by channeling it into taking care of their own bodies. I don't know too many people like that. But I do agree with you because I don't want to cut off hope. Actually, in a way, I do want to cut off hope because, as M. Scott Peck says in *The Road Less Traveled*, you have to fall out of love in order to truly love. Let me paraphrase that and say that you have to fall out of being in love with love in order to fall in love. And this is precisely what I'm encouraging you to do. I'm not saying that relationships are hopeless and there'll never be another one in your life. I'm just advising you to go into these things with your eyes open, rather than with your eyes closed.

I'd like to spend a little more time discussing agape. You must have figured out by now that I associate Aquarius and Uranus with agape. I think that the archetypal and astrological significance of the sign of Aquarius has been vastly misunderstood. To the Greeks, agape literally meant "the love of god for man." Now, if you go back to the way the Greek gods loved mortal men and women, you'd see that it wasn't an unsexual kind of loving. It was, however, an *unattached* sexual loving in which the gods and goddesses never married or formed permanent relationships with a mortal. But the Christians came along and distorted agape much in the same way that they distorted epithemia, philia and eros—they turned it all upside down. Now, when we speak of agape in the Christian sense of the term (or as *caritas*, which is the Latin sense of the term), we see the love of god for mortal humans as a sexless love. After all, there's no Mrs. God, and Jehovah was a bachelor god—the only lady in his life was the Virgin Mary and she conceived immaculately, so that means he never even laid a hand on her. Indeed, sex and touching was considered so bad that even the Virgin Mary's mother was considered a virtuous saint, thereby extending the concept of immaculate conception back to the previous generation. So Judeo-Christianity implies that sexuality is not a part of godliness, that it's a separate thing which is, of course, the result of the work of Satan and the fall of Eve. So in Christianity, we have the idea that godliness is sexlessness, whereas the Greeks made a place for sex in godliness. In Greek mythology, the gods had sex with mortals in order to bring some kind of gift or some kind of awakening to the mortal, such as a shower of gold. And what was often the outcome of a god having sex with a mortal woman, or a goddess having sex with a mortal man? What happened? They gave birth to a hero or heroine.

Agape is not a sexless kind of love, nor is Aquarius a sexless sign. Aquarius brings with it everything that has been learned in epithemia, philia and eros, but it goes a step further by incorporating the feeling that "I love you enough to leave you to be who you are." This is what is meant by detached love. It is the love of the awakener for the awakened. Agape or Aquarian love is Uranian, bringing in that zap of awakening and awareness that breaks and shatters the ego. In its own way, it can be just as painful as the erotic Plutonian kind of love, because agape shatters and awakens you to truths about yourself that you've never had before. I don't consider Aquarius to be the sign of friends. If you've ever really known Aquarians, you will have observed that they are superficially social, that they know how to play those games. Libra is more the party-goer; Libra is a much more social sign than Aquarius. Aquarius carries the feeling of "I want to be alone or involved with the entire world community rather than just engaging in a one-on-one chitchat kind of thing." As I have said, Aquarius represents agape, the kind of detached relationship that exists between the awakener and the awakened. Agape is a form of love that says, "I love you best when you are being who you are—even if that means you have to leave me." Eros couldn't handle this kind of openness, which is why agape is one step beyond eros. In order for a therapist to let a client go, he or she must be able to get to agape, to feel agape toward the client. Agape says, "I love you most by freeing you," and there are a number of therapists around who can't do this: "Oh, you must come back now for your twenty-fifth year of therapy because we're still getting into some deep, dark stuff." Eros can transform itself into a lifelong relationship if it can reach the level of agape, a more airy kind of love than watery eros. Agape says, "I love you enough to give you space and distance." But the question is, does that distance imply entirely breaking up the relationship? This seems to be the case for most people in our culture today—the belief that when distance begins to happen in a marriage, it means that the marriage is over. What has happened to the fiery courtship period of philia? Where has the powerful emotional and sexual connection of eros gone to? With philia and eros gone, it seems as if the relationship is finished. The truly long-lasting relationship must include agape, where you have this lovingly detached relationship. But this does not mean that the relationship has to be nonsexual. Agape means that I love you enough to let you more fully and completely be who you are. Indeed, the more you are fully and completely yourself, the more I love you; and this is because the more you are fully and completely who you are, the more I can be fully and completely who I am. Do you see how this differs from philia? Philia says, "You must be my hero or heroine, you must be this beautiful idol sitting up there, this archetypal vision of my inner golden heart, and you must never fall off that pedestal because to do so would be to destroy my image of myself and my image of who you are." So although Aquarius is sexual, it's still nonbinding.

Aquarius and agape are very different from eros, which is possessive in and of its own nature because eros always seeks to continue the feelings of ecstasy associated with it. Epithemia is possessive in the same way that a dog is possessive of its bone, or in the same way that a child is possessive of its mother. A little baby does not love his mother because she's a virtuous, well-educated, sympathetic and compassionate person. The little baby likes mother because mother means warmth, mother means milk, mother means being held and comforted, and because mother means safety. These are the reasons why a baby loves its mother. A baby's love for mother is epithemia at its most pure and honest, and it's a right and good thing. Every relationship has some degree of epithemia in it. Have you heard of the pheromones? These are sexual hormones that we all give out in the form of a smell. Animals find out who they are attracted to through their sense of smell. And if the truth be known, so do humans, but the problem nowadays is that the deodorants, perfumes and after-shaves that advertisements encourage us to use actually hide and camouflage the smell of the pheromones. What I'm saying is that humans would find out who they are attracted to by using their sense of smell, that is, if Madison Avenue hadn't tried so hard to convince us that they know better what we should smell like. Smell is the primary sense I associate with Taurus and with epithemia. The people you are attracted to are the ones whose smell you like. Smell is one of the original contact points. When we are sexually aroused, we give off a very potent smell. But after we've put on our extra-dry deodorant or whatever, the natural smell we give off when we feel sexual is banished from the world. So again, part of our cultural inheritance is the idea that people shouldn't smell like people, and they especially shouldn't smell like sexually-aroused people.

I have a few more points to make about agape. The image associated with Aquarius is the water bearer, a god pouring water or a fluidlike substance from an urn. The urn and its contents represent love as a gift from the gods. Agape awakens and frees us at the same time, and this is why I consider Aquarius the symbolic sign of the archetypal Holy Grail, or more specifically, the upturned grail. Heroes and heroines—whether we are referring to Parsifal or Jesus—go through their heroic journey and then bring back the gifts of truth, freedom, enlightenment, cleansing or redemption to share with humanity. The hero goes off on a journey, trial or test, but then returns home to share and pour forth what has been learned or gained from the journey. The urge of agape is for each one of us to offer as a form of love those things we have learned through our individual journeys and through our suffering. Leo, philia and the Sun represent the hero awakening to his godhead, embarking on his journey toward redemption; but this journey is not complete until he brings something valuable back and offers it forth for everybody to share. I repeat, agape is not sexless; it can be sexual, but in a way which is nonbinding. I must have made my point by now. Let's take some time for questions.

Audience: I find it interesting that you associate the Greek idea of the four kinds of love with the four fixed signs.

Richard: Yes, the reason for this is that fixed signs are signs of manifestation. They bring something into focus that begins in a cardinal sign and that will be changed and transformed in a mutable sign.

Audience: Does the sexual form of agape contain the element of pain that is associated with erotic love?

Richard: If both partners are in touch with agape, it shouldn't, in theory at least, entail pain. But agape can be painful. I'm reminded of a triptych depicting the Annunciation as painted by Grünewald. This triptych shows an angel coming down to tell the Virgin Mary that she is with child, and that this child is the son of God. This was a popular theme among Renaissance artists. Normally in such paintings, the angel is standing there and telling Mary the good news. But in the Grünewald rendition, the angel Gabriel is looking at the Virgin Mary much in the same way as Lucifer looked at Eve. In effect, the angel is saying, "This is going to change your life forever, lady. It's a gift from God, but it's not going to be easy for you." Uranus can have a Humpty-Dumpty effect on us—it hits us and off the wall we fall. God's gift will transform Mary, but it's a two-edged sword. By the way, Grünewald's Virgin Mary is rather luscious. She's voluptuous, full-breasted, and her gown is cut so low that she's almost coming out of it. She wasn't shown as this kind of narrow, thin, sort of wormy-looking creature which was in vogue in medieval renditions of her. In the Grünewald painting, you can see why God wanted her! Here is the Virgin Mary sitting at her toilette with a mirror in her hand (quite the child of Aphrodite), turning around to look over her shoulder as this angel of the Annunciation magically manifests in her boudoir, and her response is to put her hand out in a gesture that suggests she's rather alarmed at what she has gotten herself into. Mary Mater Dolorosa, the perpetually suffering mother, suffered terribly with this mixed gift that came from God. So, yes, agape can have painful qualities. And you should remember that no relationship is purely one thing or another, so you can have some of agape mixed in with some of eros. The eros part explains the jealousy you might feel. As a matter of fact, a lot of people don't know they're in love until they feel jealousy, which means that they have defined love in terms of eros. And when they don't feel jealousy anymore, they assume the relationship must be over. But no, maybe it's just that they have now moved on to agape.

Audience: You said that eros is best experienced by a group of people in order to ground its potent energy. I also think that the group serves to spark off eros as well.

Richard: Yes, that's true. I'm glad you brought this up. The reason we need a group of people is that a critical mass of energy is necessary in order to evoke anything Plutonic. I guess it's possible to have a critical mass of two. In some cases, you can have a critical mass of just one person. I'm thinking of Michelangelo who said that his reason for sculpting was to release the form hidden within the stone, and this certainly implies eros at work. So you can have an erotic relationship between one's self and one's creations. As a rule, however, you need a mass of people to arouse the full energy of Pluto and eros. You can see it right now, here in this room: eros is being sparked off here in this group. You also can see it happening in mob scenes, and in crowds in a state of panic. Theater requires an audience. Have you ever gone to a movie when there were only three people watching it with you? It can be a very powerful movie, but something will be lacking. If you view the same film with a whole crowd of people, you'll get a much more powerful experience. You can pretty well count on a crowd getting highly sparked off and aroused, but you can't always count on this happening in a one-to-one relationship. Another thing I wanted to stress about eros is that romantic love is very often a forbidden love. Romeo and Juliet didn't get to spend much time together. Eros thrives on taboo, on that which is forbidden. If I can have you easily at anytime, then the pain and ecstasy of our coming together and separating again is lost. The concept of romantic love thrived in medieval times, but it was romance based upon frustration.

Audience: Can you comment on the role of agape in a therapeutic situation?

Richard: Therapists can feel a lot of eros between themselves and their clients, but hopefully the therapist is carrying enough of agape to love their clients with an open hand. Therapists should be aware of the erotic energy that exists between healer and patient, and it is the therapist's responsibility to make sure that agape is always controlling the situation. If this is not the case, the therapist will be caught in an erotic countertransference that is bound to hinder the healing process.

•   •   •

Let's complete our discussion of the four types of love — Taurean epithemia, Leonine philia, Scorpionic eros and Aquarian agape. I know that it's a rather painful thing to realize and accept the idea that we are not going to satisfy all these levels of love with the same person all at the same time, and yet this is what I have to tell you is the case. People think that if they could just find the right person, or if they could just get more evolved, or if they could get their act together and clear up all of their problems, they'd be able to experience all the levels of love simultaneously with the same person. I'm sorry, but I just don't believe this is possible, although I do think the only way such a thing might happen is by giving up the idea that it can happen. As I said before, in order to find love, you must fall out of love. Falling out of love means falling out of love with the expectation that there is going to be some kind of particular pot of gold at the end of the rainbow for you. Because we are so hooked into romantic ideals of what a relationship should be, we often miss the beauty and opportunities right in front of us. It's possible to experience all these kinds of love, but not all of the time with the same person. Perhaps we can have it with the same person, but not all at the same time. If we are truly living in process, if we are growing and evolving, we must expect and accept that change is part of life.

Demeter's problem was that she could not accept change, and for this reason, she had to lose her daughter. If you want to look at it one way, this was also Jehovah's problem in the Old Testament.

He creates Adam and Eve in the hope that they will live happily ever after in the Garden of Eden, but this projection onto them doesn't leave much room for change and growth. A relationship may begin with philia or idealization as its predominant mode, but mutual idealization cannot last forever. What I'm saying is that relationships go through phases, and we must honor whatever phase is dominant at any given time. A relationship that starts off quite erotically can change its face into one that's based more on agape, the kind of love that is given with an open hand, the kind of love that is no longer jealous and possessive of the partner. I've always thought that the glyph for the sign of Scorpio—the sign of erotic love—looks like a rollercoaster, with all those peaks and valleys, all those ups and downs. When eros deserts a relationship, we shouldn't try to bring it back in artificially or by force. Paradoxically, the only way to possibly retrieve eros is to let go of the predominant desire for eros within one's primary relationship. If you are living a relatively self-actualized existence, you have work that interests you, you have other relationships with family and friends that are meaningful and important, you have compelling hobbies or an outlet for your creativity, and you also have your spiritual life. With all of these things in your life, there is no need to try to fulfill all your needs through one special other person— which, of course, puts less demands onto the relationship and frees the other person to be who he or she really is. Having said all this, it still is very difficult to let go of the notion that someone will eventually come along who will change your life forever.

The myth of romantic love comes from the medieval and Renaissance idea of courtly love handed down by the troubadours and minstrels. I'd love to go into all this in more detail, but we just don't have the time. I suggest you get hold of Robert Johnson's book We,[3] in which he views courtly love as the merging or blending of the idea of romance with the ideals of Christianity. For instance, idealizing an unattainable woman is similar to the adoration of the Virgin. You could say that the collective anima of the medieval and Renaissance period in history was this divine, untouchable Virgin. The strange thing about it is that the Virgin

---

[3]Robert Johnson, *We: Understanding the Psychology of Romantic Love* (San Francisco: HarperCollins, 1985).

was allowed to be married. Although this is not something that was talked about very much, Mary was in fact married to Joseph. In general, however, there were three main rules governing romantic or courtly love—rules that you can see in stories like the triangle between King Arthur, Lancelot and Queen Guinivere, or in the classic tale of Tristan and Isolde. Rule one is that you should never be sexually involved with each other, so courtly love could never be consummated, much in the same way as our love for the Virgin Mary can never be consummated. God never consummated his love for the Virgin Mary; instead it was carried out by a third party, the angel. Unlike Zeus, God didn't incarnate himself into an ox or bull or swan or shower of gold in order to mate with a mortal woman. Not becoming sexually involved with the object of your love means that she will always remain immaculate. It doesn't matter that she might be married to someone else and having a sex life with that person. As far as you're concerned, she's still immaculate and perfect. The second rule is that you must never be married to each other; indeed, you are usually married to someone else entirely. The third rule is that you must stay perpetually aflame with passion.

It's interesting how these three rules work together: you can stay aflame perpetually with passion so long as you never become sexually involved with your heart's desire, and so long as you are not married to one another. These are the rules. An element of suffering is also involved in all this. So-called romantic love is a very Neptunian situation in which you can never consummate or completely satisfy all of your desires. Yes, there's perpetual courtship, but it doesn't go much beyond that. If you can imagine it, the good knight chose his fair lady and proceeded to worship and adore her forever, harboring this tremendous passion for maybe 50 to 60 years. Now, a lot of this comes out of the Christian ideal that it is better to sublimate something than to experience it, which takes us directly back to St. Paul, who seems to have had pretty bad feelings about his own sexuality. He said that it was better not to have sex at all, although he also stipulated that if you craved sex, it was "better to marry than to burn" in hell. What Paul seems to have meant was that conjugal sex is preferable to extramarital sex, so that if you must have desire, it should at least be channeled into a vehicle ordained and sanctioned by God or a rabbi or a priest.

That way the distraction or destructive quality of rampant sexuality is contained.

The Romantics wanted it both ways. They wanted to marry one person and burn for another, which is how they kept the flame of desire alive. Eros doesn't mind this, because eros thrives on impediments. Eros loves triangles. If you were to picture eros as an astrological configuration, it would form a T-cross with you as the focal point. The Christian ideal of sublimating the sexual drive into something higher had a major influence on the nature of romantic love. In medieval times, nobody expected to consummate a romance. In the King Arthur legend, everybody—including Arthur—knew that Lancelot and Guinivere were madly in love with each other, and that wasn't considered taboo. What was taboo was the fact that they consummated their relationship. The other thing they did that was taboo was getting caught doing it. Such a consummation of courtly love was considered an act of treason, which is why Guinivere was sentenced to the stake. It wasn't the act of love in itself that was punishable, it was the fact that they broke the strict code associated with courtly love.

In our society, we tend to see romance as a direct prelude to marriage. There's nothing wrong with this, except for the fact that most of us also believe that romance should be kept alive between you and your mate even after you've married. If we no longer continue to feel romantic after we've taken our vows, then we think something is wrong with the marriage. But you can't keep that kind of romance alive within a marriage, because romance is kept alive by the frustration, deprivation, agony, distance and sub- limation arising out of the fact that it's a taboo to consummate the relationship and actually live with your beloved. Can you see what we've done? We've set ourselves a double bind that is essentially unresolvable. We're hungry for this idea of romance. Just look at the kinds of stories published in romantic magazines, which always end with living happily ever after in the state of marriage. The publishers and writers of these stories don't tell us how the relationship actually develops after the marriage, because they don't want us to know that. In other words, these magazines feed into the idea that romance always magically results in marriage and all that happily-ever-after stuff. Frankly speaking, until we can let such notions go, we cannot have a real relationship. This ideal of romantic love also interferes with other relationships we might have, because if we're so busy looking for and waiting for that *one* special person to come along and carry our epithemia, philia, eros and agape, then we can't give very much to our friendships or to developing the creative side of our nature.

I'm certainly in a bubble-popping mood today, and I hope that you don't see what I'm saying as too negative or depressing. I hope that you see all this as hopeful. For me, it is hopeful, because part of individuation and coming into adulthood entails letting go of the illusions of childhood and adolescence.

Another bubble I'd like to burst concerns the myth surrounding the idea of family as we have known it since the days when we were all gathered together in caves serving up a leg of saber-tooth tiger. The family as we've known it since that time is on the way out. When we talk about family, we're normally referring to a mother, father and children in spite of the fact that right now in the United States 26 percent of the children are being raised by one parent, and the divorce rate is well over the 50 percent mark. The projection is that by the year 2000, 50 percent of the children will be living with and raised by one parent, most likely the mother. Fifty percent, that's half of us! Usually, when we talk about family archetypally or astrologically, we're talking about the family historically — the old notion of family based upon tribes and clans of interrelated people all living within the same area. We're talking about uncles and aunts and grandparents and cousins and cousins and more cousins, once and twice and three times removed. In other words, we're still seeing the family as this great nurturing mass of people all bonded together. Currently, in most cases in what we choose to call the first world (the United States, Western Europe, Australia and possibly even Japan to some extent), this outdated historical notion of family is starting to fall apart for reasons that I won't discuss in great detail just now. But briefly, these reasons include the falling apart of structured religion, the tremendous expansion of communication, traveling and transportation, along with the ever-popular idea that the way to individuate and find ourselves is to leave our nests and our family in order to discover more fully who we are. So we put on our hats and grab our suitcases and say, "Bye, bye chums, I'm off to find myself." For all these reasons, the family is falling apart. I'm not saying that this is bad or wrong, but I am saying that this is the state of the things right now.

The falling apart of the old kind of family network is another reason why we have difficulties with relationships. The idealized other—the one who comes along and is meant to carry everything for us—now has to serve as a father and mother to us, as a best friend and companion, as a critic and teacher, as the fulfillment of our anima and animus projections, as well as the one who helps us resolve all the problems that we've not completed with our parents, while graciously allowing us the freedom to discover ourselves. On top of all this, we also want the relationship to be an open one (which usually means I want you to give me freedom rather than the other way around), although we don't mind if our partner gets jealous from time to time because that proves how much they still love us. You see the horrible paradoxes we've landed ourselves in? My point is that we're asking our relationship with that one special other to carry more weight than it can possibly bear, and such an overloaded relationship is bound to come tumbling down around our ears, which explains why we have such a high rate of divorce. The tremendous fantasy life we have around finding this idealized relationship keeps us perpetually searching for that one right person.

Audience: So you're saying that our society has built up this myth about finding *the* one. Don't similar myths exist in other cultures?

Richard: Actually, I don't really think it's a myth, I think it's a hope. There's a difference between a myth and a hope. But let me cover the cross-cultural thing for a moment, just very briefly. The idea of romance certainly exists within most cultures, and the idea of eros exists within most societies. But most cultures do not assume that the person we fall romantically in love with is the person that we're going to eventually marry and share a life with. This is because most cultures do not consider falling in love as the main reason for marrying and being together. In many parts of the world, marriage is seen more as a legal commitment, an arrangement classically undertaken between two fathers. The father owns the daughter; she is his chattel or property and he is free to give her away as he chooses. Many marriages are still arranged astrologically in India, and the choice of marriage partner also depends on the caste system or the position of the parents. Prince Charles isn't a typical case, but he is someone who would have had very little latitude to marry where his heart lies. I remember my grandmother asking, "What is all this stuff about marrying for love?" She said that in her day, the fathers got together and struck an arrangement: hopefully they picked a nice boy for you, and if you were lucky, you'd both later learned to love one another. Do you recall that wonderful song in *Fiddler on the Roof*, the one Tevye sings with his wife Golda? He has three daughters close to the marrying age, and shockingly for the times, they all want to marry for love. What is this? What about tradition? Then he has this great scene with his wife in which he asks, "Golda, do you love me?" And his wife replies something like "Do I love you? For 25 years I've lived with you, slept with you, raised your children, cooked your meals. What do you mean, do I love you?" And they both agree that if that's not love, then what is? Arranged marriages are the rule in India, China, throughout most of tribal Africa, and other tribal cultures, and probably throughout most of the Islamic world. This may seem shocking and backward to the Western mind. In actual fact, the idea of romance and the notion that we should marry for love is a relatively rare and modern phenomenon.

It's interesting to look at the different astrological houses in terms of the kinds of love covered by them. The 8th house, which has to do with eros, passion, death and transformation, and other risks of that nature, is not the same as the 5th house, which describes our heart's desire, the awakening of romantic love, and what we choose to call creative self-expression. The 5th house is the arena in which philia is most likely to be acted out, and it carries a very different meaning from the 7th house, the house normally assigned to marriage. The natural ruler of the 7th is Libra, a sign that can be associated with contracts and diplomatic bargaining, such as a carefully thought-out marriage arrangement.

Audience: Is it right to say that a lot of people seem to be searching for a divine or transpersonal experience through a love relationship rather than through a religious path of devotion to one's idea of God?

Richard: Yes. We all have a part of us that wants to reach out for the divine, but because the old religious precepts no longer work for us, we now translate the medieval idea of romantic love into the search for a living, incarnated person who is going to come along and transform our lives. The other day I quoted you a byline from a movie advertisement that said something like, one day someone will come into your life who will transform it forever. Five hundred years ago such a sentiment would have referred to finding God or Jesus. As I've been saying all along, the problem is that we look for the transpersonal within the interpersonal. We keep hoping that we'll contact and experience the magical, mystical and numinous through the agency of an interpersonal relationship. Not only that, but we want this experience of the numinous to stay alive continually through a marriage situation. That is the problem. We keep looking for our deepest Self, for Jesus and redemption in a one-to-one love relationship. We keep looking for a love that will transform us, heal us, help us discover ourselves and make us whole again. We keep hoping for that relationship that will make all our pains go away and leave us self-actualized. We think we will become enlightened when that special person finally comes into our lives. We keep looking for the person who'll do this for us, who'll make us a full human being. We wait and wait and long for a love of this nature. When it doesn't come our way, we think that maybe changing our hair color will change our luck and bring that special divine person to us.

I have a few points to make about the story of Tristan and Isolde. Tristan has a divine experience when he meets and falls in love with Isolde, but he can't have her because she's already married to the King of Cornwall, and is therefore untouchable. Her unavailability is the very thing that keeps his eros perpetually flaming and burning. He could have the hand of another woman, but he does not want her. The reason he doesn't want her is because he can have her. Basically speaking, the main problem with romantic love is that once you actually have the beloved, he or she then loses that romantic glow and aura. What keeps you aflame is the thing that you can't have – the minute you can have it, its magical aura is lost. This is what happens when you project the transpersonal onto another person. The transpersonal is infinite and unbounded. It's an injustice to try to force the numinosity of the transpersonal onto something that is basically relative, finite and material. In his book *We*, Robert Johnson defines sin as the act of calling something by its wrong name.

Another thing about romantic love is that it doesn't necessarily entail wanting the beloved to be happy. Tristan doesn't want Isolde to be happy in her marriage. He suffers because he cannot have her, and he would like her to suffer as much as he does. This isn't love. This is not agape, which says I love you enough to let you go. At best, Tristan's love for Isolde is a very schizophrenic kind of love. He is in torment and therefore she shouldn't be happy either. The only thing that will solace him is that she be as miserable as he is. Something similar happens in the finale of the Arthurian legend. Arthur has long since died, and Guinivere has entered a convent. She has not seen Lancelot for many, many years. Eventually, Lancelot is compelled to find Guinivere again. It's important for him to know that she is still suffering as painfully as he. However, when they meet, she tells him that she has finally found salvation through devotion to Jesus, something that St. Paul would have applauded right from the start. Guinivere had finally gotten it right, because the proper place to put the transpersonal is onto the transpersonal. You can't find the transpersonal in the interpersonal because they are different things. Leo, Virgo, Libra and Scorpio are social signs, interpersonal signs. Sagittarius through to Pisces are transpersonal signs. We would like to have the transpersonal in the interpersonal, but it doesn't work that way. You might think you have found the numinous and transpersonal in a romantic relationship, but I can assure you that it's a projection. This dream we have about finding the person who can satisfy our need for the numinous is a dream that dies hard. I hear a lot of kicking and screaming about it.

Audience: Couldn't we find the transpersonal in the most important relationship of all, the relationship which we have with ourselves?

Richard: Yes, that is precisely what I'm getting at with this whole thing. We cannot find all the different levels and kinds of love within one human being. If you're trying to do this, you are doomed to unhappiness, because you are always searching outside yourself for someone who just doesn't exist. If you want to keep hanging onto that dream, fine, that's your business. Indeed, a lot of people don't know they're alive unless they have that kind of suffering hope. I'm not saying that you shouldn't love passionately or erotically, but I am saying that you shouldn't try to hold onto that kind of love forever. The problem in our society about this issue is twofold. First, we think that we can actually find one relationship that simultaneously satisfies all of our love needs; and second, we think we can permanently maintain such a relationship once we've found it. I'm not saying that there is anything wrong with the god Eros coming along and piercing us with his arrow. In fact, I consider it a great gift from the gods when this does happen. This kind of passionate love can happen between two lovers; it can happen between a teacher and a student; it happened between Michelangelo and his stone; and it happened between Beethoven and his music. Beethoven was so attached to his music that he had to be tricked and lured out of his house in order for anyone else to get hold of manuscripts that he refused to part with.

Do you hear what I'm saying? I'm saying yes, go out there and experience eros. Go for it, go for broke. Feel as deeply as you possibly can. If you are lucky enough to be chosen by the gods to have such a thing, then take advantage of it. You are among the blessed if you are chosen to be impaled by one of Eros's arrows. It's a wonderful experience to have. But I'm also saying that you shouldn't expect to marry it and live with it forever, because this is not the nature of eros or erotic love. So much of the suffering and disappointment we feel in relationship has to do with the fact that we hope to capture and maintain the intensity of eros forever. If you do manage to capture eros, it is only for a moment in time, because the gods won't allow it any other way. So bless the moment, go completely into the moment, surrender to the moment. However, please remember that you can't surrender to the moment if you're desperately trying to clutch it and hold onto it forever. Accept it with an open hand, but freely let it go. When you do experience it, you are experiencing what the Greeks referred to as "divine madness"—they would have seen it as a daimon coming to possess you. Something similar happens when you're in the throes of creative ecstasy, only in this case, it's a slightly different form of daimon that possesses you. Passionate love and passionate creativity are erotic things that you cannot permanently hold onto.

When you've finished writing a book, you have to let go of it, you have to hand it over to the publishers. An erotic experience is like the breath of God flowing through you, but you can only be inspired in this intense Plutonic way if you are ready not to have it. That's the paradox of it all. I know that what I've been saying has triggered an awful lot of stuff in you, and these are precisely the kinds of issues I'd like you to be taking up in your workshop groups. There is no right or wrong answer to all this. I'm not saying I'm right; however, I am saying that this is my experience, this is how I see it. Do with it what you will.

• • •

Let's move on. Now, I'd like to say a little bit about how the Moon, Mercury, Venus and the Sun archetypally go into and experience relationship. We've already talked a great deal about the lunar type of love, which is an umbilical kind of love even in adults. What lunar love says is that if you love me, you'll nurture me, you'll be my mommy, you'll be my daddy. I was quite shocked to hear that President Reagan calls Nancy "Mommy." This wouldn't be so bad if Nancy called Ronnie "Daddy," but she calls him Ronnie. It makes me think that we're in bad trouble! There is nothing wrong with lunar love – it's a component in every relationship. We have the need to nurture each other, and if the nurturing lunar part of us is not met by the other person, we cannot experience safety, security, love and comfort. We'll be discussing synastry in greater depth in the coming lectures, but suffice it to say for now that one of the most important planets to look for in a synastry contact is the Moon. This is because the Moon depicts the inner child in us, and that inner child must be fed. Lunar love only becomes a major problem if we are hooked into it at the expense of other kinds of love, or at the expense of other facets of our nature which are more solar, mercurial or Venusian. In other words, we are still so attached to the umbilical cord that all we want out of relationship is for the other person to constantly give us all the nurturing we need. There's also a Mercury level in love relationships. Mercury love works by trial and error. It's when we experiment without feelings to discover who we are, and we do this by trying on various relationships. I call this "the relationship as therapy syndrome," that is, I really don't know who I am until I spend time with another person, and through experimentation, trial and error, and through figuring things out, I begin to find out not only something about you, but also something about me.

Lunar love operates on the level of the infant (notice that I'm trying to avoid saying the word infantile which sounds like a judgment), while Mercury love correlates to the *puer* and *puella* in us, the masculine and feminine versions of the eternal youth. This is the stage when we are Peter Pan or Alice in Wonderland. Peter Pan is a classic puer because he doesn't want too much closeness and dependency in relationships, and yet he is constantly attracting and pulling people toward him. Pinocchio is another puer: he's artificial, a puppet, and his dream is to become a real boy. This mercurial phase of finding ourselves by trial and error in relationship is a very normal stage or part of all our relationships—we do it in childhood, we do it with the original friends we make, and we probably also do it in our first sexual encounters. The Mercury stage is going on when a seven-year-old boy and a seven-year-old girl, or two kids of the same sex, go behind the barn and play doctor. They are curious about how they differ, they're curious about what each other has got. You show me yours, and I'll show you mine. This differs from the Venus stage, which might occur around the age of 16, when the two people who go behind the barn not only want to see how they differ, but also want to take these differences and put them together. Seriously, this is the difference between Mercury love and Venus love. Mercury is still separate and it is propelled by a desire to understand the world. Archetypally connected to the air sign Gemini, Mercury love says, "I want to stand back and observe myself in different situations in order to discover who I am, and I do this best by comparison, by comparing this with that, or by comparing myself with other people." Virgo does something similar on an earthy level: "I need to stand back, discriminate and compare one thing with another in order to decide what's what and which is which." I associate Venus with the adolescent phase of love—a period in which our ideals are awakened. Venus, especially through its connection with Libra, is very sensitive to what our particular culture deems as ideal or beautiful, and we seek this in a partner in order to feel complete, in order to feel good about ourselves. For instance, if you were a young man living around the turn of the century, then you'd probably want a woman who looked like Lillian Russell, someone with a tiny waist, wide hips, and enormous bosoms. Mae West was the perfect example of this kind of figure. However, if you are a man growing up today, you'd probably prefer a woman who looks anorexic, because this is what our culture currently upholds as the divine ideal. Boy and girl adolescents, still in the process of finding out who they are, are extremely sensitive to this kind of peer pressure. So we have Joe Jock, the high school football hero, and we have Marjorie Majorette, the curly blond-haired, blue-eyed, dimpled thing. He is the guy most of the girls are in love with, and she is the girl most of the guys are out to get. Joe Jock carries the animus projection for most of the girls in high school, and Marjorie Majorette carries the anima for most of the boys. Usually Joe Jock is looking for Marjorie Majorette, and Marjorie Majorette is looking for her Joe Jock. When they get married to one another, everybody sighs and says how inevitable it was. And as far as I'm concerned, it's fine for these two beautiful people to get together so long as they're still living in the adolescent Venus stage of intense projection. But the chickens come home to roost when he begins to develop a potbelly and is unable to find a good job, and when he sees her with her hair up in curlers and discovers that maybe she's a bit of a shrew who doesn't cook all that well. So this kind of idealized relationship has a tendency to fall apart as the years go by.

Romeo and Juliet are the perfect example of the archetypal Venus phase of relationship during which we search for our ideals of beauty in another person. Of course, Shakespeare had to kill Romeo and Juliet off in order for them to live on as beautiful in our imagination. In truth, this Venusian phase of projecting the ideal simply will not and cannot last forever. However, there are many people who try to hang onto this Venusian phase forever in their relationships, just as there are many people still trying to live relationships on the infantile level. If we're stuck in the infant-based lunar phase, we are looking for somebody to be our perpetually perfect mommy or daddy. If we're stuck in the Venusian phase, we hold onto adolescent ideals within a relationship and what we're saying is that we must have the perfect beautiful other in order to feel complete. Much of Venus love is hooked into the physical and surface ideals of what a person should be. He should be tall with broad shoulders, he should be dark and have a powerful personality, he should have a deep voice and make lots of money as a high-powered executive or something like that. She should always be young and beautiful. You see this happening around you all the time: men project their Venus onto women, while women project both their Venus and Mars onto men. What happens when a man is projecting his Venus onto a woman, and she starts to grow a little older? He often dumps her for a younger woman, which, as you know, is a classic fear held by a lot of women. Men, generally speaking, don't own their Venus, which means that they aren't in touch with the beauty and loveliness inside themselves and therefore seek these qualities through a partner who can carry Venus. Since Venus is the archetype of a young, nubile woman, the Venus projection fails when the woman gets older or if she becomes too motherly. Indeed, many men fall out of love with their wives when she has their first child and becomes a mother, because she no longer fits the Venus archetype. A man may be happy enough about having a motherly type wife, but he will have to go elsewhere to shop for his Venus. I think that women know this on some level, and they also know that it puts them in a very difficult position. How can they be both the Moon and Venus? How can they be a mother for a man while still being the perpetual Aphrodite?

A man who succeeds in reclaiming his own Venus frees his partner or wife from having to carry that load, and she is then permitted to grow older and change. It's the same thing the other way around for the woman and her Mars. If a woman is projecting Mars onto a man, he has to be her conquering hero, her knight on the white charger, the kind of guy who goes out there and tackles the world, the one who will defend and protect her against the many dragons she fantasizes are lurking about just waiting to get her. If he fails to do all this, she might provoke a conflict in order to see if he loves her enough to fight with somebody over her. Aphrodite, who in her pure form was a real troublemaker, was always provoking men to play the warrior, ready and willing to clash antlers with his rivals in a fight to win her love. A friend of mine is a good example of this. She has Sun conjunct Mars and Pluto in Leo in the 12th house, with Venus rising in Leo right on the

Ascendant. She's an extremely beautiful woman who always manages to get herself embroiled in emotional triangles. Actually we shouldn't call them triangles, we should call them T-crosses. She's very clever at getting herself involved in T-crosses where she is the focal point. For instance, she dated two different men, both of whom loved her and wanted to marry her. She somehow set it up so that she had a date with both of these guys on the same night. When the two of them turned up at the same time, she suggested that it was possible for everybody involved to love each other and go out together. The men didn't like this idea. Joe said something like, "Listen, you have a date with me and this other man can just get lost." And Sam said to her, "Look, it's now or never; make your choice because I'm not going to put up with this." She then moaned about what an awful position they were putting her in. She just couldn't understand why the two men couldn't work it out between themselves. Of course, this was not the first time this sort of thing had happened to her. You could say that Aphrodite is turned on by blood. After all, she did choose Ares, the god of bloody warfare, to be her lover. Conflict turns her on, and she is constantly provoking it. So the true Aphrodite female is one who has not integrated her own Mars and therefore seeks it in a man.

Audience: Wasn't it Aphrodite who indirectly started the Trojan War?

Richard: Yes, the Trojan War is a good example of what I mean. You probably know the story, but I'll review it very briefly. Two mortals are getting married and all the gods are invited to attend the wedding except for the goddess Eris, the goddess of strife and discord. Eris is not pleased, and when all the gods and goddesses are seated for the marriage feast, she rolls a golden apple down the table. The apple is inscribed with the words "for the fairest," and it lands midway between Hera, Athene and Aphrodite, who all reach out their hands for it at the same time. Trouble. Zeus, copping out as usual, decides to settle the matter by having Paris, a mortal man, select which of these three goddesses is the most beautiful and therefore deserving of the golden apple. It's no accident that Paris is chosen to be the judge in this matter. The story goes that Priam, the King of Troy, was told by an oracle that he would have a son who would cause the fall and destruction of his city and his whole family. In a futile attempt to prevent this fate from happening, King Priam abandons Paris, his first male child, on a mountain, where he ends up adopted by shepherds and kept far away from other people. Paris is so isolated that he has never seen a young, beautiful woman. Because Paris is so pure, unsullied, and innocent in this respect, he is chosen by Zeus to judge the beauty contest. The three contestants then proceed to bribe Paris as a way of influencing his choice. Hera says if you choose me, I'll make you very powerful by giving you the governorship of all of Asia. Athene says if you choose me, I'll make you the greatest warrior that ever existed. Aphrodite simply stands up, loosens the cords of her tunic, which drops seductively down to her waist, and says if you choose me, I'll see to it that you have the fairest woman in the world for your wife. Of course, Paris gives the golden apple to Aphrodite. (Did you know that Aphrodite was often portrayed with a mirror in one hand and with a golden apple in the other?— which implies that Aphrodite was a classic narcissist, totally in love with herself.) The most beautiful woman in the world at that time was Helen, who just happened to married to King Menelaus of Greece. With the use of her magic girdle, Aphrodite arranges Helen and Paris to meet and fall in love. Paris brings Helen to Troy, and this sets off the Trojan War. So the Trojan War—12 years of tragedy and destruction—was actually caused by Aphrodite's desire to win the beauty contest at any cost.

Believe me, you've got to watch this idea many of us have of Venus being all sweetness and light, bonbons and candy. That's a big, big mistake, because Venus (Aphrodite) has a very dark side. It is essential to accept the dark side of Venus so that you can face it and work through it, rather than live it out unconsciously or indiscriminately. You could say that Mars without its opposite (Venus) is a monster, and that Venus without her opposite (Mars) can also be monstrous. Along with the Moon, Venus is a prime anima figure for men, while Mars is a prevalent animus figure for women. What prevents Venus and Mars from becoming destructive is their integration and balancing. By the way, this is true for all other archetypal, complementary pairs of planets. Integrating the Moon with its opposite, Saturn, takes the monster quality away from both of them. The same goes for other complementary planetary pairs, such as the Sun and Uranus, Mercury and Jupiter, Mercury and Neptune, and Venus and Pluto. If we don't find a way to integrate, balance and blend each of these pairs of planets, our behavior is likely to turn pathological.

Audience: So complementary pairs of planets are based on the planetary rulers of opposite signs.

Richard: Yes, Venus rules Libra and Mars rules Aries, so Venus and Mars complement one another by virtue of being the rulers of opposite signs. The Sun rules Leo and Uranus rules Aquarius, so the Sun and Uranus are complementary planets that need balancing. The Moon rules Cancer and Saturn rules Capricorn, so the Moon and Saturn are complementary opposites. Since Saturn is a co-ruler of Aquarius, you could also include the Sun and Saturn in your list of complements. If the two sides of a planetary complement are not integrated and balanced with one another, the most neglected side will be projected outwardly and met externally. An unintegrated planet is usually experienced in an archetypal or mythical form, and very often in an extremely monstrous form. Part of anyone's healing process is integrating the archetypes of the six complementary pairs of signs and their corresponding complementary pairs of ruling planets. For example, if Kore—who was archetypally an innocent Venus figure—had been in touch with her Pluto, she wouldn't have needed the experience of summoning him in such a monstrous form from underneath the earth. We could even interpret her rape and abduction as a gift from the gods, because it enabled her to get in touch with a part of her psyche that she hadn't as yet included and acknowledged in her life. Venus (in the form of Kore) attracted her opposite, Pluto, much in the same way that Eve attracted her opposite in the form of Lucifer. If Eve had already accepted and integrated her own Pluto and taken a bite of the apple on her own volition, she wouldn't have polarized and manifested the need for a Lucifer-type creature to tempt her into it. A similar dynamic is alive and well within many, many relationships.

I would say that solar love is an adult love. Please, don't put a value on this as a good or better kind of love, it's just another different kind of love. The solar kind of love says, "I'm an adult, I know who I am, I know where my boundaries are." The glyph of the Sun tells us something similar: "I am in the center of my being," although in some cases this can also mean self-centeredness. If we take the symbol of the Sun and put 12 lines through it, we've turned it into the astrological chart. And if you picture yourself standing in the center of the chart, then in whichever direction you turn, you will see another part of yourself. The person who is in his or her center as an adult is capable of an adult kind of relationship that says, "I know who I am. I don't need you to define who I am. I don't need to play roles of mommy, daddy or child with you. I'm not using you as an experiment to discover myself." As I explained earlier, Mercury love, unlike solar love, uses relationship as therapy, as a way of growing: "God, this relationship is terrible but aren't we learning an awful lot through it." And solar love is not like Venus love, which is full of projections and idealizations, and which can be based on surface things that are not actually tangible. Solar love is unlike the love associated with Mercury or Venus. Solar love says, "Since I love and value my own self, I am capable of loving you for who you are, rather than what I want you to be or what I imagine you to be." Solar love says, "I choose you," rather than "I need you." Moon, Mercury and Venus need the other person, unlike Sun love, in which you consciously choose a partner from your own center.

Now, nobody experiences love solely and purely on the level of the Sun. You can only get to the solar level when you have turned inward, reclaimed, and integrated your lunar projections. Actually, I should say you can only get to solar love when you have integrated your Moon-Saturn axis, because we should look at planets as complementary pairs. So when the Moon-Saturn axis is integrated and well-balanced inside us, when we can reasonably take care of our inner child, then we are more prepared for solar love. And when we've grown through quite a bit of the Mercury love experimental phase of trial and error, and when we've to some extent integrated our Venus and Mars and are no longer putting strong projections onto the idealized other, then we are beginning to be free enough to tune into the level of solar love. People tuned into the solar level are quite capable of being content and happy on their own. They recognize their separateness and individuality, and they do not *have* to be with you or with anybody. This is a very hard place for most of us to get to, because the Moon, Mercury and Venus parts of ourselves need to be with somebody else. Can you be alone and not turn the television on? Can you be alone and not have to read something to keep you occupied? Can you just be alone with yourself? It's not easy. Adult solar love not only says that you can be alone, but it also says that you mostly like who you are. This doesn't mean that you are not accepting of the fact that there are certain ways in which you need to change or grow, but it does mean that you basically do love and accept yourself for who you are. In other words, you don't need someone else to love you to prove that you are lovable. Solar love says, "I choose you," not "I need you." Solar love can see and accept a partner's faults, because people coming from the solar level of love are capable of still loving themselves with their own imperfections. "If I can accept my imperfections and still love myself, then I can accept your imperfections and still love you."

If you are still busy projecting parts of yourself all over the place, then you can't realize solar love. A lot of people have this myth that they cannot really love somebody or allow somebody to love them until they've finally achieved perfection—until they've finally lost that 10 pounds, until they've finally gotten that college degree, until they're finally earning enough money, until they've finally done whatever. Everything is constantly kept waiting for that magical time of perfection, which, of course, never comes. A lot of people are also under the illusion that love has to wait until they find that perfect person out there, that person who is all together, all wise and beautiful.

Audience: I've been thinking that Woody Allen has really presented us with a whole new type of culture hero. He's so open about himself and he's not afraid to show himself in his work, especially when it comes to his foibles in love. I can't think of a single astrological archetype that defines what he's doing. He's not the Sun, he's not Mercury, and he certainly isn't Mars.

Richard: Do you want me to give you some feedback on what you've just said? Okay, the truth is that Woody Allen drives me crazy. I confess that I am a New Yorker and that's why he makes me crazy. Although I consider him a genius, he is what I call an overly psychoanalyzed man, constantly laying his psychoanalytic trip on everybody. I find that boring. When I watch his films, I feel as if I'm being trapped into watching him psychically masturbate, which might be interesting once or twice, but after a while it becomes a bit much. I do think he is wonderfully funny in many ways, and I agree with you in that he touches on some kind of archetype, but I think that archetype has to do with complete and total self-involvement. I think he's a total narcissist. Nonetheless, it is educational to see some of his stuff. He's an extremely creative man, and I thought *Annie Hall* was wonderful, but after a while I get so tired of his self-involvement.

I know that much of the stuff about love and relationship that we've been discussing in the last few days is not easy to take. Working through it is hard, painful and slow. I would say, however, that half the battle is the "ah ha" that happens to you after you've been jolted by some new insight and awareness. This is Uranus, Neptune and Pluto in operation—something has been shocked or dissolved or blown up inside of you, and there's often a long period between the shock and the "ah ha," between the realization of something and the change that comes about as a result of that realization. During this period, it's important to be patient and gentle with yourself. Don't beat yourself and think that you're stupid because you haven't realized something sooner. It doesn't help to be hard on yourself in this way. Many of us think that change follows immediately upon realization, but this is not the case. A lot of what happens in the psychotherapeutic process is that we go round and round over our basic ground until we have explored the parameters of all the stuff inside. We go circuit after circuit until we finally say, "Wait a minute, I know this area. I know this space, so why am I going round and round again?" Although we may be trembling and full of fear, what we ultimately need to do is to take one little baby step outside the parameter of our usual circle, and look to see what lies beyond it. It's at this point that it's really helpful to have an ally with you—whether that's a good friend, a partner, or your therapist. In the Middle Ages, when it was thought that the Earth was flat, cartographers used to draw in dragons just outside of the area marked by the borders or boundaries of the world. They thought that when you came to the edge of the world's borders, you could fall off and land yourself in a terrible and frightening place. In this respect we are like jackrabbits, terrified of venturing beyond our known world. I think it's true that there are dragons out there; they aren't just a figment of our imagination. The dragon may be your mother, or it may be your fear of freedom, or it may be the self-realization that you're growing up and having to own your projections or integrate your planets. However you wish to say it, there are dragons out there beyond the borders of your known world, and it takes a great act of courage to face them.

One of my first psychology professors used to say that you can go round and round the merry-go-round in the endless search for *why*. He used to say that *why* is like the brass ring on the merry-go-round. If you've ever grabbed for the brass ring on a merry-go-round, what happens? Another brass ring pops up right there in its place. We can go perpetually round and round and round seeking why. I'm not implying in any way that one of our goals shouldn't be to seek why, but the perpetual seeking for why can get in the way of taking that step outside of the magic circle into the world where the real dragons are waiting. What I'm saying to you is to be patient with yourself. I have a big sign on my wall at home in the room where I counsel people. It's a quotation from *Hamlet*, and it simply says that *readiness is all*. Sometimes you just have to leave it at that, but if you're in process, please trust that the point will come when you're ready to pick up a sword and go after your particular dragons. But it is a mystery: you don't really know if and when you'll reach that point — transits and progressions can't even tell you this in any definitive way. A certain transit or progression may indicate that a god is knocking at your door, but who's to say whether or not you'll be there to answer it.

I hope that you're beginning to see, or that I'm beginning to make clearer, that the path of integration, astrologically speaking at least, is to own within yourself the complementary pairs of planets and signs. To the extent that one side of a complement is out of balance, the other side must equally be out of balance; but it also follows that as you begin to integrate one side, the other side automatically must integrate. Do you see what I'm saying? Take the Moon and Saturn, for instance: the more you integrate your own parent (and let's assume that it's a loving parent), the more you are integrating the hungry child who's on the other side. Or take the Sun and Uranus: the more you are comfortable with who you are, the more you can accept the Uranian experience of shattering, falling apart and rebuilding yourself. In spite of the fact that your existing ego identity has been shattered through some new breakthrough or awareness, you know that it will regroup again in some other way. I'm not going to run through all the pairs of opposites with you right now; just remember that each sign and planet has its complementary opposite.

So how can you tell where you are in all this? Start by taking a close look at your life, and a close look at your relationships. I named this conference "Through the Looking Glass" because the people in our world are the mirrors of ourselves. Because it's very hard to be objective and subjective at the same time, it's not easy to see yourself clearly and objectively. But it is a fact that the objective world is very clearly represented by the kinds of people we have chosen to bring into our lives. One indication that we are embarking on a process of change and integration occurs when various important relationships in our lives begin to break or shatter. This isn't easy, because part of us would like to stay within our basic ground; part of us doesn't want to change and grow and let go of our projections. Jung once said that change is hard, that change is painful. Maybe we don't change until we've suffered enough. When you are beginning to grow and change and become better integrated, certain relationships may fall away or go through a very testing time. This doesn't necessarily mean that the whole relationship need dissolve or come to a closure, but it could be the case that the projected part of the relationship is ready to fall away. When you take back things you've been projecting onto another person, it's possible that the other person may not be able to follow along with you. I'll explain what I mean in more detail. By reclaiming your projections, you become better integrated and balanced. Let's say that you're a woman whose game is to play the little girl or child bride in a relationship with a man who's playing daddy for you. In other words, you're the Moon and he's Saturn. And let's say that a time comes in your life when you are ready to integrate your own Saturn, when you're ready to become your own parent to some extent. You discover your own aims, ambitions and goals, as well as a destiny that is uniquely your own, which extends beyond the parameters of your marriage or family. Now, what happens is that as you reclaim your Saturn, your husband must reclaim his Moon, which, up to now, he has been projecting onto you. If he isn't up to reclaiming his Moon, you may reach a crossroads where you have no alternatives but to say to him, "Look, either you start to move with me, or I must move alone," and this can mean a very hard parting. Relationships are like aspects in your chart, and aspects are like chains of energy. You can't have a transit over one planet without it ultimately affecting any other planet it aspects. A similar dynamic applies to relationship. If something happens to you, it causes a chain reaction that affects everyone who's involved with you, and the people most closely in conjunction or opposition are the people who are going to be most affected by your changes. All I can say to you is that changing and growing is often very hard. It's often painful, and yet it's also hopeful. Don't forget that there are people around to help you through it. We're all in the same boat; we're all in the process of moving toward greater integration, and not one of us has yet achieved complete wholeness or integration. So please be very gentle with yourself in this process.

MARS: SELF-ASSERTION IN RELATIONSHIP

I want to talk a little bit about anger and about Mars in the chart. This is another loaded area that I'm pretty sure will provoke some strong responses in you, and I wish I had much more time to cover it thoroughly. Actually, I like provoking you, because I have more than a bit of the provocateur in me.

Audience: In that case, do we have to hold our questions until the end?

Richard: Yes, hold the questions. Suffer with them. Live with them a little, let them percolate inside you, and we'll have great fun letting them all out later.

   Naturally, I connect anger with Mars, because Mars is the ruler of Aries, and the fundamental archetypal quality of Aries is to survive. Aries represents one's own survival – the survival of "me." I believe that the first and most fundamental principal of life is that of one's own survival. Out of Pisces we come into Aries; out of chaos and nothingness we come into somethingness. The fundamental life urge is to keep that somethingness manifesting, and this is why I call Aries the fundamental sign of survival. If you want to look at the sign of Aries in a Freudian or somewhat Jungian way, you can see it as the force for life, the life force or life wish, the urge to go out and exist in the world. Aries is so primitive and archetypal, it's almost impossible to describe. What I can say is that Aries represents the survival instinct, and that Aries does this through assertion. Taurus is also an archetype of survival, but Taurus survives through preservation. So Aries survives through assertion, and Taurus survives through preservation. These two modes of survival are quite different, and yet Aries and Taurus need to work together. Assertion says, "I go out after what it is that I want, and what I think is right for me." The opposite of Mars and Aries is Venus and Libra. In themselves, Mars and Aries are very primitive—you could say that they are presocial, and that they essentially are capable of being extremely bloody. The *Iliad*[1] is an example of a work of literature that I consider to be clearly and purely Martian, with all its lust for blood, slaughter and glory. You see something similar in the Vikings—the joy of pillaging and raping just for the pure life of it. I know that I'm most alive when you're dead. Jehovah is constantly commanding the Israelites to burn houses and slay the women and children. Here we see a very raw, primeval kind of Mars, and it's obvious that we couldn't live in a civilized society if we were all operating on this purely asocial Mars principle.

So balanced against this is Venus and Libra, the complementary opposite to Mars and Aries. Libra gives us a sense of mores and social control, and is there to help us achieve greater balance in the way we behave in society. Of course, the idea of what constitutes moral or "nice" behavior does vary from society to society, but whatever the case, Libra helps to balance out the primeval quality of Aries. Those people who are terribly unbalanced on the Aries side of the polarity usually aren't among us in society for very long. We lock them away in mental institutions and prisons. We call them antisocial, or asocial, or sociopaths, because they haven't developed enough social awareness or social conscience to enable them to live within society. And there is a small percentage of our society which is, perhaps, permanently antisocial. So this is the Aries side without the Libra side balancing it out.

However, most of us have managed to become nice little boys and girls—we've learned our Libra roles very well. We know what it is to be nice, to be considerate of the other fellow, to be objective and to see the other guy's point of view, and to have good manners. Libra is the sign of manners, and manners are used to balance out the raw and primitive energy of Mars and Aries. In ancient Rome, the way they shook hands was for each person to grab the other person's arm up to the elbow. The Roman handshake wasn't like this because they liked to feel each other's elbows; it was done

---

[1]Homer, *The Iliad*. Many translations are in existence, one of the most recent being a 1989 verison published by Doubleday, New York.

like that because grabbing the arm that a person used to wield his sword was one way of guaranteeing that he wasn't going to suddenly reach for his sword and go for you. Bowing is a way of offering your neck up for the chop to someone, and it communicates the idea that you have no harmful intent. The tipping of the hat comes from the days when knights lifted their visors to show their faces, and this action was a way of saying, "I'm not the enemy, I'm a friend." When a knight closed his visor in a certain way, it meant get your sword out because I'm ready for a fight. The curtsy has interesting origins. Women never carried swords in court, but they often carried daggers, and maybe you can guess where they hid them. The curtsy position insured that a hidden dagger would fall from its hiding place. Go home and try it. The curtsy is also similar to the bow in that you're offering your neck. As a matter of fact, when men wore tunics in ancient Rome, the also were obliged to curtsy. So what I'm saying is that many of the things that we call manners and mores were directly derived from ways of showing other people that you don't intend to harm them. Even the smile, the famous Libran smile, is a way of saying I don't mean harm to you. Now the problem is that most of us have learned our Libran lessons so well that we are tipped to that side of things, which leaves our Aries side slack and underdeveloped. We're afraid of assertion, because we think that if we are assertive then other people won't like us, that we'll be seen as pushy and then rejected for it. Of course, this is a much greater problem for women than for men, because Mars is fundamentally an animus kind of planet, and Aries is the most primitive, archetypally male sign. Generally speaking, women experience more problems with their Aries side, just as men have more problems with Taurus, which is fundamentally a feminine sign. Men have more problems than women when it comes to sensuality and their ability to tune into the world of nature; and women tend to have more problems with their assertiveness and their ability to go out directly after what it is they want in life.

To be assertive is to know what it is that you want, and then to go after it. It's important, however, to understand the difference between assertion and aggression. Assertion says, "I ask for what I want, but I also recognize that there is a not-self out there who has his or her or its own interests in mind, so I'm also ready to accept that I may not get what I want." Aggression says, "I get what I want and you don't count." There's a big difference between the two. If people call me assertive I'd have to agree with them, because I normally consider myself pretty assertive. If people call me aggressive, I don't agree with them, because I really don't think of myself as aggressive. I'd be sad to think that I was aggressive, because it's one thing to say, "Hey, I want something from you," and it's quite another thing to say "Gimmee." The opposite of aggression is placation. Aggression arises when Mars is not connected with Venus, when the bond is broken between Mars and Venus; the reverse is also possible—the placating Venus that is totally cut off from Mars will never know what it wants. If you're totally tipped to the Venus side of the scales, you can't be assertive, you can't give clear messages about what it is you want, and you constantly try to walk the Libran tightrope, believing that if you stay neutral enough and don't commit yourself to anything, then somehow you are going to be safe. This is Libra trying to keep its Mars shadow at bay. Assertion, however, comes about when Mars and Venus are better integrated, and to repeat, it says, "I am able to state clearly what it is I want at the same time as being aware that there is a you out there. And I'm also aware that what may be right for me and what I want from you, may not work for you."

It might be fun to illustrate what I'm saying by acting it out with one of you. I need someone from the group to do this with. Any takers? Okay, Phyllis, come up to the podium and sit on this stool. In this impromptu drama, we're going to act out Aries and Libra, and we're also going to illustrate the difference between aggression and assertion. You'll see what I mean. First, I'm going to be Aries without an integrated Libra side, so watch what happens. I'll start by approaching Phyllis in this way.

Richard: Hi, how you doing? Great. My name's Richard. You really look nice. Want to go out?

Phyllis: No.

Richard: Oh, yes you do. I'll pick you up at a quarter to eight. We're going to have a good time. I mean, you are going to find me the hottest guy in the world.

Phyllis: I'm busy.

Richard: So what? Just cancel it. I mean, I'm better than whoever your date is anyway. I'm just the kind of guy you like.

Phyllis: I'm not going.

Richard (to the audience): So do you see the kind of role I'm playing? I'm being Mars without Venus. You can see how I scare her when I'm behaving that way. Of course, I'm illustrating it in a very raw form—I could be a much more charming Aries and not be quite so aggressive about it. I could walk up to her and say, "Hi, how you doing?"

Phyllis: Okay.

Richard: Good, my name's Richard.

Phyllis: My name's Phyllis.

Richard: Glad to meet you, Phyllis. I just got in from California. I'm an astrologer out there. You know, I study the stars. I could do a chart for you sometime if you'd like. By the way, I really dig your red hair. God, redheaded women are absolutely the greatest!

Phyllis: Well, thank you.

Richard: Yeah, you're welcome. So tell me . . .

Richard (to the audience): One of the things you'll notice about Aries unconnected with Libra is that Aries has no real sense of anybody's body space. If I'm that kind of Aries, then there is only my will— you don't exist, you're an object. Phyllis, were you starting to feel like an object?

Phyllis: Yes, definitely.

Richard: Yes, this is how Aries tends to make other people feel when it's not connected with Libra. Another thing that out-of-balance Aries does is that IT'S ALWAYS SHOUTING AT YOU, because pure Aries unconnected with Libra has no sense of space or distance. Did you notice that in the last sketch, all the conversation came from me? Although I approached her, I was not the least bit interested in her as a person in her own right. Did you feel that?

Phyllis: Yes.

Richard: And did you feel that I had some kind of ulterior goal in mind?

Phyllis: Yes

Richard (to the audience): Okay, now I'll run through the same scenario, but this time I'll be Libra.

Richard: Hi.

Phyllis: Hi.

Richard: How you doing?

Phyllis: Good.

Richard: Good. (Longish pause.) You come here often?

Phyllis: No, this is my first time.

Richard: Oh, really? What's your name?

Phyllis: I'm Phyllis.

Richard: Oh, that's a nice name. Where are you from?

Phyllis: Denver.

Richard: Denver. That's a beautiful city. What do you do there?

Phyllis: I'm an astrologer.

Richard: An astrologer! Wow! Tell me all about that. Or are you here on holiday trying to get away from it?

Phyllis: Uh-huh.

Richard: That's wonderful. How do you like it here?

Phyllis: I love it here.

Richard: Really? What have you been doing since you've been here?

Phyllis: Well, I've been acting passive a lot.

Richard: Oh, far out. I can't quite hear you. Do you mind if I come a little closer?

Richard (to the audience): Libra can be just as assertive as Aries, but it's done in an entirely different way. Notice that in my last conversation with Phyllis, she ended up knowing nothing about me. Libra is perpetually mirroring, and Aries is perpetually asserting. When Libra is not integrated with Aries you can get total stasis, as if the scales become frozen. I'll give you an example from my caseload. I was working with a couple who were considering divorce—all the "magic" had gone out of their relationship. In the first session I worked with this couple, I observed that there really seemed to be a lot of love between them. By the way, he has the Sun and Moon in Libra, and she has Sun in Libra and Venus in Libra conjunct her Libran ascendant. So their synastry isn't too bad. I accidently left the tape recorder on just after the session was finished, and they were discussing what to do with the rest of the day. She said to him something like. "Well, honey, what do you want to do tonight?" And he said, "Well, I don't care. Whatever you want to do is all right with me." She then replied, "Well, we could go to a movie." And he said, "Well, if you'd like to go to a movie, we could go to a movie." Then she said, "Or we could go home because the kids are with my parents and you know we've been away for a long time." He says, "Well, if that's what you'd like to do, we could do that. Whatever you want is all right." Then he added, "Well, we could go for a drive and go to the beach. How about a walk on the beach?" And she says, "Well, if that's really what you want to do, then I guess it's okay with me." Do you see what was going on?—both of them looking at each other desperately and saying, "Tell me what you want so that I can know what it is I want." This is what happens when too much Libra is around—without anybody being able to be assertive, the relationship falls away. So you could say that an assertive relationship is an erotic relationship; an aggressive relationship is a destructive relationship; and a placating relationship is a boring relationship.

The next question is what do we do with anger in all of this, because most people see anger as an aggressive act. I promise you it isn't, but the way most people practice anger, it does come out aggressively. Anger is a great shadow culturally within our society. It's an even bigger shadow for women than it is for men. Most of us have not had anger modeled to us in a correct way. What we've seen happen in our families and around us is anger distorted into violent and aggressive acts, which probably have terrified us. For this reason, as children, our little child minds deduce that anger must be bad stuff and we should have no part of it. Mars tends to be one of the most projected planets of them all, and probably the most common planet to fall into the shadow (as is the sign of Aries). But this is a real problem, because if we are afraid of assertion, or afraid of the possibility of our assertiveness turning into aggression, and if we are afraid of anger coming at us from other people, then what happens is that our whole instinct toward survival becomes suppressed. And when this happens, our ability to defend ourselves starts to fade away. As I said earlier, this is a big problem, particularly for women, because many women believe that if they can be placating in a Venusian type way, nothing bad will ever befall them. I have a rather unfortunate example of this. A client of mine was raped in New York. She was on the subway, and this guy sat opposite her and started to stare at her. She confessed to me that her instincts told her she should have gotten out of her seat, moved away, or gone for help. (By the way, if you're in touch with Mars, you're in touch with your survival instinct.) But she told me that she didn't act on these impulses, because she was afraid of hurting his feelings, and that he might really have been a nice person. These were more or less her words,

"He smiled at me, and of course, I felt, well, I can't be unfriendly. I mean, I shouldn't be cold, so I gave him a little smile back." And so on and so on. Her stance to the world is basically placating. The smile she had given to the man on the subway was a pained smile which was actually saying, "I'm tired, leave me alone, don't stare at me," but that placating message only served to encourage the aggression he had stored inside him—which is why I'm constantly telling women to honor their Mars, even if this means taking up a martial art or something along these lines. There may never be a need for a woman to put a martial art into action in her life, but just to know that she could do so if necessary helps her to have a more positive relationship with her Mars.

Audience: So what you're saying is that placating actually triggers aggression in other people?

Richard: Yes, placating triggers aggression, and you can see this going on all the time. Have you ever watched male and female animals courting? When the female acts in a placating way, she triggers aggression in the male. Some women believe that being placating makes them appear disarming, when what they're really doing is being charming.

My definition of anger is assertion plus passion. Anger is eroticized assertion. Anger says, "Because I care so deeply about this situation, a great deal of emotion is touched off in me." One of my counseling teachers used to say that anger is a gift of love, which is a beautiful way to put it. The people that I express my anger toward are the people whom I care passionately about, and one of the people I care passionately about is me. So I can express anger when something is being done to me that I object to and want to stop. This is why anger is an important component of our survival instinct. Of course, when anger is distorted or masked by some other form of behavior such as sulking or pouting, then it may not be serving your survival instinct in the positive way it does when your anger is clean and direct.

I consider anger to be the language of love. You could say that one rule in an erotic relationship is that anger leads to passion, caring, intimacy and clarity. One of the things that anger does (provided it's not distorted anger) is to bring you greater clarity.

Anger can give you clarity right away. Hear me, I'm not talking about blaming, I'm not talking about sarcasm or violence. Anger says, "Look dammit, you're my husband, and when I go to a party with you and see you trying to seduce other women, it makes me bloody angry. I want you to stop it, and my telling it to you in this way says that I love you and I love me, and it also says this is the way I feel when you act that way at parties." As I've said, I believe that anger brings clarity. In the little scene I've just described, for instance, the husband may turn to his wife and say, "Golly, honey, you're right. I'm sorry, I'm really going to have to watch that. Sometimes I run on automatic pilot at parties and forget myself, but you must believe I really do love you. I'll try not to be that way again." So her anger has made him aware of something he hadn't seen before, and this has opened things up for discussion. Of course, the husband in this case could turn to his wife and say, "Screw you, I'm going to do what I want." This kind of reply, if you are truly open to hearing it, will also give you clarity, because it says an awful lot about the relationship you're in. Or the husband might respond to his wife, "You're always imagining things." Even this reply can serve to give you greater clarity, because it tells you that he simply isn't hearing you. Or he might say, "You're one to talk. Remember 3½ years ago at Susan's party, you flirted like mad with some guy." This response also gives you clarity, because it informs you that he is holding onto something that is not yet resolved inside him; and it could also signal that he's still out to get revenge on you. Or he might answer, "I'm sorry, I don't want to talk about this," which will also give you clarity, because it brings to light the fact that you're in a relationship with someone who really doesn't want to communicate with you, and it raises the question of what you're going to do about it. So every time you assert, you get some kind of clarity, even if it's not the answer you'd like to hear. The passionate kind of assertion that comes with anger has the effect of bringing clarity by forcing issues out into the open.

Expressing anger can be a problem for both men and women, but it's usually more of a problem for women, because they are culturally taught that it's wrong for them to express their anger. Unfortunately, the rule is that denied or repressed anger turns toxic. I think that bottled-up anger is one of the fundamental causes of depression. Even the symbol for Mars is saying, "I want to go out of myself toward something." If for some reason you can't give expression to your Mars, it turns back in on the self and manifests either in active self-hate or in the form of depression. Do you find yourself tired a lot of the time? If you do feel pretty constantly exhausted or depressed, it could mean that there's a lot of Mars energy that you're bottling up and not channeling properly into the direction it wants to go. People usually bottle up their Mars if they're afraid that expressing it would threaten the stasis or security of a relationship. They're afraid that asserting themselves or voicing their anger will topple the relationship. You may be afraid that you'll get answers that you're not ready to hear, so you don't dare ask the question or say what you want, because you aren't sure you could handle the consequences. Please be clear, I'm not telling you that you should immediately get out there and unleash any pent-up anger, but I am saying that learning to express your anger is something you should think about working toward and developing. I'm not saying that you should go home and practice it on your spouse immediately, but you can, at least, start finding ways to be more comfortable with the expression of your anger.

Another rule about anger is that it needs to be served hot out of the oven, like a soufflé. Watery types of people or people with Mars in a water sign, may suppress their anger because they're afraid voicing it will make them fall apart, break down or cry. People with Mars in an air sign may think, "Well, I'll put off voicing my anger until I've thought about the situation for three or four more days, which will give me time to consider all sides of the issue to see if my getting angry is really justified or called for." The problem with this way of handling it is that the anger gets cold, and cold anger tends to come out in a distorted fashion. People with Mars in an earth sign do not enjoy the experience of being ruffled in any way, so their tendency is to sit on their anger until it manifests in the form of an ulcer. Or they displace the anger into overeating, or they sublimate it into something like housecleaning, or into some work or project that they can throw themselves into. Mars in fire is probably more directly prepared to express its feelings, although people with this placement could be afraid that their anger will come out too explosively or cause too great a commotion. Not daring to express anger because of the explosion it might cause, suggests a lack of self-trust—which is unfortunate, because living a conscious life or a solar life or an erotic life ultimately depends on knowing and trusting the self.

Audience: I've observed that fire doesn't always give it that much thought, that they just go POW.

Richard: Well, some people with Mars in fire actually fear going POW because they're afraid of hurting others or hurting themselves in the process. But if you have self-trust, you know how far to go, you know the limits, you know that you're not going to pick up a golf club and start swinging it at people. I believe that the quicker anger is expressed, the less toxic it becomes. Conversely, the longer it's held in, the more distorted and worse it becomes.

In the past, I've run workshops in which we've used exercises to learn more about cleanly expressing anger, but unfortunately we won't have enough time to do this. One of the best rules for expressing your Aries or your Mars is to start with the statement "I want" or "I feel." Stick to that and you can't go far wrong. For instance, rather than attacking your husband and calling him a son-of-a-bitch or a selfish bastard, you could say, "I feel neglected, and as if you don't care for me when you do . . . ." This is Mars speaking clearly. As babies, we probably started out expressing our anger instinctively, but this gets quashed in us fairly early in life. Most of us have to learn how to express our anger cleanly, because most of us grew up with no role models around who could teach us how to handle anger in a healthy way. But I warn you, any relationship (not just love relationships, but even friendships or the relationship between a parent and child) that does not permit assertion or anger will eventually become static and passionless. Relationships that don't allow room for anger or assertion will eventually turn flat; the affect goes out of it because one or both of the parties involved are sitting on a whole load or list of things they haven't voiced and about which they're still angry. Some therapists call this "stamp collecting," each stamp representing something that's been left unsaid. I'm thinking of the play *Who's Afraid of*

Virginia Woolf?,[2] which some of you must have seen. The two protagonists, George and Martha, are in this classic, vicious, vindictive relationship. All of the toxic stuff that's never been brought out into the open in their long relationship comes to the surface in the last act, which I believe is called "The Death of the Gods." When couples get to the point of starting some kind of couple or marital therapy, they usually have already reached that phase where all the poison is beginning to surface. By that stage, they have taken things so far, and so much toxic material is spewing out, that the relationship is almost inevitably doomed, which can be a very painful thing to watch or go through. We call Venus the planet of relationship, but Venus has no existence without Mars. They are two faces of the same thing. And, as I've just explained, Mars is a common shadow area of most birth charts.

There are many distortions of anger, and we don't have the time to describe each of them in great detail. Generally speaking, we distort the expression of anger in an attempt to keep a relationship in stasis: we don't want to risk losing face or losing the relationship, or we want to keep things under control and not give any power away. What normally happens is that we get into blaming, which is one of the most common distortions of anger. How come you always make me feel so bad? How come you always hurt me? Blaming is a way of holding the other person responsible for what you're feeling, when in actual fact, what you're feeling or how you react to what someone is supposedly doing to you is your own responsibility. So blaming is a Mars distortion, and it's usually done as a way of making the other party feel guilty. I've seen this with people who have Mars-Saturn combinations or who have aspects between the Moon and Mars. Sarcasm is another distortion of Mars and anger. You are angry at your partner, but the anger is not expressed cleanly or directly and comes out as sarcasm instead—usually in the form of caustic swipes or remarks directed toward the person you're angry with. Even playing practical jokes on someone can be a distortion of anger. I heard about a groom who had put itching powder in his wife's panties on the day of the wedding ceremony. And he just couldn't understand why she got so upset, because it was just a joke.

---

[2]Edward Albee, *Who's Afraid of Virginia Woolf?* (New York, Macmillan, 1962).

Another common distortion of anger is known under the heading of passive aggression. Getting sick as a way of making the other person feel guilty is one form of passive aggression. Burning the dinner, forgetting an anniversary, or even gaining weight can also be manifestations of a passive or indirect expression of anger. Passive aggression is a great weapon of children. Children who feel powerless often learn quickly how to be passively aggressive. They are constantly forgetting to do things they promised to do, or they're always turning up late for things, or they regularly spill their milk. Have you ever watched a kid doing that? They'll sit there in their highchair watching you, and they'll wait until you're looking away, then they accidently on purpose knock over the glass of milk on their highchair. Boom, like that! Then they'll say things like, "Oh, I didn't do it, I really don't know how it happened, or my elbow must have jerked of its own accord." Passive aggression is a trick of the powerless, and a lot of women turn passively aggressive when they feel powerless: they get sick, they faint, they get hysterical, they cry, they sulk, they turn inward. You really can't blame them, because society is largely responsible for teaching them this way of behaving.

Viciousness and vindictiveness are also distortions of anger. Vindictiveness is one of the quickest ways to distance yourself from someone. It usually hits below the belt, is most likely done in public, and is very often about sexual things. A partner who's being vindictive will zap you right in public with the most private and vulnerable things you've revealed in moments of confidentiality. I'm reminded again of a scene in *Who's Afraid of Virginia Woolf?* where Martha really has George on the ropes. She's given him one after another, and when he finally cries uncle and pleads with her to stop, she says something like, "For Christ's sake, George, when are you going to realize that you married me for this?" Violence, both the physical and the psychological kind, is another distortion of anger. In essence, the violent person is saying, "I'm going to win at any cost, and you're going to lose. I'm not risking exposing my vulnerability. I'll go to any means to have power and control over you."

I've noticed something very interesting about violence—almost every time a violent act is about to be committed against you, your instinctual Mars tries to warn you that this is coming. But placating

Venus (that part of us that wants the relationship to remain in stasis) will usually butt in with, "Don't worry, it will all blow over and settle down soon, and everything will be okay again." I want to give you one rule about violence: if someone you're close to has been violent toward anybody or anything in the past, chances are that it will eventually be directed at you as well. So if you observe somebody being violent toward anybody or anything, you shouldn't think that somehow you are magically protected—one day it will eventually be your turn to get it. The person you've seen lose his temper and punch someone in the face for not giving him his way will probably do the same thing to you when you don't let him have his way. The man who kicks the dog will eventually get around to kicking his wife or children, unless, of course, he's worked hard in the meantime to resolve the eruptive side of his nature. Violence is always presaged by something, there are usually clear warning signals. If we're in touch with our Mars, we know how to take steps to deal with impending violence. In the Casteneda books, Don Juan tells Carlos that we must always be like a warrior, which means that, without being paranoid about it, we should walk around in the world with our antennae out. In other words, we should always stay conscious of what is going on around us, and we should be especially conscious of the fact that death may be waiting for us at any time. So instead of walking around in a fog, we really should stay aware of what's happening around us. I lived in New York's Harlem for 12 years, where I was the only white person around for blocks. I loved it, and I learned an awful lot from the experience. It was a dangerous situation, but when I was out on the streets I kept my antennae well tuned, and if something inside me said don't walk on this side of the street, I would cross over to the other side. I like to look at people, but with certain people I instinctively sensed that I shouldn't look directly at them. Or if someone was approaching me about whom I felt something funny or strange, I would do a U-turn and walk quickly away in some other direction. This is what I mean about staying in touch with your Mars instincts, because Mars is the planet of the survivor. I might add here that if you've had violent parents, then violence will be part of your myth about what relationships are like, and you'll be prone to attract it from other people or act it out yourself. There's a lot more to say, but I think it's time for some questions.

Audience: Could you list some of the kinds of martial arts?

Richard: The ones that immediately come to mind are kung fu, karate, wrestling, boxing, judo, aikido and tai chi.

Audience: Something bothers me. I heard you implying that passive women invite violence and other forms of aggressive behavior. I'm not comfortable with that statement, because it seems too much like blaming the victim. I know cases where women have fought back and ended up being beaten much worse. It seems like a double bind.

Richard: It is.

Audience: I also got angry when you said that women often act in a way that invites aggression. I really don't think that's true in a lot of cases, and yet they still get men being aggressive toward them.

Richard: I hear what you're saying and it's a legitimate point. I can understand your anger about all this, but I still think that the idea of being a victim is a bad myth to hold onto. It's too easy to project blame. What I'm offering is another way to look at this whole situation. If a woman upholds that society or something outside of herself is responsible for turning women into victims of men's brutality, then she is pretty much stuck in the role of a victim. I believe that when a woman seriously starts to integrate her Mars, something changes on a psychic, inner level. She begins to walk with a different orientation toward the world, and she sends out different messages from those she sent out when she was in the habit of disowning and projecting her Mars. Any one of us could become a victim. Look at the people whose plane was hijacked in Lebanon. In this case, I don't think their getting hijacked really had much to do with whether or not they had an integrated Mars, and yet they all ended up victims. But if you have integrated your Mars to a fair degree, it would be a great help in getting you through a situation like that. Mars is your inner warrior. An overcompensating Mars might say, "I don't care, I'm going to kill one of those guys even if this results in the rest of us on the plane being killed." A totally passive Venus will fall apart and be incapable of doing anything, and will just wait for somebody else to take action.

Audience: I think it's better to have Mars so integrated in you that you walk around with an active survival mechanism, rather than just bringing it out when you have to fight back.

Audience: I think it's important to integrate Mars in a physical way. Besides having your antennae out, it helps to walk around with square shoulders and a look that says don't mess with me. It's like you're an actor at that point; you may feel insecure inside but what you're showing to the world is a strong presence that will usually deter others from attacking you in some way.

Richard: I knew this topic would bring up a lot of discussion. I'm glad that you're all talking about it with one another, but there really is no right or wrong answer, and that's because it's a very emotional issue. I just want to tell you one story to illustrate how I see things in this respect. When I lived in New York, I studied acting with a woman named Uta Hagen, who, by the way, was the original Martha on Broadway in *Who's Afraid of Virginia Woolf?* She is a very centered woman, who has managed to integrate her Mars without coming over as "ballsy," competitive or dominant. I've noticed that people who have begun to balance Mars and Venus often become quite androgynous. This doesn't mean that a woman loses her femininity, but there's something about her that is strong and self-sufficient. I think it's very unlikely that someone like Katherine Hepburn is going to get mugged. It could happen, but I think she's naturally going to send out messages that say, "Back off, Charlie, you're going to be in big trouble if you mess with me!" and she doesn't have to hit somebody to communicate this message. Anyway, Uta Hagen is this type of woman. I'll never forget an incident that happened in a class she was leading. She was sitting there with her little poodle that she always brought with her to class, and with her hair up in a bandana. While one of the students was doing an improvisation, the garbage men outside were horsing around and making a lot of noise during their lunch break. It was so hard to concentrate with all that ruckus going on that Uta stopped the improvisation and asked the class secretary, a pleasant young woman, if she would please go outside and ask the men if they could be a little quieter. The secretary went out to do this, but her efforts only provoked a lot of loud banter and laughter from the men, and the noise continued even worse than before. Uta then said that we should just try to put up with it and continue with the improvisation, because their lunch hour would be over quite soon. But the noise became so bad that Uta sent out the school's treasurer, a very tall man, to try to talk them into keeping it down for the sake of the class. Well, he went out to the street, and, once again, all you could hear were the guys laughing at him. He reported back to us that there were eight of them, and they all were very big. Uta said that we should try again to carry on with the improvisation, but sure enough, the noise outside got worse and worse. So Uta got up, handed her poodle to someone to hold, took off the little glasses she wore on the end of her nose, marched out the door, and within half a minute, the noise stopped and all you could hear was silence. Uta returned and we went on with the impro. Somebody finally asked her what she had done to get them to quiet down. She answered that she didn't do anything except look at them. This is an example of the kind of warrior power you have when you have achieved a high level of integration. It's an inner quality, an inner aura that communicates *don't mess with me*, and it doesn't necessarily mean you have to have the physical power or strength to fight someone off.

It's time to end now. I suggest that you get together with your workshop groups sometime today in order to discuss the kinds of issues we've been examining—in particular, anything around anger. Look at your charts, see where your Mars is by house and sign. Explore what you do with your anger or your assertion. If you have time you can also talk about the four kinds of love—epithemia, philia, eros and agape. You could also examine your projections in romance, and delve deeper into anima and animus issues. Be sure to correlate what you're talking about with placements in the astrological chart.

PART THREE

PRACTICAL
APPLICATIONS
OF SYNASTRY

RELATIONSHIP SIGNIFICATORS IN THE NATAL CHART

I want to begin by talking about some of the things you would look for in a person's chart to get an indication of what relationships will be like for that individual. This will lead us directly into synastry and chart comparison, but I think it's very important that you study the charts of each person separately before you even begin to compare the two in terms of their relationship and interaction. Relationship is a function of who we are: in order to do a proper synastry between two people's charts, it's important to know what each of these individuals is like as a person, and also to have some idea of what kinds of things each of them is likely to look for or get up to in relationship. Jumping in and comparing two charts without first having studied each one separately is like trying to interpret a transit or progression before you even know what the natal chart looks like.

Although where you start isn't that important, I'm going to begin by talking about *missing functions*, which are one of the first things I would look for in a chart to glean a sense of what relationships would be like for that person. I use the term missing function to describe a situation in which there is no planet in one of the elements (fire, earth, air or water), or no planet in a particular polarity (no planets in a yang sign, or no planets in a yin sign), or nothing in a particular modality (nothing in a cardinal sign, or nothing in a fixed sign, or nothing in a mutable sign), or no planet in a particular orientation (that is, no planet in one of the personal signs, or no planet in one of the social signs, or no planet in one of the universal signs). Something I also do, which you may want to follow or not, is to look at houses in terms of their orientation. The first four houses are personal houses, the second four houses are social, and the last four are universal houses. So if you didn't have any planets in the first four houses, then you'd have a missing function in terms of the personal houses. If you had nothing in the second four houses, then you would have a missing function in terms of the social houses, and so on. (For the record, I don't consider houses to have elements or modalities. A house can be angular, succedent or cadent, but I wouldn't refer to a house as being a fire house, or an earth house, or an air house, or a water house. I say this because elements describe a typology or way of perceiving the world, while houses represent arenas of experience, and I don't think the two necessarily mix. However, if you personally feel it's okay to mix them, then go ahead and do so.) Missing functions indicate an area that is likely to be projected in relationships. Indeed, you'll see that the most dynamic relationships are not ones in which you have like seeking like, but the ones in which *unlike* seeks *unlike*. Please don't put a value judgment on this. When it comes to chart comparison, you should remember that there is nothing good or bad per se. Something that might seem like a very difficult aspect for you, may be just the sauce that stimulates another person. For instance, I consider Mars-Saturn contacts to be one of the most dynamic aspects that can occur between two charts. Classic astrology wouldn't agree with this, but I find it to be so. It's certainly been true in every case I've seen.

As I was saying, a missing function is an area that is likely to be projected onto another person. I use the term *dominant function* to describe where you have the most energy. For instance, if most of your planets are in air signs, then air would be a dominant function for you. Let's say you have seven planets in air signs, which leaves only three remaining planets to be divided among earth, fire and water. Looking at it in this way, those three functions would then be less dominant or *inferior*. Take heed, I'm not intending inferior to be interpreted as less good than something dominant—it just means that there is less of it. A dominant function is an area in which we function comfortably; it's an area that comes naturally to us, where we feel at home. The person with a dominant air function will usually feel comfortable or at home with communication. Someone with air as an inferior function still needs to communicate, but there's an obsessive or compulsive quality underlying that need. (By the way, I include a singleton—one planet of a kind in any group—under the heading of an inferior function.) Psychologically speaking, inferior functions have a driven or compulsive quality about them, and they are much more likely to have psychological defense mechanisms—such as denial, repression, projection, sublimation or compensation—clustered around them. I don't want to be throwing a whole lot of psychological jargon around the room without you understanding what I'm talking about, so I had better try to encapsulate very quickly what I mean by some of these terms. Denial is the refusal even to admit the possibility that there's a particular quality existing inside me. Repression, however, means that some part of me recognizes that I have a certain trait or quality, but I repress it or try to keep it out of my conscious awareness because I don't really want it to come to the surface. In other words, something repressed is a little closer to consciousness than something in denial.

I think I should say a little more about denial. Denial is a defense mechanism, and we use it when we absolutely can't bear to face something that's in us. Some astrologers dive into a client's chart and start talking about all the different problems, complexes and defenses they see in that person through the chart—which is a bit like unzipping the client's psyche in such a way that it spills out all over the place. Even though the astrologer is sure of the correctness of the interpretation, the client may protest and deny the truth of the reading. What I'm saying is that you should tread carefully if you run up against denial in people, because it's there in order to armor or protect them against things they are not ready to acknowledge or handle. A trained therapist knows that a lot of work may have to be done with some people before they are ready to let go of denial, whereas some astrologers tend to jump in there and blitz a person before he or she is really ready to hear certain things. Which is why I strongly believe that people who want to work as counseling astrologers should obtain a proper training in counseling skills. This belief has not made me very popular among some astrologers in North America. I know that it's a rather heavy and loaded area for lots of people, but I feel very strongly about it, and it comes straight from the heart. I call myself a born-again astrologer because I started out as a traditional astrologer, and then went back to school to train in psychology in order to deepen and improve my astrological work. If you are already working as a counseling astrologer or if you plan to, you owe it to your clients as well as to yourself to get a good training in psychological skills and technique.

Anyway, the dominant function is an area that functions rather easily and where we feel at home. The inferior function indicates an area of stress and strain. There can be an enormous amount of power and psychic juice associated with an inferior function. Beethoven was short of water in his chart, and yet he was compelled to write powerfully emotive music. And I'm thinking of Michelangelo with his missing earth. Or poets like Byron and Keats with no fire. The fiery Latin lover, Rudolph Valentino, had no fire in his chart, and the same goes for Errol Flynn, another daring and adventurous fiery lover. In a roundabout way, what I'm saying is that some people take their inferior function and sublimate it into a creative outlet or into some kind of outstanding feat or achievement. In other words, they sublimate or redirect their inferior function into an area that differs from the primary direction in which it would naturally express itself. Compensation is another defense mechanism that comes up around the inferior function, and this occurs when we compensate for a sense of weakness or lack in ourselves by working extra hard to prove our worth and capability in the area where we feel inadequate or underdeveloped. Our society tends to approve of sublimation and compensation, because these defense mechanisms often manifest in a superlative performance of some kind, and yet, the person who is doing the sublimating or compensating often experiences great psychological pain or duress in the process.

I can't repeat it enough: the inferior function is the one most likely to be projected, and, for this reason, it's what we commonly meet or attract to us in relationships. Please remember that projections can be both positive or negative, and we often have a love-hate relationship with what we project or with whom we project it onto. Think about this in terms of the astrological signs. Many people, when they first start studying astrology, are surprised to realize that the signs they are most attracted to are the very ones that turn them off the most. Do you think Leos are pompous, egotistical and self-centered, or do you experience them as playful, jolly fun-loving and warmhearted? Well, my friends, the answer to this question is entirely in the eye of the beholder. And you may find that, at some point, your negativity toward Leo undergoes a big change or switch when you begin to own in yourself the archetypal qualities associated with this sign. When you have integrated more of Leo within yourself, you'll probably find that the wild polar swing between the horrible, terrible, selfish and egotistical Lion whom you hate, and the playful, charming, creative Leo whom you love, comes into better balance. One of the ways you can tell how well you have integrated a particular sign is to observe your subjective reactions to people who display the archetypal behavior naturally associated with that sign.

Of course sometimes you'll come across people who aren't manifesting the qualities associated with their dominant function. The reason for this usually can be traced back to early family conditioning, where family pressure acts to disallow or inhibit the expression of someone's dominant function. For example, take the case of a woman with a dominant fire function who comes from a very traditional family which believes that women are not supposed to act in a fiery way. So the message she gets early on is that if she manifests who she is, she is mad or bad, and she'll lose the love of her mother or father or both. I strongly suspect and glean from experience that a repressed dominant function can lead quite directly to psychosis, phobic reactions or severe somatic (body and health) problems. People who suppress their dominant function will live more completely in their inferior function, and therefore will tend to project their own dominant function onto another person. And they'll usually experience some sort of crisis when faced with the person receiving the projection of their dominant function.

When considering a chart in terms of a person's expectations around relationship, you should also carefully examine the 7th house. Although I believe that we can project any part of our chart onto other people, the most classic line of projection falls across the 1st and 7th houses. The Ascendant and 1st house is the domain of the self, while the Descendant and 7th house is the domain of the not-self. Our mask or persona (the face we show to the world) is formed around the dominant stance we take toward the outer world, and this is usually signified by the Ascendant (although I feel that the Ascendant represents more than just our mask or persona, and I also believe that other parts of the chart besides the Ascendant contribute to the formation of the persona). Our psychic skin or armoring or persona is also developed partly in reaction to our perception of what is out there in the rest of the world, and this is signified by the Descendant and 7th house. The sign on the cusp of the 7th and the placements in the 7th house indicate those qualities we don't believe we have in ourselves, as well as telling us a great deal about how we perceive the external world. For example, if Sagittarius were on the cusp of my 7th, my perception might be that the world out there is full of teachers – wise people who can tell me what to do with my life. And the way I invoke this wise teacher in other people is through my Gemini Ascendant, by presenting myself to the world as a young or eager, bright-eyed student of life, full of questions. In other words, I play the archetypal student in order to invoke the teacher in you. At least, this is the positive way to project it. I could also project it negatively. For instance, I might see most people as pompous windbags (the negative side of Sagittarius on the 7th) and decide to play the Gemini rising trickster or prankster in order to challenge, provoke and irritate all the know-it-alls of the world. There is a kind of chemistry at work by which we attract people into our lives who are working through and dealing with issues similar to those suggested by our own Ascendant-Descendant axis. Now, this doesn't mean that you're necessarily going to hook up with someone whose Ascendant sign is the same as your Descendant sign, although you'd be surprised at how often this is the case. The point you should remember is that your Ascendant-Descendant axis line is a very potent force for you in relationship. When you meet someone who plays into this axis, something in you goes click and immediately recognizes a strong connection or interplay between the two of you. You realize that both of you are somehow operating on the same wavelength, and it's possible that you might dislike this sort of person intensely, because they are living out aspects of your nature that you haven't yet owned in yourself. Historically, however, this kind of connection often leads to romance. Kate and Petruchio in Shakespeare's *The Taming of the Shrew* are good examples of how loathing can lead to love, and the reason for it is that apparent opposites are often more alike than they think.

It's very easy to look at the nature of a planet in the 7th house and say this isn't me, although I see it a lot in other people. Of course, we don't do this consciously, but what happens is that anyone who manifests the qualities of this planet causes us to get all excited and charged up. For example, if you have Mars in the 7th, you may find it difficult to accept your own assertiveness, your own anger, your own libido, or your own sexuality (this could be especially true for women with this placement because Mars is such a yang planet). Then along comes someone who obviously manifests strong Mars energy—someone with Aries rising, or a Sun-Mars conjunction, or with Mars on the Midheaven or in strong aspect to the Moon, Venus or Ascendant in your own chart, and whammo, you fall in love with that person although something in you also resents them or finds them difficult. If I were to make up a chart for Kate in *The Taming of the Shrew*, I would say she is the perfect example of a 7th house Mars. And, of course, whom she most loathes and at the same time most loves, is this Mars-like Petruchio, who after three minutes bends her over his knee and spanks her bottom. Oh, I hear you saying to yourselves, listen to that male chauvinist pig who thinks how great it is that Petruchio spanked Kate's bottom. I don't think it's a particularly wonderful thing to do, but I do think that it worked well in that particular relationship.

Major planetary configurations that show up in a chart tend to be areas that are constellated in and through relationship. The grand trine, the T-cross, the yod and the grand cross are the most obvious major configurations to consider, although the kite and the grand sextile are examples of two other major configurations you might also look for. I find the T-cross and the yod the most interesting in terms of relationship dynamics, because they are out-of-balance major configurations. In the T-cross, planet A and planet B are in opposition, and planet C is the focal point receiving the square from both of them. In this case, C becomes a very psychologically stressed planet. The same thing applies to the yod: planet A and planet B are now in sextile to each other, and both are quincunx to planet C, which again puts planet C under a great deal of stress. In both these cases, the focal planet C is so sensitized that it behaves almost like a child who is special in some way—perhaps special because of his or her potential for genius, or special because of his or her potential for madness. When it comes to synastry, you'll notice that important or powerful relationships often correlate with a planet or angle in one person's chart touching off the highly sensitized focal point of a T-cross or yod in the other person's chart. Relationships based on this kind of interaspect often have a compulsive quality about them. Another thing to watch for occurs when one person has a planet (we'll call it planet D) in his or her chart that makes an opposition to focal point C in a T-cross in the other person's chart. In other words, when you do the synastry between these two people, you find that planet D in the chart of one of the parties involved turns the other person's T-cross into a grand cross. This has the effect of balancing out or completing the T-cross, which, by itself, is an incomplete or out-of-balance configuration. When this is the case, you can be sure that there will be some kind of powerful dynamic going on between these two people. Something similar applies to the yod. If one person has a planet D that opposes another person's planet C (the focal point for that person's yod), then the yod is somehow made into a more complete or balanced configuration through the interaction of these two people. What would you call a yod that is completed by an opposition to the focal planet? You might call it a boomerang. Or how about calling it a grand yod—I like that, it sounds very elegant. Anyway, whether we are talking about a T-cross or yod, the planet at point D, by virtue of completing an out-of-balance configuration in the other person's chart, serves to close an open circuit.

Stationary planets are also something I would look for in someone's chart to get a sense of what relationship might entail for that person. A stationary planet is a planet that is stuck in one place or moving only very, very slowly, going from retrograde to direct, or from direct to retrograde. (In terms of the natal chart itself, it doesn't matter much to me whether the planet is stationary turning direct, or stationary turning retrograde, although this does have a lot of relevance when you are considering progressions.) What is important is the fact that a stationary planet is hardly moving at all, especially if it's a normally fast-moving planet like Mercury, Venus or Mars. I'll use a metaphor to explain its importance. Imagine that the movement of my hand represents the movement of a planet, and there is a candle burning just below where my hand is passing. If my hand represent a fast-moving planet traveling at its normal speed, it will pass pretty quickly over the burning flame—the candle might flicker and I might feel some warmth from the flame, but otherwise, not a lot is going to happen. Now, if I slow my hand down, when it passes over the flame I would probably feel a little burning on my hand. But if I held my hand stationary just over the candle flame, I would feel a pretty intense burning. Something similar would happen if I held a lens or prism stationary in line with the sun's rays. As I held the lens steady, the sunlight would continue to filter through it, and eventually would start a fire. All this is by way of illustrating that there is something highly concentrated and intense about the nature of a stationary planet. In fact a stationary Mercury, Venus or Mars in a natal chart can have the same kind of power and intensity which you would normally associate with a heavy outer planet. There is something more to a stationary planet (especially a normally fast-moving one) than meet the eye. For instance, I've seen a stationary Mercury manifest in cases of dyslexia, and also in cases where a person with the stationary Mercury is definitely some kind of mental genius. I remember working with one boy with Mercury stationary in Pisces who actually couldn't speak unless it was in rhyme! He was a natural rhymer, and everything had to rhyme—I tell you, there was amazing stuff coming out of that kid. So, as a general rule, stationary planets in a person's chart summon some kind of psycho-dynamic energy or force which is going to affect anyone with whom this person has close contact. I also like to compare a stationary planet with a pot of soup over a burning flame. As you turn the flame higher, the soup will come to boil more quickly, and when it does, all the stuff that's been hidden at the bottom of the pot starts to rise to the top. In a similar way, the intensity of a stationary planet has a way of stirring up quite a lot of deep stuff in us in terms of the area of the chart it affects.

You also should consider a person's natal squares, oppositions and quincunxes in order to get an idea of what he or she might meet in relationship. Oppositions immediately imply polarity, and any two things in polarity will complement one another. However, because we live in a very linear society in which we are supposed to choose up sides and be either a *this* or a *that*, there is a tendency for us not to live out both sides of an opposition; so what happens is that we own one side of the opposition and project the disowned side onto someone else. By the way, which side we own and which side we project can vary from relationship to relationship. The side that you project also can vary depending on one's sex; for example, a man with a Moon-Mars opposition is more likely to identify with his Mars and project his Moon. Although this is certainly not going to be true in every case, I would more likely expect it to turn out this way, rather than a man identifying with his Moon and projecting his Mars. But, yes, it does sometime happen the other way round.

Squares are an extremely psychodynamic aspect, and in some ways, they resemble and irresistible force meeting an immovable object. A square is an aspect of conflict and confrontation, and often an area of pain for people. But don't forget, of all the major aspects, I also consider the square to be the most creative. One of the ways we deal with a square is to decide which planet involved in the square is the closest to our social role or family myth, and then we identify ourselves with this planet and project the other planet involved in the square onto other people. In other words, we identify with one of the planets and we scrap the other. The result is that we're left incomplete, and therefore have to import what would make us more whole or more complete via the agency of another person. Let's use a man's chart as another example. Given the role of men in our society, a man with Mars square Venus is much more likely to identify with his Mars and project his Venus, which means he probably will be very attracted to Venusian or Aphrodite-type women, although it's almost inevitable that he will fight with them because of how Venusian they are. The scenario is pretty familiar: the kind of man who is attracted to gorgeous, voluptuous, showy women is also likely to argue with them about how provocatively they dress—"I don't like it when you wear such low-cut dresses when we go out on the town. You should only dress like that in the privacy of our own home," that sort of thing. And yet, I also would strongly expect that he kind of likes it when she looks sexy and gorgeous in public, because that's probably a large part of what drew him to her in the first place!

Quincunxes in themselves are very paradoxical aspects, because what you have here are two signs trying to connect where there is no natural connection. Let's take an Aries/Virgo quincunx as a typical example. Aries is cardinal and Virgo is mutable, so you have different modalities trying to get it together. Aries is fire and

Virgo is earth, so you have conflicting elements trying to get it together. Aries is a personal sign, while Virgo is a social sign, so you have two different orientations trying to get it together. Now, you might think that because of their differences, there would be no real area of attraction, but I actually consider the quincunx to be one of the most erotic of all planetary aspects. As I see it, eroticism is more often sparked by differences rather than by sameness, and the quincunx is very much like trying to fit a square peg into a round hole. Above all, I understand the quincunx to be an aspect of problem-solving and crisis: problem-solving stems from its natural 1st house–6th house connection, and crisis stems from its natural 1st house–8th house connection. In other words, if you drew a line in the natural zodiac from the 1st house to the 6th house (from Aries' natural house to Virgo's natural house), you'd get an angle of 150 degrees, and the 6th house is an area which, in my opinion, represents problem-solving. And if you drew a line in the natural zodiac from the 1st house to the 8th house (from Aries' natural house to Scorpio's natural house), it would make an angle of 150 degrees, and the 8th house is a crisis-engendering area. As with the square and opposition, there also is the tendency with a quincunx to identify with one end of it, and to project the other end onto the relationship.

It's also important to look for any hard aspect or any conjunction that is a singleton. This occurs when you only have one set of planets in a square aspect, or only one set in opposition, or only one conjuncton in the chart. (A singleton trine or a singleton sextile usually won't wield the same amount of power as a singleton conjunction or a singleton hard aspect, although there may be exceptions to this rule.) A singleton aspect has a powerful effect on the psyche, because it's something that stands out psychologically from the start as an area likely to be projected onto relationships.

The 12th house is another area of the chart that can influence what you attract or experience in relationship. Because the 12th shows what lies right beneath the persona, planets there (or the sign or signs spanning the 12th) often symbolize archetypal qualities or characteristics that your persona deems unacceptable. Or you can look at it this way: if the Ascendant represents the mask we show to the world (which is just one of the many things the Ascendant signifies), then it could be said that our mask is a compensatory reaction for what is hidden behind it in the 12th. The 12th house is one big psychic closet, and if you look in the 12th, you'll see what is hidden behind your mask. Because we normally are reluctant to integrate or accept what's in our 12th house, we tend to project these qualities onto other people, or, in the name of completeness and wholeness, we attract these qualities to us through the kinds of people with whom we get closely involved. I'd like to elaborate a little more on this point in terms of the astrological signs. I believe that each sign is derived from the material related to the sign before it. Aries, for example, comes out of Pisces. If the sign of Aries could speak, it would probably want to say something like, "I am not chaotic. I know what I want and I go for it. Forget all that Piscean stuff about compassion, and adjusting to or blending in with the cosmos or with what other people need or want. I'm looking out for Number One." If you think about it for a minute, you'd see that the archetypal energy represented by Aries is a kind of compensation for Pisces, the sign just before it. Each sign evolves out of and in reaction to its previous sign. Taurus can be understood as a compensation for Aries. If Taurus could speak, it might say, "What's the need for all this pushy and aggressive Aries energy? Just sit still and wait, and everything will come to you." Are you getting a sense of how each sign defines itself in reaction to the previous sign? Scorpio reacts to Libra by saying, "What good is all that Libra fence-sitting? What's all this Libran stuff about sweetness and light, fairness, objectivity and detachment? I'm going to come from my deeper feelings and emotions, even if this doesn't seem fair and reasonable to you. I'm going to go for what I want, even if it means invading your space."

Any sign or planet in the 12th indicates the kinds of things we pick up on or pull in from the collective unconscious. Because anything mediated via the collective unconscious tends to express itself in a way that is archetypal, mythic and larger than life, we might have difficulty integrating it into our everyday ego identity. This is another reason why planets in the 12th (or the planet ruling the sign on the 12th) often represent energies or qualities that we project out onto others, or which we attract in someone we get close to. For instance, people with Neptune in the 12th could have difficulty accepting the numinous, the mystical, the passionate or poetic, or accepting that part of themselves that is willing to lose control and be taken over by something bigger or greater than the self. If this is the case, they will be drawn to someone who is a good hook or projection for these qualities. Along these lines, I've noticed that people with Neptune in the 12th often attract someone who is chaotic or helpless into their lives, and then they try to heal or look after that person. They might even make a profession out of caring for Neptunian types—for helpless, confused or lost people. As in this instance, you can see how the 12th house could be a very subtle indicator of career choice. Finally, you should take special note of any planets in the 12th that are parental indicators (in particular, the Sun, the Moon or Saturn), because people with such placements are often looking for someone to play the role of parent for them—whether it's a caring and nurturing parent (the Moon), or a strong, dazzling, heroic-type parent (the Sun), or a strict authoritarian parent figure (Saturn). The same thing applies if the ruler of the 12th house is placed in the 4th or 10th, or if the ruler of any of these houses is found in the 12th.

You will be powerfully attracted to, or strongly put off by, people whose Ascendant or Midheaven manifests something that is a shadow function for you. For example, let's say you're not very happy with your Moon, which means you have difficulty accepting that part of you which is infantile, helpless and needy. If someone comes along whose Ascendant or Midheaven falls in the same sign as your Moon (which means that this person outwardly manifests an aspect of your nature about which you're very uncomfortable), you'll find yourself massively attracted to, or tremendously turned off by, that person. Interestingly enough, this kind of experience is one way of discovering what areas of your chart fall into your shadow. If you're constantly complaining that the behavior of people with a Virgo Ascendant or Midheaven makes you want to climb the walls, you're actually revealing that you find the Virgo part of yourself unattractive or unacceptable. If you say things like, "People with Virgo rising make me cringe, I can smell them a mile away. I know they can't wait to criticize me and analyze everything I do," you can be sure that your buttons are being pushed. And if Virgo types push your buttons in this way, you should look to your chart to see what planets you have in Virgo or Pisces (because opposite signs often have trouble integrating with one another), and if you don't have a planet in the Virgo-Pisces polarity, look to see if these signs are angular in your chart. If none of these things apply, I would advise you to check out the house (or houses) with Virgo on the cusp or contained within it, because this house is likely to represent a sphere of life where your shadow is operative. Or you might even look at the position of Mercury (Virgo's ruler) in your chart as a way of discovering what area of life your Virgo shadow is most affecting. If Virgo or Mercury are linked to the parental houses (4th and 10th) or to the 7th and 12th, you could be projecting your disavowed Virgo qualities onto parents, partners or others with whom you have close contact.

Another area which is potent within relationships is the 4th-10th house axis, because these houses represent and hook into parental issues. Planets in the 4th and 10th, the signs on the cusps of these houses, and the planets that rule these signs, become charged with umbilical issues. You can't say just by looking at the chart whether or not you've resolved these things, but signs and planets connected with the 4th and 10th describe the kinds of family myths you carry around. People who touch off your 4th-10th house placements will evoke powerful responses in you. To the extent that your parental issues are still unresolved (and nobody really ever completes all the business with their parents), you create a powerful psychic magnet that pulls the right people into your life to trigger your parental complexes. If you don't finish or pass the second grade at school, you'll have to take that year over again. Similarly, if your parental issues are still spewing all over the place, you'll keep attracting people who activate these issues until you've learned your lessons. People will inevitably come along to challenge you in this way—in other words, you have to keep facing it over and over again until you successfully resolve the bulk of your unfinished parental business. You might think you'll never graduate, but through conscious awareness and effort on your part, you can grow, change and move on.

There is one more topic I wish to discuss concerning areas in the chart that affect relationship, and this has to do with the nature of natal planets and their aspects. I'm about to classify the planets in a way that is quite arbitrary, but you might find it useful. The schema I'm going to show you should not be taken too literally, so try to understand it as a metaphorical or archetypal kind of thing. I divide the planets into yang planets and yin planets. In our society, at least, the yang planets correlate with the masculine or positive planets and generally rule masculine signs. So I would classify the Sun, Mars, Jupiter and Uranus as yang. The nature of yang planets is to express, and, by nature, they're usually uninhibited and extroverted. Of course this can vary—put Mars in Cancer and it could lose some of its yang quality, and yet the innate nature of Mars is to be extroverted and to give out from inside the self. Yin planets are normally introverted and inward-turning, so I place the Moon, Saturn, Neptune and Pluto in this category. Yang planets tend to be expressive, while yin planets tend to be receptive. Now, this leaves two planets—Mercury and Venus—without a category. Mercury can be understood as a neuter planet, because it easily slides from one direction to another, and takes on the color of the sign it is in and the aspects to it. However, I believe that in our society Mercury tends to be more yang than yin. (I've never been comfortable with Mercury as the ruler of Virgo. I think something is amiss here. Nor am I comfortable connecting Virgo with the asteroids.) Like Mercury, Venus is also neuter or bipolar. In other words, I feel that, by nature, Venus is a bisexual planet even though it is associated with Aphrodite. Interestingly enough, if you put Mercury together with Venus, you get Hermaphroditus, which was the name given to the child conceived by the union of Hermes with Aphrodite. Eros, himself, was another extremely androgynous god, normally portrayed as a rather feminine-looking young man or as a rather masculine-looking young woman. Venus is bipolar. Venus says, "I am a mirror and I will reflect you, so what do you want me to be?" although in our society, Venus does have a predominant yin function. When I say that Venus is bipolar or bisexual, I don't mean that Aphrodite is literally into sex with both men and women, although she would be perfectly capable of it because she likes anything that feels good and she isn't all that concerned with morals. Venus represents the desire to please and reflect the other, and yet it is also a very argumentative planet as well. If you're the kind of person who is always giving perfectly logical arguments for everything, you are expressing the Athene face of Venus. Venus has a strong Athene component, which is reflected in its desire to continually redress imbalance—but this is another issue we'll go into at a later time. For the time being, I'll put Mercury in the yang column, and Venus in the yin column, although they both frequently switch around.

As I've said, yang planets are extraverted and expressive. If you get an aspect between a yang planet and another yang planet, the desire to express is multiplied and enhanced. The nature of the aspect really doesn't matter here—any aspect between the Sun and Jupiter is not likely to inhibit very much. The Sun says, "I allow my light of consciousness to shine on you, Jupiter," which means that the ego is giving Jupiter permission to express itself fully. Jupiter says back to the Sun, "Go for it baby, you're wonderful, keep expanding; the more of you there is, the more I love it," By comparison, two yin planets in aspect have a kind of hidden contract which says, "Hold it in, don't let it out. You really don't know what the outer world is going to be like, so proceed with caution." Take Moon-Neptune as an example. The Moon says, "I'm a sensitive little child in a big frightening world, and I'm not quite sure how to deal with it all." Neptune goes, "I agree with you completely. Things are seldom what they seem. Life is full of illusion and mystery, so we had better hang back and watch everything for a while before we proceed any further." Do you see what I'm saying? Yang is in agreement with yang, and yin is in agreement with yin. Now, the fireworks start to happen when you have a yang planet in aspect to a yin planet. For instance, Mars is naturally yang and Saturn is normally yin (although it can have its yang side). Put these two planets together by aspect and you have an irresistible force meeting an immovable object. The reason that a square is such a dynamic aspect is because it brings a yin sign into conflict with a yang sign (unless, of course, it's an out-of-sign square). The only other major aspect that does this is the quincunx. For this reason, natal squares and quincunxes indicate major stress points within the chart, and this tension is likely to spill over into relationship. Similarly, squares and quincunxes formed by interaspects in synastry create a lot of attraction/repulsion-type energy between the two people involved, and therefore can be quite potent erotically.

Audience: Does the same thing apply if you have a yang planet in a yin sign, or vice versa?

Richard: Yes, that's a good point and I should have mentioned it. What arises in this situation is a relationship by disposition, and it evokes a dialogue between the planet and sign involved. Take Mars in Cancer for example. When you have yang Mars in Cancer, a yin sign naturally associated with the Moon (a yin planet), there is a need for Mars and Cancer to work out a modus vivendi, a way of living together. The same thing applies when you have Mars in aspect to the Moon. If the Moon and Mars are in trine, they are equal partners who have the same degree of potency as one another. Mars in Cancer also evokes a dialogue, but a different kind of one. In this case, Mars is in the area where the Moon is most naturally at home, and therefore the obligation rests with Mars to somehow accommodate itself and be comfortable there. Let me put it another way. If I were to travel to the Soviet Union, I would have to accommodate myself to the way of life I find there, rather than the Soviet Union accommodating itself to me. This doesn't mean that I'm not going to affect the Soviet Union in any way, because I certainly would, or at least I hope I would. But it is me who must make the biggest adjustment. This also brings us back to the whole argument about whether it's good for a planet to be in the sign it naturally rules. When I'm in my own home, I'm a slob. I'm certainly comfortable there, but I don't think that it's necessarily good or evolutionary for me to feel that way. Now, if I came to your house, I would be on my best behavior, believe me. Likewise, a planet that is placed in an uncomfortable position is often provoked into greater psychological development, while planets in their own sign can be rather "naughty," as one friend of mine would put it.

Jung once said that consciousness or individuation is stimulated and triggered by the constantly shifting and changing dynamic between conscious and unconscious. And I think we see this very clearly expressed when you have a yin planet in aspect to a yang planet, either natally or by synastry. Generally, speaking, two yang planets are so naturally expressive that they offer little resistance to one another when they are connected by aspect. Two yin planets in aspect are so naturally impressive, that they tend to agree with each other, and they'll quietly hide below the surface level of consciousness for a great many years until something yang comes along to push them into awareness or action. Because the

Sun, Mars, Jupiter, Uranus and, to some degree, Mercury, are yang or masculine planets in our society, we could say that these five planets are the ones that comprise a woman's animus, and, therefore, are the ones she is most likely to project. So when planets in a man's chart aspect the yang planets in a woman's chart, she will feel charged up in those areas, especially if they've been dormant or unactualized for a long time. It doesn't even have to be a man touching off her yang planets. A woman could have her yang planets triggered off by another woman. If Woman A meets Woman B whose planets activate her yang energy or her animus, Woman A is going to react strongly to Woman B (negatively or positively), because Woman B is living out the unexpressed animus side of Woman A. In a man's chart, the Moon, Saturn, Neptune, Pluto and Venus are most likely to form or constellate his anima. If he has not integrated his anima, he is going to be looking for a woman onto whom he can project his unexpressed feminine energy.

All this leads us to some rather interesting points concerning chart comparison. Trines and sextiles between two charts tend to give rise to a feeling of comfort in the relationship, facilitating communication and increasing mutual understanding. One person starts to say something, and the other person finishes the sentence, as if one knows how the other thinks and what the other is going to say. In other words, the two people involved think in similar ways. When you find this kind of connection in two charts, the relationship has a brother/sister/companion/friend quality to it, and a lot of marriages are based on this sort of thing. There's really nothing wrong about it being so cozy and comfortable, and it often tends to make agape the dominant mode of the relationship—the ability to understand one another and love with an open hand. But instead of thanking one's lucky stars for having this kind of relationship, the people involved often complain that it lacks eros or passion. And because of this, one or the other person might want to end the relationship in order to find someone with whom there is more charge, passion and excitement. However, if the synastry between two charts mainly involves squares, the relationship tends to be more erotic. Remember, squares bring together yin signs with yang signs, and the constant dynamic between yin and yang can be rather exciting and tempestuous, although you might then yearn for something more calm and peaceful. A whole bunch of squares between charts often results in the kind of relationship where you feel you can't live with, but can't live without, the other person. I've seen this happen between parents and children, where the relationship is one of fairly constant, grinding tension.

The nature of a natal chart can tell you what kind of relationships a person is prone to. A heavily dynamic chart—one in which there are missing functions, lots of singletons and singleton aspects, stationary planets, and many squares, oppositions and quincunxes—denotes the type of person who opts for tremendously stressful and erotic relationships. They get off on it, they need it, this is what is reality for them. However, these are the kinds of people who also come to you for counseling and complain that they never seem to find the right person to make everything all wonderful, or they keep asking you when their current relationship is going to settle down and work peacefully. It's as if they want to turn their squares, oppositions and inconjuncts into trines. By golly, if they ever did succeed in turning the relationship into something cozy and peaceful, they would probably leave it to find a more exciting one, because they thrive on stress and conflict. I mean, if Kate and Petruchio had ever managed to turn their relationship into a trine-type situation, one or the other or both of them would have been off in a shot to look somewhere else. By comparison, the person who has a largely relaxed, balanced and easy chart without singletons and missing functions, and without a lot of squares and oppositions but with a predominance of trines and sextiles, would be more inclined to a static relationship rather than an erotic one. These are the kind of people who often moan about a lack of excitement in their lives, although if they should find an exciting, tempestuous relationship, they'd only end up complaining that it's too much for them to take. In other words, be careful when people tell you what they really want, because what they say or think they want is not always what they really want. Part of being a sensitive therapist or counselor is to see through what clients are saying and discover the reasons why they are saying it, a technique I call "peeling the onion," which involves finding out what lies behind what's being said. Winston Churchill once said something like, "Who you are speaks so loudly that I can't hear a word you're saying." So therapists need to examine closely the way their clients lead their lives, because what they actually do with their lives is a truer picture of who they are than what they say about themselves. Are there any questions before I move on?

Audience: What about conjunctions between charts?

Richard: One person's yang planet conjuncting another person's yang planet has a tendency to encourage expression. For instance, if my Jupiter were conjunct your Mars, I would have the effect of arousing and bringing out your Mars, probably in a positive way. If one of my yin planets conjuncted one of your yin planets, we would tend to be in agreement about things related to those planets. But the situation is much more dynamic and loaded when one of my yin planets hits one of your yang planets or vice versa. Let's say it's my Moon and your Uranus. This could mean that I crave intimacy and closeness in our relationship (the Moon), while you opt for freedom and autonomy (Uranus). You'll stimulate my need for closeness or arouse the child in me (your Uranus on my Moon), but I'll elicit or bring out your need for independence (my Moon on your Uranus).

You've probably guessed by now that I don't see security, peace or comfort as the goal of life. I think that comfort causes stasis, and that discomfort keeps us alive and growing. This doesn't mean that we shouldn't ever have moments of peace and serenity, but if things get too staid and peaceful, we can get stuck and lose the impetus to keep growing and developing. If Beethoven had been totally happy with his first symphony, he might never have written two, three or four. I think it's tension and challenge that keeps a relationship dynamic. If you've said everything you have to say and there are no stresses and strains between you and your partner, then you may see no point in being around that person. A good relationship ought to provide some peace and comfort, but I don't think that comfortableness should be the be-all and end-all of existence. Growing and evolving doesn't feel easy and comfortable. I mean, life isn't comfortable after you've bitten into the apple and are thrown out of Eden. I don't really know how you can unbite the apple. Probably the most comfortable world we ever experienced was in the womb, and even the womb might not have been all that comfortable for some of us.

Audience: What about synastry contacts to the outer planets?

Richard: Contacts to the outer planets always bring in some element of the transpersonal or the mythical. You'll usually notice, archetypally speaking, that Neptune and Pluto constellate feminine figures, although Hades can also be a masculine figure. Uranus always tends to be more masculine and yang.

Audience: You were talking about the 12th house as representing the qualities that the ascending sign is trying to mask, but what if the sign on the 12th is the same as the sign on the Ascendant?

Richard: Yes, this may be the case, but if you tried a different house system, the situation could change. When I'm talking about the sign behind the Ascendant, I'm referring to it in an archetypal sense rather than literally in terms of what is on your 12th house cusp. I would say that the sign just before the Ascendant is the natural 12th house sign to the Ascendant, even if it really is in the 11th house, if you see what I'm getting at. In any case, the planets in the 12th carry more weight than the sign on its cusp. But if you have Scorpio on the 12th house cusp and also Scorpio rising, it could mean that certain qualities of the Scorpio archetype have been pushed back into the unconscious. So some of Scorpio is acceptable and used to make up your mask, but other aspects of Scorpio are hidden beneath the mask. The emotionality and eroticism of Scorpio could be on the surface, but that part of Scorpio that seeks power gets hidden and thus becomes the unconscious quality you need to integrate in the name of becoming more complete.

Audience: I've found that if Uranus is prominent in a natal chart, or is highlighted in synastry, long-term relationships can be very difficult to sustain.

Richard: Yes, I agree with you. I'm not saying it's impossible, but it is difficult if you try to play by the usual rules. If you're the kind of person who has individuated enough to become separate from the family myth and the social myths you were brought up under, you may then be able to make rules that work for you. For instance, you may decide that an open marriage is what works best for you. Or you are married to someone or committed to someone in a monogamous way, but the two of you don't live together. Or you take separate vacations from your partner if you need to. With Uranus strong (and also with Neptune and Pluto strong), the normal or the usual doesn't work. You'll also run into problems if you try to seek the transpersonal in the interpersonal. Another thing comes to mind, however. I have seen successful relationships where there has been a Venus-Uranus contact strongly placed in both charts or in the synastry, but in each of these cases, the two people worked together on some sort of creative endeavor. In other words, they channeled their creative energies into the same socket, and this served to discharge the wandering-off side of Uranus. But as a rule with Uranus, following a usual or traditional path just won't work.

Audience: The astrologer Isabel Hickey used to refer to the 12th house as the house of self-sustainment or self-undoing. Can you link this up with what you've said about the influence of the 12th house and the unconscious on our relationships and our choice of career?

Richard: Well, I can give you an example of something like that. A woman analyst was a client of mine. She had the Moon conjunct Pluto in Cancer in the 12th, and one of her presenting problems was that she experienced great difficulty separating from her clients. By the way, she worked mostly with women (Pluto was her 4th house ruler, which, in her case, I saw as more representative of the mother than the father). The woman in question had brought her Moon-Pluto into her work with women, and she really excelled at it. She's great at evoking feminine images and has even written books on the subject. However, her mother was one of those great, devouring-type Gorgon mothers, and my client had never really severed the powerful umbilical connection she had with her. In fact, her mother was living in a nursing home and was demanding that her daughter take her from the home to live with her. Not long after this became a conflict, my client developed the early stages of breast cancer. Fortunately, it was caught in time and arrested, but the whole cancer incident suggested to her that there was something cancerous about her intense need to nurture. She finally realized that she had reversed roles with her mother, and that she was bringing something of her own devouring mother into her work with her therapy patients, and this is why she had so much trouble separating herself from them. It was very, very powerful stuff. So what I'm saying is that the 12th house can be a seat of wonderful creative energy where we tap into great collective images and archetypes, but it also can be an area that is very painful and potentially destructive for us. Traditional astrology has always referred to the 12th as the house of secret enemies. But, in most cases, the secret enemy is there inside you, not somewhere outside of you. It might jump out of your psychic closet at night, but it's not something that is going to come out of your actual bedroom closet and get you. The self-undoing side of the 12th comes from the inability, or the reluctance, or the lack of courage, or whatever it is, that prevents us from integrating the material in that house. A planet in the 12th is like a double-edged sword: it's a sword with which we can kill dragons, and it's a sword with which we can kill ourselves.

Relationship Significators in the Chart of Isadora Duncan

Isadora Duncan certainly had some interesting relationships, so I thought we could use her chart (see Chart 1, page 222) to illustrate and ground some of the things we've been discussing so far. She was a woman very much ahead of her time, especially in terms of her courageous individuality, which could be seen in her life, her work and her relationships. I've heard a story about her, which might be a fabrication, but I like to think it's true. Isadora was at a party when she approached a married couple and said to the woman, "Madam, I would like to borrow your husband for the evening. I'll return him in the morning, and I'm sure we will all profit from the experience," after which she walked off with him. Let's start with they way I break down the functions in the chart.

Here is a list of the functions I take into consideration: the modalities – cardinal, fixed and mutable; the elements – fire, air, earth and water; the personal, social and universal signs; and the personal, social and universal houses. I also need to explain the formula I use for grading all this. Each planet gets one point, except the Sun and Moon, each of which gets two points, and the planet ruling the Ascendant, which gets an extra point. This means there are 13 points altogether. For example, if you had Leo rising, the ruling planet would be the Sun, and it would count for three points (two for being the Sun, and one for being the Ascendant ruler). If it were Cancer rising, then the Moon would score its usual two points, but would also receive an extra point as the ruler of the Ascendant – so the Moon would score three points in this case. By the way, this is the same system I use when training psychotherapists how to quickly pick up the psychologically potent parts of a chart. It's my own system, and you can take from it what you want. It doesn't really matter which function you begin to examine first, but I'd like to start now with the modalities.

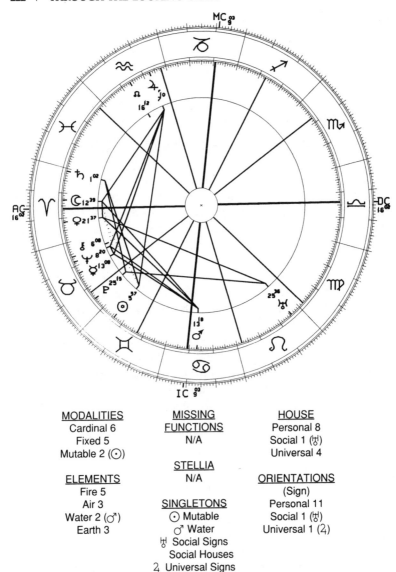

MODALITIES	MISSING FUNCTIONS	HOUSE
Cardinal 6	N/A	Personal 8
Fixed 5		Social 1 (♅)
Mutable 2 (☉)		Universal 4
	STELLIA	
ELEMENTS	N/A	ORIENTATIONS
Fire 5		(Sign)
Air 3	SINGLETONS	Personal 11
Water 2 (♂)	☉ Mutable	Social 1 (♅)
Earth 3	♂ Water	Universal 1 (♃)
	♅ Social Signs	
	Social Houses	
	♃ Universal Signs	

Chart 1. Isadora Duncan, born in San Francisco, May 27, 1878, at 2:20 A.M. LMT. Birth data from Lois Rodden, *Profiles of Women* (Tempe, AZ: American Federation of Astrologers, 1979). Chart calculated by Astrodienst using Placidus houses.

We'll begin by counting up Isadora's cardinal planets and assigning points to them. We have one point for Isadora's Saturn in Aries, two points for her Moon in Aries, one point for her Venus in Aries, and two points for her Mars in Aries, which gets an extra point for ruling the Ascendant. Altogether this makes six points for planets in cardinal signs. Now we go to fixed signs. Jupiter in Aquarius is worth one point, Neptune in Taurus is another point, Mercury in Taurus is one point, Pluto in Taurus gets a point, and Uranus in Leo is worth one point—which gives the fixed signs a total of five points. Now we come to mutability, and looking through her chart, we'll find only one planet in a mutable sign, but since it's the Sun, it gets two points. But, as you can see, the Sun ranks as singleton in Isadora's chart because it is the only planet in mutable signs, and this is something that's important to note.

Then we'd carry on in the same manner, this time considering the elemental balance. Counting up the planets in fire signs, we have one point for Saturn in Aries, two for the Moon in Aries, one for Venus in Aries, and one for Uranus in Leo, which makes five points for fire. Counting up the planets in air signs, Isadora gets one point for Jupiter in Aquarius, and two points for the Sun in Gemini, which makes three points for air. Mars in Cancer is the only planet in a water sign, and it's worth two points as the ruler of the Ascendant, so water scores two points. You should also note that Mars is a singleton because it's the only planet in water. (Please remember, when you're assessing whether or not something is a singleton, it can be misleading just to count points—as you see in this case, Mars is a singleton in water, but it's worth two points by virtue of being the Ascendant ruler). Mercury, Neptune and Pluto are the only planets in earth, so earth scores three points. Now, adding fire and air together, we come up with eight points for the yang signs; and adding earth and water together, we come up with five points for the yin signs.

Next, we can add up the number of points for planets in personal, social and universal signs. Starting with the personal signs, we have one point for Saturn in Aries, two points for the Moon in Aries, one point for Venus in Aries, one for Neptune in Taurus, one for Mercury in Taurus, one for Pluto in Taurus, two for the Sun in Gemini, and two for Mars in Cancer. That makes a grand total of 11 points for personal signs. Right away, this tells you that this area is an enormously dominant function. Obviously, if one thing is so dominant in a category, the other things in that category are going to rate as inferior. With such an imbalance as this in Isadora's orientation by sign, you can expect something unusual to manifest around it. If we count the planets in social signs, we have one point for Uranus in Leo, and that's it. Isadora's Uranus is the only planet in the social signs, so it's a singleton in this respect. Her Jupiter in Aquarius is the only planet in a universal sign, so that gets one point and is also a singleton.

Audience: Didn't you used to give one point to the Midheaven and one to the Ascendant?

Richard: Yes, but I changed my mind about it. I see the planets as dynamic, archetypal and psychological energies—they're alive, functioning and moving. The Ascendant and Midheaven are undoubtedly important and critical points in a chart, but they don't have the same dynamism as a planetary energy. But if you want to give an extra point to the Ascendant and Midheaven, then do so.

The next thing to consider is the orientation by house. The first four houses are the personal houses, and she has Venus in the 1st for one point. Neptune in the 1st for one point, Mercury in the 1st worth one point, Pluto in the 2nd worth one point, the Sun in the 2nd worth two points, and Mars in the 4th for two points— altogether, that makes eight points for the personal houses. She only has one planet in the social houses, Uranus in the 5th, so that gets one point, as well as making Uranus a singleton in this category. How interesting: we see that Uranus is a singleton in two cases (as the only planet in a social sign, and as the only planet in a social house). Automatically you want to start interpreting the significance of this, and I already can hear the "ah ha's" in the group. Looking through the universal houses, we see that Jupiter scores one point for being in the 11th, and Saturn one point for being in the 12th, and the Moon in the 12th gets two points, so altogether that's four points for the universal houses.

Let's start analyzing some of the information we've gleaned so far in terms of what we would expect Isadora to meet or get up to in relationship. First of all, we should take into account that this is a chart of a woman born in 1878, at the height of the Victorian era, which was a very repressive time for women. And yet, we know that she managed to break free of that repression and live her life in a very individualistic way. You could say she was the exception to the rule of her time, which would lead us to conclude that there must be something exceptional in her chart to indicate this. What planet do you think correlates with being exceptional? Yes, Uranus, and look what we have already discovered—that Uranus is twice a singleton. The other planets in singleton are the Sun, Mars and Jupiter. What do we know about all these planets? Yes, they are all masculine, yang planets. So what we're saying is that here is a person powerfully influenced by masculine, yang planets. What we don't know, however, is whether she is going to own and integrate this energy and live out her animus, or whether she's going to project her yang energy and look for it in a very yang man, or whether she is going to do a little of both these things. The usual type of woman of this period almost definitely would have aspired to import these potent yang energies into her life through marriage. And if she didn't succeed in marrying it, she probably would have denied her yangness, repressed it, or possibly sublimated it (although there weren't many ways a woman could sublimate this kind of energy during this period in history). Knowing something about Isadora's life, it looks as if she owned and lived out quite a bit of her yang energy, but that she also sought it in the kind of men she found attractive. And you could even say that some of it was sublimated into her pioneering work in modern dance.

I'm reminded of another story about Isadora, which aptly describes what kind of woman she was. When she danced on stage, she used to wear a kind of Grecian gown with nothing on underneath, and when the light hit her, you could see very clearly beneath her clothes. The night she opened in Boston, she was booed by most of the audience and roasted by the critics, who accused her of being an exhibitionist intent on perverting the arts. By the way, Isadora was one of those people who was adored in Europe, but pretty much unappreciated in the States—especially since she lived during a period when America was in one of its puritanical moods that it reverts back to from time to time. Anyway, she appeared on stage in Boston again the next night, and it's reputed that somebody in the audience shouted out to her that one's private parts were not art. Her response to this was to move to the front of the stage, drop down the top half of her tunic, take hold of her exposed breasts, one in each hand, and proclaim to the audience, "This, Boston, is art!" She got a round of applause and continued to dance. So here is a very, very exceptional woman with an exceptional life. Many of the most famous men of her day were her lovers, and some of the most famous women of her day were among her close friends, including the highly acclaimed actress, Eleonora Duse. My first acting teacher was a German woman who was one of Isadora's friends. My teacher described her as a dark, dumpy woman who was transformed into someone truly magnificent and magical when she danced. Often, at private parties, the dishes would be cleared off the table, and Isadora would get up on it and start to dance. Everybody would sit down and stare at her feet, because her feet moved so fast that you couldn't even see them touch the table—she literally gave the impression that she was somehow suspended in air . . . absolutely magical.

If we go back to her chart, we can see the strong emphasis on yang, masculine planets and signs, and we can see that the cardinal and fixed mode are both more dominant than her inferior mutability. In fact, her sun in Gemini is a singleton in this area. Now, just by looking at the chart, we really don't know what she is going to do with her inferior mutable function. Is she going to project it onto somebody else? Is she going to suppress it? Is she going to compensate in some way for the mutable function? Mutability can describe change, fluctuation and the need for variety, which fits with the fact that she was something of a female Don Juan, a real heartbreaker. When asked why she didn't settle down and do the typical things a woman of her time was meant to do, she replied by asking, "Does the honey bee marry the flower?" and that was the end of the subject. So you can see how her inferior mutable function played quite a dominant part in her life. She also used her mutable solar power (the singleton Sun in Gemini) in other ways. She not only performed as a dancer, but she taught dance as well. She wrote, she traveled a lot, and she was a strong backer of the Communist revolution in Russia. Mutability has a lot to do with communication, and she was always getting into trouble for what she called her foot-in-mouth disease, which took over when she would stand up to lecture her audiences on social issues in a rather unpleasantly high and raucous voice. The strong constellation of planets in Aries straddling her Aries Ascendant makes for an extremely pushy persona. What we have here, then, is an extraordinary yang woman in a society in which women were expected to be yin. One of the interesting things about an inferior function (and I'm not using this term in the Jungian sense, but in the astrological sense) is that it resembles the 12th house in certain ways: the potentiality for great creativity is there, if only it could be harnessed. Another thing is that the inferior function carries within it the tendency to want to grab the superior or dominant function in moments of crisis and shove it down into the unconscious.

Audience: Can you rewind the last two sentences?

Richard: What I'm saying is that the inferior function has great creative potential hidden within it. To the degree that the inferior function is not integrated into awareness, it also has the tendency to grab the dominant function and relegate it to the unconscious, especially at times of crisis.

Maybe a metaphor will help you understand more clearly what I mean. The inferior function is like a little child who is normally well-behaved, but who surprises you now and then by throwing a tantrum in public, usually under moments of stress. Furthermore, a missing or inferior function can provide you with a creative solution that frees you from a problem. And the inferior function often operates as a channel—for good or ill—for both the personal and collective unconscious. As I've said, you can't just look at a chart and know whether an inferior function will manifest positively or negatively. The inferior function can become a kind of driving force or daimon in the Greek sense of the word. Or it acts like a trickster figure, who periodically yanks the rug out from underneath you, which can feel frightening and awful at times, and yet which also can be a positive experience in terms of individuation and growth of consciousness. Let me give you an example of what I mean. If Mars is a singleton in your chart, it may indicate an archetype or way of being that is not integrated into your life. I'm thinking of a woman I know who has water as her dominant function, with a singleton Mars in Leo in the 12th as her only planet in fire, her inferior function. She was 68 years old and living in New York City. One day she was walking through Central Park and somebody tried to mug her. Now, she is a very tiny woman, not even five feet tall, and arthritic to boot. She ended up beating this guy within an inch of his life. Nobody was more surprised about it than she. She could hardly believe what came over her, except that she got infuriated by the attack and was determined not to put up with it. She told me that she felt as if she had turned into a tiger. So you see how her inferior function came to the fore in a time of crisis, putting her dominant water function into the background. What do you think—is what she did good or bad? After all, she could have been killed in the process. Anyway, she sat on this guy (a young teenager very much taller than she), and she yelled and screamed until some people came to drag her off him and take him away. I say, good for her! In any case, this is an example of how the inferior function can operate. Although it can express itself negatively and land you in trouble, it also has the potential to come out in a very positive way. Sometimes, it can be a little of both. Ronald Reagan is another example of someone with inferior fire. Under stress, he has been known to call up his inferior fire function in the form of enormous optimism—a kind of hail fellow, well met looking on the bright side of things. You know, shoot him with a gun and he says, "That's all right folks." Tune in the next day and he'll crack a little joke and tell you that he's feeling just fine. On the other hand, his inferior fire function seething away in his unconscious also gives people the feeling that underneath it all, he is a real warmonger. His fire—this explosive, assertive anger and aggression—is bottled up, and when it does come out, it is likely to be in a way which is over the top.

We've established that, by element, Isadora's chart shows eight yang and five yin. Being so yang is always a problem for a woman, just as being too yin is usually a problem for a man. If she had come to me for counseling, I would have been very curious about how her family dealt with her yang qualities, as shown by all that Aries stuff constellated around her Ascendant. It must have appeared pretty early on in her life, and I wonder what her family made of it. It's pretty clear that she had a mother complex, because her mother was one of those stage-mother types who pushed Isadora onto the stage and traveled with her when she toured Europe.

In other words, Isadora must have had an enormous problem breaking the umbilical connection with her mother, a very competitive, angry woman who lived out her own desires for attention and applause through her talented daughter. Isadora's Moon and Saturn in the 12th also indicate parental problems, but I'm getting ahead of myself here.

There is no strong dominant function among her elements, although fire does come out on top, which means she was essentially a fiery woman who would have needed to be creative and expressive, both of which she managed to accomplish. In addition, the men in her life were largely creative, expressive men — important people, such as politicians and famous artists — and this reflects not only her fiery side but also her singleton Mars. With a very yang planet like Mars in a watery sign, she was attracted to quite violent, crazed and poetic types. In fact, one of her greatest loves was a famous Russian poet, one of these mad, passionate, emotional poets who eventually ended up committing suicide. A question comes up for me about the way in which she actually managed to integrate her singleton Mars in Cancer. It denotes a water animus, and this makes me curious about how she expressed and dealt with her anger and her needs for self-assertion. With such a yang planet as Mars in a watery sign, there's bound to be a lot of tense, erotic feelings simmering and bubbling up inside her. Her Mars is in the 4th, and I would say that this placement connects with the mother or the nurturing parent, because I normally associate the 4th house with the nurturing, nesting part of the family background, and the 10th with the part that points us toward the future and our destiny in the world — although the whole situation of 4th as mother and 10th as father can be extremely variable. In Isadora's case, I strongly suspect that the 4th really does refer to her mother, with whom she had a lifelong love-hate relationship. She started taking lovers very early on as a way of escaping from her mother's dominance, something you can see in the chart by the 4th house Mars in square to the 12th house Moon. As we learned in a previous lecture, Moon-Mars contacts equate nurturing (the Moon) with anger and fighting (Mars), which is exactly the kind of thing she experienced with her mother: Isadora was constantly fighting this angry, submerged maternal figure who was trying to live her life vicariously through her achievements and adventures.

Isadora was born with the ruler of the 4th (the Moon) in the 12th, which, if you remember our discussion on 12th house issues, is an indication of problems breaking the umbilical connection with mother—even Isadora admitted that she always had trouble unhooking herself from her mother, and it wasn't until her mother's death that she finally felt free of her. And, although Isadora was close to some very remarkable and sensitive women, she also tended to have extremely competitive relationships with them, because they were also powerful women in their own right. Most of her friends were men—women in general found it very hard to deal with her. All in all, I would say that Isadora had a pretty well-developed animus, which is shown astrologically, in part, as a compensation for her yang, singleton Mars in water.

The singleton Mars also means that sexuality is going to be an important issue for her, and that it would have been connected (via its placement in Cancer) with a lot of watery, emotional stuff. Looking at this in her chart, my first impression would be that here is a person who is going to have very stormy relationships. Perhaps this is exactly what she needed and wanted—after all, look at the kind of baggage she carried around in terms of the fights and power struggles with her mother. Her image of love was very much reflected by her 4th house Mars square the 12th house Moon. Her life history is filled with issues around love and hurt, and love and anger, and the association of nurturing with anger and the struggle for independence. In short, she experienced a major conflict between her Cancerian need to merge with others, and her Aries need to be a free spirit.

Now, we can look at where she stood in terms of orientation—personal, social and universal. Here is where we find the greatest imbalance, because her dominant function is weighted so heavily in the category of the personal. This tells me that she was a very self-involved person, concerned with her own needs and pleasures. This would have conflicted with the social message of her time, which said that women should concern themselves primarily with what other people need, that women were meant to care for others and put their own needs aside at the drop of a hat. Had Isadora been another kind of woman, she might have compensated for her strong orientation in the personal by appearing extremely receptive to the needs of other people, but her singleton Uranus in a social sign points against her doing that. So she was, indeed, a very self-centered and self-oriented person. I don't intend to imply that being self-centered is a bad thing—as a matter of fact, some of the most creative people in the world have an enormous constellation of planets in personal signs, which means that their energy is available to use for themselves, rather than being dispersed and given away to me, you or the universe. Take a genius like Bach with four planets in Aries, and you'll see that creative genius often constellates around planets in the very elemental signs of Aries and Taurus. These signs are very busy being themselves, and not so distracted by what other people are doing, or what other people need from them.

Audience: What kinds of messages do you think Isadora gave to her two children?

Richard: I think the main message they received was that Mama was different. They frequently traveled around with her. As you probably know, both her children drowned in a tragic accident: they were driving with their nurse and the car went off a bridge, and Isadora had a complete nervous breakdown as a result. She went to the great tragic actress of her day, Eleonora Duse, for comfort, and Duse was the only person she could be with during the long period of depression that followed. When she came out of the depression triggered by her tragic loss, Isadora decided to open a school for teaching children and young people her methods in dance, and eventually established academies in Moscow, Paris and the States for this purpose. As I was saying, her strong dominant orientation to the personal means that her social and universal orientations were inferior. Her academies, which can be seen as a service to other people, came about as a result of her personal tragedy. Her inferior social orientation by sign and house (Uranus is the only planet in a social house as well as the only planet in a social sign) is an indication that she reached out to others by channeling her personal unconscious in a highly unusual, creative, ingenious and iconoclastic way.

A singleton planet in a social sign also indicates that she would have approached the whole area of relationship in a different way from her contemporaries, and this was heightened by the fact that the singleton social planet by sign was Uranus, which also happened to be a singleton social planet by house. There is no doubt that she was a woman whose very nature was totally unsuited to the normal rules of relationship that prevailed in her day. And had she tried to force herself into that mold, what would have happened? The inferior social function would have grabbed her from underneath and really have given her a hard time—especially because Uranus is involved here, a planet I associate with the trickster archetype, the kind of force that accidently-on-purpose pushes Humpty Dumpty off his wall. In other words, had she been less conscious of her need for space and freedom in relationship, and had she tried to be Mrs. Joe Smith, the barber's wife living in a small town doing what small-town people do, Uranus would have intervened and simply not allowed it to continue. As it was, Uranus intervened in her relationships whenever they became too restricting. When Isadora began to feel bound by a relationship, there was no way she'd be there waking up next to her partner the next morning. That would be it, she was gone. In many ways she was the typical, archetypal Aries, which is something you hardly ever see expressed very cleanly in a woman.

Isadora's Jupiter in Aquarius in the 11th is a singleton in the universal signs, so the dispositer of this singleton is Uranus, which is twice a singleton. This puts a strong emphasis on the Uranian and Aquarian side of her personality—indeed, you can't get much more Uranian than this woman. I connect the 11th house with causes, and her singleton Jupiter in the 11th indicates her involvement in communism and socialism, as well as the way she linked teaching dance and other creative activities to the idea of freeing the mind of youth. She used to stand up and preach to people about their corrupt conventional morals, because she believed that sex and bodies were a good thing, and that Puritanism and any other kind of repressive dogma was bad and would only lead to trouble. She was marched out of a lot of countries, literally taken to the border and told to leave. As you can imagine, she didn't go over too big in Switzerland, although they loved her in France and Russia. She was actually considered a revolutionary in a revolutionary country. The degree to which she did live out and express her own yang side meant that she led a very different life from the majority of other women around at her time.

Let's sum up what we've learned about her so far. Her chart shows a high degree of dominance of personal signs, and only a slightly lesser degree of dominance of personal houses, all of which means that she felt most comfortable with things that had to do with her personally. Social signs and houses, and universal signs and houses, pale in comparison to the emphasis on the personal. We also know that she was a woman with a strongly yang nature, and when she projected this part of her psyche, the projections were extremely powerful. You can see this in her attraction to very intense, highly charged, creative men. And even if she had found a man to carry and live out her highly charged, creative animus, stuff from her own unconscious would have erupted to topple the relationship. In other words, if she had found a man to live out her creativity, and if this meant she wasn't being creative herself, she inevitably would have gone through a constant cycle of trying to destroy the relationship, because she needed to fulfill her own Sun, Mars and Jupiter for herself. As it was, she didn't have any long-term relationships, and here we get into a question of values. What is a good relationship? I suspect that many of us judge a good relationship by its longevity, but should this standard apply to people who are strongly Uranian? Many of us dump on ourselves if we break up a relationship or if a relationship we're in fails, because this goes against the myth that relationships should be forever. So we think there's something wrong with us if we can't sustain a long relationship.

I've heard people describe themselves as two-time or three-time losers, when referring to their lack of success in relationship. What a terrible thing to say. Instead, we should say, "I'm a there-time winner because I've been in love or married three times, and it was wonderful when it was wonderful, and I've learned and grown so much from each of these relationships, and I was mature enough to know when it was over and the time had come to move on, and all this has been part of my individuation process." But if your society myth says happily ever after, then you're in trouble. A lot of people hang onto a relationship long after it's gone dead, lest they start to feel there's something wrong with them because they couldn't make it work.

Let's move on and examine some other factors in Isadora's chart. The Descendant and 7th house are important in terms of relationship, and we find Libra there in her chart. She used to say that the only kind of man she wanted was a pretty man, because she felt ugly enough for two. She also said that her gifts were in her feet, not in her face. So with Libra on the 7th, it's as if she sought to import more beauty into her life through the men with whom she became involved. In actual fact, she was very attractive. In her autobiography, she writes that "Aphrodite smiled at my birth," and apt description of her rising Venus. There is very little going on in the western side of her chart. Couple this with the emphasis on the personal orientation by both house and sign, and you can deduce that it was very difficult for her to give an awful lot of herself to other people in an interpersonal way, and what she was really looking for in relationship was someone to be a mirror for her. Venus, the planet ruling her 7th, is placed in the 1st house—everything comes back to her. From all the information we have gleaned from looking at the chart so far, it strikes me that it would be very difficult for most men to sustain a relationship with her—especially a traditional type of man of her time. Even the ruler of the 7th gets pulled back into the 1st, which says it all comes back to me. She was attracted to very pretty, fiery men, but there was always a struggle about who was going to be dominant within the relationship. She kept saying that her dream was to find a man who could harness and control her. She obviously never found one, because that is not what she really wanted. How could she have really wanted it, when she would fight like a tiger to make sure she didn't lose power and control in her close relationships? For years, she bullied one of her lovers to marry her. When he finally agreed to give in and marry her, she immediately left him. To justify ending the relationship, she invented some excuse for his offending her. He was an alcoholic, and not too long after the split-up with Isadora, he killed himself. She felt very badly about it, but, without a doubt, the way she went about ending relationships left a wake of very damaged people behind her. All this is typical of what a strongly Uranian and Martian person would do.

What other significators would we want to examine in her chart in terms of relationship?

Audience: There's a clear lack of oppositions in her chart.

Richard: Yes, that's something important to look at when it comes to relationship. Oppositions give balance, objectivity and the ability to see things with some clear perspective. Oppositions give the ability to see the other. A lack of oppositions suggests that she really couldn't see other people objectively, or detached from her own needs and wants, a quality that is further emphasized by the strong Aries-Mars personal orientation. As I said before, even the ruler of the 7th (the house of the not-self) is placed in the 1st, the most personal of houses.

Audience: Would you say that she had a stellium in Aries, because she has three planets and the Ascendant in this sign?

Richard: Actually, I consider a stellium to be a group of four or more planets, but many people settle for three. What I do find interesting is that she has three planets in Aries and three planets in Taurus—the two most primitive and primeval signs of the zodiac. Please don't mistake my use of the word primitive to mean unevolved. By primitive, I mean fundamental and close to nature, and in touch with one's libidinal energy. All the messages that the society of her time were giving out about women suppressing their libido and dedicating their lives to serving the needs of others, simply fell on deaf ears in her case.

Audience: Where's her empathy? I can't find anything in this chart that shows it. The Moon in the 12th is a possibility, but there it is in square to Mars. And the lack of empathy is also shown by the lack of oppositions. She probably had little awareness of what she was doing to other people. She probably wondered what was wrong with other people, because they weren't just like her.

Richard: I agree with what you're saying. The singleton Mars in Cancer also verifies her self-centeredness. She undoubtedly was sensitive to her own mood changes, and she was prone to fly off the handle if somebody did something that bothered her, but most likely she was unable to understand this kind of behavior in other people—she couldn't understand why certain things wounded them or why they would sometimes fly off the handle. After all, Mars is a very self-centered planet and Cancer is a personal sign.

Audience: She has an out-of-sign quincunx between Saturn and Uranus. Could you comment on this?

Richard: Saturn in the 12th means that a part of her secretly wanted to be controlling, and this was paradoxical because the Uranian side of her preached the doctrine of freedom, free love and letting everybody go off and do their own thing. It's almost as if she were saying, "It's fine for you to be free and do your own thing, but I still want to have some control over you." This quincunx would also indicate an innate conflict within her between her need for security and stability versus her strongly Uranian need for autonomy and independence. By the way, she never knew her father. His absence is indicated in the chart by the fact that Saturn, the ruler of her 10th house (father), is situated in the 12th, the house of what's hidden or mysterious. Her mother more or less became both a father and a mother to her. Isadora intensely disliked authority figures—she saw fathers and father figures as bad and projected this complex onto people who had power in government, or who ruled over the establishment. In other words, her rebellion against the establishment could be traced back to the anger she felt toward her absent father, and her rebellion against her mother's attempt to rule her life. Isadora usually sided with revolutionaries—more than that, she encouraged them. I would attribute this whole dynamic to the Saturn-Uranus quincunx.

Audience: What orb do you use for a quincunx?

Richard: I use a five- or six-degree orb for quincunxes, but it really is up to you to choose the orbs you find that work.

We haven't even put up a chart to compare with hers, and yet, through the kind of analysis we've been doing, we already have a good sense of what relationships would be like for her. What we've done is to set the stage for synastry by finding out what she was like as a person and how this would affect the way she set about making relationships and the kinds of problems she would encounter in the process. Synastry will now be a lot easier because we've already gathered so much information about her just from her own chart. So let's continue to examine her chart for relationship factors. It's always worth taking a close look at Venus in this respect, because archetypally, Venus shows the qualities we are seeking in another person that would make us feel more complete. And Venus is an exceptionally important relationship significator in Isadora's chart, because it also happens to be the ruler of her 7th. You can learn a great deal from the planet that makes the closest aspect to someone's Venus, and in her case, this is a trine from Uranus. This, in itself, tells us that she was looking for magic within relationship and marriage.

Transpersonal Uranus in aspect to interpersonal Venus means that she was looking to be awakened through love, or, conversely, that she would be the one to play the role of the awakener for other people. Things that are magical, translucent, shimmering, shocking, freeing, awakening and nonbinding formed a large part of her myth of what love and relationship ought to entail. And, in actual fact, she managed to live this out a lot better than most people do.

There are two other aspects that are reasonably close to her Venus—the Moon is 9 degrees away from a conjunction to Venus, and her Mars makes an 8-degree square to it. Mars square Venus reflects the fact that her relationships were charged with passion, sexuality and power conflicts. We spoke quite a bit about Moon-Venus aspects in earlier lectures, and related these to an inner conflict between a woman's lunar, mothering side and her sensual and creative Venusian or Aphrodite side. Moon-Venus also manifests quite often in conflicts and competition between mother and daughter—what I call the poison apple syndrome. This is exactly what happened between Isadora and her mother: when Isadora started to blossom into adolescence, her mother became psychologically violent toward her.

Audience: Can you say more about Isadora's feminine side?

Richard: Both of the primary feminine planets—the Moon and Venus—are disposed of by Mars, so even her femininity was strongly colored by her assertiveness and the qualities of a yang, warrior-type person. The Moon and Venus square Mars suggest much the same thing. She was a sensitive woman and very creative in a feminine way through her dance, but she didn't really evince many of the other qualities we normally associate with "the feminine." Her stance in relationship was largely masculine, and she was very often the pursuer and the seducer, instead of the one who pursued and seduced.

Audience: Would you call her an animus-dominated woman?

Richard: That's a tricky question, and I'm not sure I have the answer to it. Jungians would probably consider that she was animus-dominated: she had explosive rages, she would physically attack people who disagreed with her, she had fistfights with most of her men, and she was usually the one who provoked angry responses in them. On the other hand, you could say that it wasn't a case of animus domination, but rather more the case that her feminine side was very masculine by nature. In other words, her femaleness was expressed in quite a forceful way.

Audience: How was she with her children?

Richard: Don't forget that she had Uranus in the 5th house. She rarely saw her children, and I wouldn't say she was very nurturing toward them. Mostly they were looked after by nursemaids. Isadora would dash in and mother the children with love, and then not see them for a week. But she certainly did love her children—in fact, she loved all children in general. She started a school to work with children, but she wasn't loving and nurturing in the way we classically expect a mother to be with her children. She didn't have much of the Great Mother archetype in her, but this doesn't mean she was animus-dominated. I think, in many ways, she was a fairly individuated woman, but a very troubled one. I don't think that anybody can have a chart this much out of balance, and not have a troubled life.

Audience: Aphrodite was very strong in her.

Richard: Yes, she had Aphrodite (Venus) hovering close to her Ascendant, and she was primarily Aphrodite in her sexuality. She would say, "I like you, I lust for you, and I want you to do things that pleasure me," but at some point she would usually say, "Thanks very much, I'm done with you. Next, please." So she was very much like Aphrodite. Aphrodite, in my mind, is one of the archetypes of the feminine, although it's not an archetype that social consciousness generally considers feminine. But it is feminine in a Venus-type way. We often get femininity confused with the Moon, and forget that there are other aspects to it.

Audience: A lot of the way you look at dominant and inferior functions doesn't really fit with Jung's way of viewing dominant and inferior functions.

Richard: Yes, I guess it's best if I come out of the closet on this one. I disagree with a great deal of Jung's typologies, and specifically with the way he classified the functions, which I believe was done too narrowly. I believe there is greater variability to the human psyche than Jung gave credit for. I am familiar with his system, but the system I'm using here offers many more possibilities. For instance, I don't believe that a dominant intuitive function necessarily means an inferior sensation function. It's a nice theory, but I'm doubtful that things are so fixed or set in that way. I don't even like correlating Jung's four functions (intuition, sensation, thinking and feeling) with fire, earth, air or water. Jung had some great ideas about the psychodynamics of intuitive types, sensation types, thinking types and feeling types, and he expressed them beautifully, but I think that the astrological elements say it all much better. The system I am showing you today opens up many more possibilities, because it allows someone with a dominant intuitive or fiery function to have an inferior thinking function. And as I just said, strict Jungians would say that this wasn't possible, that someone whose superior function was intuition would automatically have sensation as the inferior function.

Audience: As a general rule, do singletons always imply overcompensation?

Richard: No, not necessarily. It depends on which planet is the singleton, and how the person mythologizes the situation. Some people don't overcompensate for singleton planets—instead, what they do is to deny the singleton planet altogether. I've seen many people with a Mars singleton who simply deny they feel any anger, rather than overcompensating for their singleton Mars by acting in a very yang and pushy way.

Audience: Can you explain the difference between orientation by sign and orientation by house?

Richard: A sign is an archetypal energy, it's a deity or force that must be honored. A house is simply an area of life in which the archetypal energy represented by a sign is manifested. Signs show drives and needs, and houses show the sphere of life where these drives and needs are acted out. For example, Eleanor Roosevelt had lots of planets in the personal signs, but they were in universal houses. Her personal urge and need was to take up causes and do something for the good of the greater whole. As a matter of fact, her dominant function wasn't personal but social, which she also lived out in the area of life represented by the universal houses. She used to call herself her husband's mouth and legs. FDR had an inferior social function, and she carried this for him. He only had one planet in a social sign, which was Uranus right on his Ascendant. Everybody saw him as this great, charming person, but he wasn't—he was extremely private and had very few friends. Eleanor carried the social function for him, but she did it through the kinds of causes associated with the universal houses.

THE ART OF SYNASTRY:
COMPARING THE CHARTS OF
ZELDA AND F. SCOTT FITZGERALD

We are going to look at the synastry between the charts of Zelda and F. Scott Fitzgerald (see Charts 2 and 3 on pages 242 and 243). I think one of the best ways of learning astrology is to read the biography of someone who interests you and follow it along with the chart. It's a nice informative, harmless thing to do, especially if the person is dead! There is a good biography of Zelda written by Nancy Miford,[1] which I used to gain information on her life. Let's spend a little time looking at each chart separately to see what shows up in terms of potential relationship indicators. We'll start with Zelda. (Please note the breakdown I've done of her modalities, elements, polarities and orientation by sign and house—it's the same system we used when we analyzed Isadora's chart.) So, in terms of relationship indicators, what strikes you first when you look at Zelda's chart?

Audience: Missing earth.

Richard: Yes, she has no planets in earth, but she does have five planets in fire. In fact, according to my system of giving points to placements, fire and air tally to ten points, while she only gets three points for earth and water. This means she is much more yang than yin. Like Isadora, Zelda was a very strong woman. Zelda's yang side could be seen in the way she took the initiative in choosing her men friends (something we also saw in Isadora's life). When she met Scott for the first time, Zelda decided that he was the man for her and she was determined to marry him. She had always fantasized about marrying an important man, and the

---

[1]Nancy Milford, *Zelda* (San Francisco, HarperCollins, 1983).

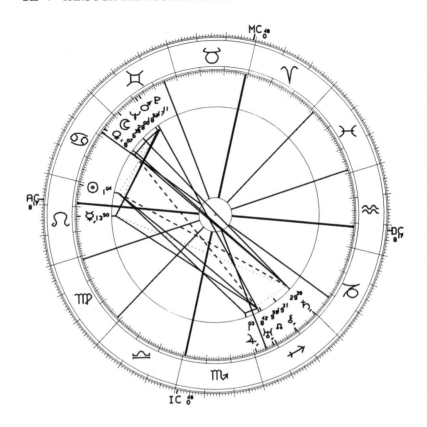

MODALITIES	MISSING	HOUSE
Cardinal 3	FUNCTIONS	Personal 2
Fixed 4	Earth	Social 2
Mutable 6		Universal 9
	STELLIA	
ELEMENTS	11th	ORIENTATIONS
Fire 7		(Sign)
Air 3	SINGLETONS	Personal 6
Water 3	N/A	Social 4
Earth 0		Universal 3

Chart 2. Zelda Fitzgerald, born in Montgomery, Alabama, July 24, 1900, at 5:33 A.M. CST. Birth data from Lois Rodden, *Profiles of Women* (Tempe, AZ: American Federation of Astrologers, 1979). Chart calculated by Astrodienst using Placidus houses.

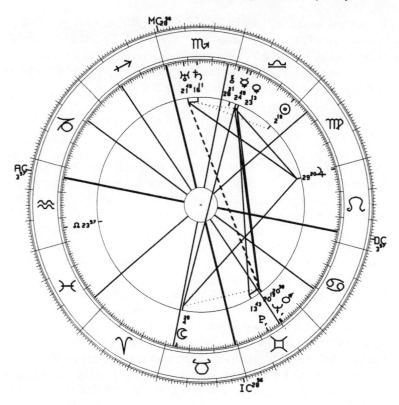

MODALITIES	MISSING FUNCTIONS	HOUSE
Cardinal 4	Universal Signs	Personal 3
Fixed 6		Social 7
Mutable 3		Universal 3
	STELLIA	
ELEMENTS	N/A	ORIENTATIONS
Fire 1 (♃)		(Sign)
Air 7	SINGLETONS	Personal 5
Water 3	♃ Fire	Social 8
Earth 2 (☽)	☽ Earth	Universal 0

Chart 3. F. Scott Fitzgerald, born in St. Paul, Minnesota, September 24, 1896, at 3:30 P.M. LMT. Birth data from birth certificate. Chart calculated by Astrodienst using Placidus houses.

handsome and successful F. Scott Fitzgerald, already established as an important writer of this day, fit the bill. In this sense, Zelda was looking for a man to live out her powerful and dazzling animus energy, which is clearly shown by her Sun in Leo in trine to her Jupiter-Uranus conjunction in Sagittarius.

Audience: Isn't her yang side at odds with her Moon-Venus conjunction in Cancer?

Richard: Yes, I agree, but let's look more closely into this. Remember that Moon-Venus aspects can indicate a mother complex, or what I called the poison apple syndrome. Zelda did have a complex relationship with her mother, which I'll explain to you. Zelda was raised in Alabama, and her parents came from a very genteel southern family. Her father was a judge, and rather distant (Zelda has the Sun in the 12th and that can indicate an absent father). Zelda's mother was devoted to her, to the point that she tried to live her own life vicariously through her daughter. Zelda was the belle of Montgomery, Alabama, and she really did play the coquette, very much like Scarlett O'Hara in the beginning of *Gone with the Wind*. Zelda was sexually precocious, and she had many beaus. Even though Zelda's mother was a very proper Daughter-of-the-American-Revolution type of lady, she actually encouraged Zelda's romantic episodes. But she also was ambivalent about all this, and she often turned around and condemned Zelda for being so promiscuous. Zelda had two sisters, and her mother made it very clear that she wanted all her daughters to be closer to her than to their father. She would tell them that their father was a very important judge and a busy man, and they should leave him alone to get on with his work.

Anyway, Zelda did marry Scott Fitzgerald, and the two of them became the living archetype of the golden years of the Roaring Twenties. They lived fast, they lived well, they jet-setted around, they drank a lot, they settled down in Paris, and they knew everybody who was worth knowing. But both Zelda and Scott were very weak in earth. She had no planets in earth, and he only had his Moon in Taurus, so, between them, there was only one planet in earth. Their missing earth is an indication that, as a couple, they were sloppy with money. Even though Scott earned a bundle through his writing, they ended up squandering it all. Zelda was the prototype of the flapper, and she seemed to embody some archetypal image for the collective, which is shown by all those planets in the 11th (the house of groups and society) and also by her Leo Sun in the 12th (the house of the collective unconscious). Although she had many different artistic interests, she never got her own creativity off the ground, which probably relates back to the lack of earth in her chart. But it's also true to say that Scott vampirized her. He used her as a model for the leading female characters in his writings. He would literally read her diary and take lines from it and use them verbatim in his novels. In a sense, he was constantly plundering who she was in order to create his magnificent characters.

I connect the 5th with creative self-expression and you can see that her 5th house planets opposed her 11th house planets. As with any opposition, there is a tendency to identify with one side and project the other. She seemed to be consumed by the 11th house—parties, society and embodying a collective image—while her 5th house Sagittarian creative energy and sense of individuality was picked up by Scott. Zelda's ego almost disappeared entirely. The one time she finally managed to finish writing a novel, Scott did everything he could to prevent it from being published. She also tried to launch a career as a dancer, but he kept stifling her. They were tremendously competitive with one another, and somehow, Scott always succeeded in diminishing her. Her difficult 5th house was also reflected in the problematic and estranged relationship she had with her daughter, their only child. As time went by, Zelda was diagnosed as a manic depressive and had numerous nervous breakdowns. She and Scott finally separated, and she ended up dying in a fire in a sanitarium.

Audience: Don't you think that Zelda's Sun in Leo in the 12th contributed to her self-destructiveness? It certainly fits with dying in a fire in an institution.

Richard: Yes, I agree with you. Her 12th house Sun indicates a natural urge toward entropy, as if some part of her didn't want to take form or take shape, and would have preferred never to have emerged from the womb at all. It's a "to be or not to be" issue. The

12th house Sun also can be tremendously creative, because its permeable boundaries give the ability to mediate collective images or to embody collective ideals and archetypes, which she lived out in her role as the archetypal flapper. And yet, that same placement gives a very weak and shaky ego identity, and trouble with self-definition. In this respect, the Sun in the 12th is a double-edged sword: it offers the gift of great creative potential, but at the same time, it can indicate terrible confusion when it comes to one's sense of personal identity.

Now, just for a moment, let's turn our attention to Scott's chart. Notice that he only had one planet in fire, Jupiter in Leo in the 7th house. His lack of fire meant that fiery people attracted him—they had a kind of energy he needed—and Zelda had five planets and her Ascendant in fire. He also had the Moon as a singleton in earth, and a singleton Moon is often an indication of the importance of the anima, women and mother in a person's life. You frequently find a strong mother complex when the Moon is a singleton. In a way, Scott was a classic *puer* (eternal youth). He was very tied to Mama's apron strings, and had a tremendously hard time breaking away from her. His mother was the archetypal Terrible Mother. She dressed him as a girl until he was four or five years old because she had desperately wanted a daughter. It's also interesting to note that although Scott was quite yang (he had eight points yang to five points yin), Zelda was even more yang than he was (she had 10 points yang to three points yin). Zelda used to accuse him of homosexuality. Indeed, I've seen a picture of Scott Fitzgerald dressed in drag for the Harvard Hasty Pudding Club. He's dressed up like a Gibson Girl, with one of those big bonnets and everything. I've covered up the caption, shown the picture to classes, and asked students who they thought it was. And they'd say, "Oh, one of those beautiful 19th century singers or actresses."

He was a very pretty, rather effete man. He had an intense relationship with Ernest Hemingway, and many people who knew them thought the relationship had strong homosexual undercurrents. I'd also like to point out the inconjunct between his Libra Sun and Taurus Moon. You would think that because both these signs are ruled by Venus, an inconjunct between them shouldn't be a big problem. But these two signs can represent a conflict between two different images of the feminine. His Sun in Libra side is pure, cool, aesthetic and distant, more interested in clothes, fashions and the ideal of feminine beauty than with an actual, corporeal woman. This conflicts with his Moon in Taurus side, which is interested in flesh, but which also embodies his mother in some way. Besides his Sun-Moon quincunx, the only other major aspect to his Moon is a trine to his 7th house Jupiter, which suggests to me that he is looking for something lunar or maternal through his partner. I imagine that Scott hoped to get some positive mothering through Zelda, unlike the kind of mothering he received from his actual mother. But even if Zelda did succeed in mothering him in a good way, Scott has a very hungry singleton Moon, so no matter what she gave, it wouldn't have been enough, and he would always be demanding more and more. His Moon also is semisquare to his Mars-Neptune conjunction in Gemini, another indication of the frustration he felt in trying to get his lunar needs met. I remember reading that while in Paris, Zelda used to drag Scott along on her shopping sprees. He loved this, in the beginning at least, because he thought she was marvelously self-indulgent (his Moon trine Jupiter). He enjoyed telling his friends endless, wonderful stories about the crazy things Zelda spent money on. In fact, his heroines often displayed this same compulsively self-indulgent quality that fascinated him in Zelda. However, as time went by, he began to criticize and blame her constantly for draining their resources. So while she exhibited qualities that fulfilled his needs in certain ways, these same qualities could also irritate and annoy him.

I'd like you to note a few more things. Jupiter in 29 Leo and Uranus in 21 Scorpio is the only square in his chart, and it's a wide one. I sometimes think that people without squares have difficulty handling conflict when it arises. It's not that conflict never arises, because it does. It's just that they don't feel equipped to deal with it when it does. They have a tendency to crack under strain and stress. You should also take notice of his 7th house Jupiter, which is in the 29th degree of Leo. I have found that planets in the 29th degree of a sign can be very tricky, as if they're teetering on the edge and about to change into something else. In any case, as I mentioned before, that wildly expansive Jupiterian energy is in the 7th house of the not-self, the house of what we project out onto the world, and the house of partners. You can see how this picks up on

Zelda's Leo Sun and Ascendant. In fact, her Ascendant is in the same sign as his Descendant, and his Ascendant is in the same sign as her Descendant. This double-whammy kind of thing usually indicates a very strong attraction based on mutual projection.

Audience: I'm drawn to his Sun and Venus in the 8th house. I've noticed that people with planets in the 8th often find these planets to be somehow out of reach, or that they can't easily connect with these energies in themselves. The Sun represents father, and Venus is the ability to have a conscious relationship. This says to me that, as a child, Scott probably had very little contact with his father, and therefore never developed a very strong ego identity separate from his mother. He needed to find and redeem his 8th house Sun and Venus. His inability to redeem these lost archetypes is shown by the way he stole from Zelda, by the way he stole from her diary and ripped off her psychic energy.

Richard: Yes, that's a very good point. I would agree that he psychically vampirized Zelda and eventually drained her. I hate to say it, but such things do happen in a relationship. His singleton Moon, sitting all alone near the bottom of his chart in Taurus but conjuncting Zelda's Midheaven, could also have something to do with this. When I say that he vampirized her, I don't mean to say that she was an innocent victim in it all, because I think that it takes two to do that dance. I think that the "suckee" and the "sucker" do a dance together. If you've seen the film of Bram Stoker's *Dracula*, you can't help noticing that there is something very sexual about having your blood sucked by a vampire. The victim is always wearing a flimsy nightgown running through some Gothic countryside, a bit reminiscent of the dance between Lucifer and Eve. Although I somehow do feel more sorry for her than I do for him, I can't honestly say she was the totally innocent victim. We tend to feel sorry for Zelda, because she ended up such a wreck. And yet, Scott's life was not so nice either. He finished up as a burnt-out alcoholic in Hollywood, writing for cheap films, and he died penniless. So he suffered a great deal as well.

Let's do some analyzing of their cross-aspects and see where that takes us. When doing a synastry, I make a point of not prejudging what an interaspect might mean. I don't necessarily agree that the man's Mars on the woman's Venus is always going to signify sexual ecstasy. There are other ways a Mars-Venus contact can manifest. In terms of relationship as well as everything else in life, the whole is greater than the sum of the parts. So please be careful of judging too quickly how certain contacts are going to manifest. I have the feeling that most people tend to think of a relationship as an entity in itself. Although it's true to say that a relationship is something in and of itself, I also believe that both people involved are still playing by their own rules. Each person has his or her own agenda and contract, which, in most cases, is never stated, and can give rise to a lot of the difficulties people encounter in relationship. For instance, I may think I'm your father, but you may think I'm your son, or need me to be your son more than your father. Many people spend years in a relationship not knowing what the real game is that's going on.

Why don't we pick a planet in one chart, and see how it aspects the planets in the other chart? Let's start with Scott's Saturn. His Saturn is at 16 degrees of Scorpio in the 9th house. In his own chart, his Saturn is quincunx Pluto, Neptune and Mars, and conjunct Uranus. Now, let's see what aspects it makes to Zelda's chart. Does she have anything around 16 or 17 degrees of a sign? Yes, his Saturn is quincunx her Mars-Pluto conjunction in Gemini, and in square to her Mercury and Ascendant in Leo. We should also note that both of them have Mars in Gemini conjunct Neptune and Pluto, which means that the Saturn inconjunct to these planets in his own chart is replicated in hers. This must mean that she brings out his own inner frustrations and paradoxes reflected in his Saturn quincunx to his Pluto, Neptune and Mars. The quincunx is always a paradoxical aspect. I imagine that he sets her up to be the coquette (the Gemini energy) by buying her clothes and introducing her to all these interesting men, and then he sits back and vicariously gets off on watching her flirt with and attract these men. But with Saturn in Scorpio inconjunct the Gemini energy, you can be sure that he makes her pay for it later. By the way, I tend to find that a natal Mars-Pluto contact is an indicator of sexual problems in itself. In some way, Pluto intensifies the sexual charge of Mars, and gives it an underworld quality, which suggests that there is something dangerous about the sex drive. So both Scott and Zelda have this Mars-Pluto issue in themselves, and their relationship is such that it brings it out because his Mars-Pluto conjuncts her Mars-Pluto. What do you have to say about his Saturn in square to her Mercury and Ascendant?

Audience: Wouldn't that aspect indicate that they had a very karmic relationship, that they were still acting out something from a previous life they had together?

Richard: I never know how to respond when people tell me that they're in a very karmic relationship, because either every relationship is karmic or no relationship is karmic. I don't think that some relationships are especially chosen to be karmic, while others are not. I also think that bringing the idea of karma into a chart reading can be a tricky and dangerous thing to do. I would never bring up the idea of karma in a consultation. I might think it privately to myself, but I wouldn't say anything along those lines to a client.

I believe that his Saturn squaring her Mercury and Ascendant in Leo could be very stimulating to his career. These cross-aspects are an indication of how he used her persona—her Leonine, extroverted Sun and Mercury rising in Leo side—to stimulate his own creativity, such as raiding and stealing from her diaries (her 1st house Mercury in Leo). However, her very extroverted Leo personality, although stimulating for him in terms of his work and career, would have made his Saturn in Scorpio seem even more inhibited that it already was. So, while he's getting something he needs from her, he also resents her for these same qualities.

Let's look at her own Saturn for a moment, and see things from her point of view. What do we have? Her Saturn is in 29 degrees of Sagittarius, so here we are again with the 29th degree of a sign, which I always feel to be an indication of instability in terms of the planet and sign involved. Remember Scott's 7th house Jupiter in 29 Leo, which I felt indicated something unsteady and unstable that he projected upon his partners. And we find something similar in her chart, with her Saturn in 29 degrees of Sagittarius, which certainly says something about her father projections and father issues. Now, her Saturn squares his Sun in early Libra, trines his Moon in 4 Taurus, sextiles his Venus and Mercury in Libra, trines his Jupiter in Leo, and opposes his Mars and Neptune in 20 Gemini. This tells us that her Saturn is much more activated by his chart than the other way around. I would definitely say that her Saturn has to do with her father issues. She had a very emotionally deprived childhood in terms of her relationship with her father, and there would be a tendency to reconstellate this in her marriage. In other words, she would unconsciously and compulsively look for a type of man with whom she could set up the same kind of deprivation she felt with her father. Also, it's interesting to note that her Saturn in 29 Sagittarius is exactly trine his Jupiter in 29 Leo. Even though these two planets are connected by a trine, his Jupiter seems to encourage her Saturn in a negative way, by feeding into her own lack of self-confidence. It's as if his Jupiter spurs on her Saturn to express itself more, but in the process, he also sets it up that she should fail or not be good enough. In essence, he is telling her to try things, to stretch herself and take the lead, but when she does do this, he makes her feel as if she hasn't done it well enough. It's as if his Jupiter encourages her Saturn to venture into an area in which she feels fragile and vulnerable, and which she can't handle when she gets there.

Audience: What about the trine of her Saturn to his Moon?

Richard: Well, she did parent (Saturn) his inner child (the Moon) in some ways. She spent a lot of time editing his work, going through it with a fine-toothed comb and helping him rewrite bits, for which he never gave her any credit. And then we have her Saturn square his Sun. This could be stimulating for him, because her Saturn (her insecurity and vulnerability) touches off his solar power and creativity. However, I wonder if, from her side, she felt belittled or put down (her Saturn) by the recognition he received for his creativity (his Sun), while hers remained unrecognized.

Audience: How did having a child affect them?

Richard: Scott was a classic puer, and Zelda was a classic *puella* (the feminine version of the eternal youth). When a puer and puella get married, they both want to play the child in the relationship. Puers and puellas are not well-suited to be parents, because producing a child means that they each must acknowledge their responsibility to be a parent, and therefore have to give up jockeying for the position of child themselves. The real loser in this situation is the actual child, who may end up being resented by both parents. Zelda first started manifesting symptoms of manic depression shortly after her daughter was born.

Let's take a minute to look at the relationship between their respective Suns and Moons. Zelda's Sun is 1 Leo and Scott's Sun is 2 Libra, which means that their Suns are sextile. Her Moon is 6 Cancer and his Moon is 4 Taurus, which means that their Moons are also sextile. But you will notice that his Sun in 2 Libra squares her Moon in 6 Cancer, and her Sun in 1 Leo squares his Moon in 4 Taurus. Because their Moons are sextile, I would say that their inner females got along well. The sextile aspect between their yin Moons also suggests that initially they must have been attracted to each other's inner child, as if they felt a sense of safety or security together, or they played together well. The fact that their Suns also are in sextile makes me think that their inner males got along quite harmoniously. However, real problems show up when we analyze the square between his Sun and her Moon, and the square between her Sun and his Moon: the mutual squares between these planets means that his male side (his Sun) and her female side (her Moon) didn't get along with each other, and her male side (her Sun) didn't get along with his female side (his Moon). So their inner females got along well together, their inner children played well together, and their inner males could relate to one another, but his male side had trouble with her female side, and her male side had trouble with his female side.

We'll have to leave it here for now, but I hope our discussion has given you some insight into how to approach the art of synastry. I think we can explore synastry further through group discussion, and I can handle your specific questions.

GROUP DISCUSSION AND CONCLUSION

As promised, this session will be devoted to questions and group discussion. You might want to ask "what if" questions about synastry, such as, what if Mars in the chart of one person makes an opposition to Neptune in the chart of another person? It would be helpful if you could specify what kind of relationship you are asking about. I don't like labeling relationships, but knowing whether you're talking about the charts of a mother and son, or a husband or wife, or two lovers, or two friends, gives me a structure in which to answer your question.

Audience: What if Venus in one chart conjuncts Pluto in the other chart, and the two people are lovers?

Richard: The Venus person would stimulate the other person's Pluto, which means that the kind of love that person A (the Venus person) had to offer would touch off deep fears, repressed material or issues to do with power and sex in person B (the Pluto person). The Pluto person might frighten off person A, or could put person A through a lot of heavy trips, which, in the end, could transform person A in some way, possibly leading person A into a deeper understanding of themselves and of relationship in general. Certainly, three would be some kind of obsessive, compulsive or passionate quality to their relationship. Because Venus and Pluto are archetypal complements as the rulers of Taurus and Scorpio, respectively, there is already a dynamic attraction or dance going on between these two planets, so the people who had them conjunct in synastry would probably feel irresistible to one another in many ways.

. If Pluto is the seducer or the violator (and I don't necessarily mean this only on the physical level), then Venus would be "the seducee," the one who is being seduced or violated. But it's highly likely that Venus wants to be violated or seduced. If you've ever watched animals mating, you see a wonderful dance between Venus and Pluto. When the male approaches, the female usually reacts by moving away, but then she will look over her shoulder and glance back at the male. Then she might roll over on her back, and the male, who may not even have been all that interested in the beginning, starts to wonder what's going on. He runs over to her and takes a sniff, and she swats him as if to say "leave me alone." Then he thinks, wait a minute, I'm getting double messages here. Then she runs away a few paces again, and looks back at him, and he begins to chase her again. There's something of a Venus-Mars type thing going on here, but it also has a strong flavor of Pluto, because the male (who is Pluto in this case) ends up forcing Venus into the act of consummation. However, I would argue that the female (Venus in this case) really wanted to be seduced all along, but needed someone more demonstrative to make that happen. So, in this sense, Venus is the provacateur, the one who provokes and seduces Pluto into seducing her. Venus's apparent innocence has a way of exciting Pluto to take action, just as in the story of Kore and Hades. As a general rule, Pluto wants to lure us out of our basic ground – that's his agenda. A Venus-Pluto aspect between two charts can be a very tricky, difficult contact, especially so if it occurs between a parent and a child, because it invariably gives an erotic flavor to the relationship.

Audience: What if the synastry between two people shows quite a few inconjuncts?

Richard: With quincunxes between two charts, there can be an endless feeling of the two people trying to reach out and communicate with one another, but neither is quite sure how to go about doing this. So, when I'm talking about rhinoceroses, you're talking about pineapples. And yet, there can be something intriguing and compelling about the mismatch that lends an air of fascination and mystery to the relationship and to each of the people involved. It's as if you're constantly trying to understand one another. You think you've made yourself clear or that you've figured out the other person, but then something happens that creates doubt and confusion in your mind. You have a conversation that you think clarifies something, but it's like a Chinese meal, and a few minutes later you don't feel as if you've really communicated at all. Quincunxes between charts can be a very erotic or sexual kind of aspect in many cases, because we often find mysterious people alluring. But it can also make you feel continually frustrated and dissatisfied, as if you're trying to get a square peg into a round hole.

Audience: What if my Moon inconjuncts your Mercury, and, at the same time, your Moon inconjuncts my Mercury, so we're getting it both ways?

Richard: Quincunxes often provoke crisis, and they are the juice out of which an awful lot of creative solutions can be extracted. The quincunx is a paradox, like sailing west to get east, if you know what I mean. It's like the idea of inoculating somebody with the germ of a disease in order to prevent them from getting the disease. There's something that seems so off the wall about doing this, and yet when you stop to think about it, it actually makes good sense. So if we translate this in terms of the Moon inconjunct Mercury, it would mean difficulty communicating feelings to one another. You might think the other person is getting what you're trying to express, but really the other person is understanding what you're saying in a completely different way from what you mean. For this reason, Moon-Mercury quincunxes make communication difficult, and yet, this kind of problem can lead you into finding rather ingenious ways of getting the other person to understand how you feel.

Audience: What about a Pluto-Moon contact between two charts?

Richard: The Moon is a nurturing kind of planet, and it could feel violated by Pluto when Pluto aspects it in synastry. So the erotic side of Pluto might feel threatening or invasive to the inner mother or the inner child of the Moon person. Moon-Pluto interaspects are especially difficult in the charts of a parent and child, because there is something potentially incestuous that happens when these two planets get together. It's as if nurturing becomes contaminated with eros, with sex and power, with the desire to seduce and overcome. My guess is that people born with a natal Moon-Pluto aspect carry around some kind of tape or myth with regard to nurturance. If your mother's or father's Pluto hits your Moon by synastry, you could feel erotic or incestuous messages coming from them, or you might experience them as power trippers. In other words, it's not just milk that comes in your bottle, but something Plutonian is being transmitted as well. The problem is enhanced if your mother, for instance, is not getting her erotic needs met by your father, and therefore turns to you (the child) for that kind of fulfillment. Or if your father is not getting his erotic needs met by your mother, and he then looks to you for that kind of involvement. Normally, it tends to go cross-sexually—mother to son, and father to daughter. In any case, it indicates that the person who is meant to nurture you is also giving you messages of a sexual or erotic nature. As a child, you will find this very confusing, because of the incest taboo. Your adult relationships could be complicated by this issue, because you'll feel uneasy about sex with anyone you are close to.

Audience: What about Venus in Aquarius in a woman's chart in an exact semisextile to Venus in Pisces in a man's chart? The two people are lovers.

Richard: I find the semisextile an intriguing aspect, and, frankly, I'm not quite sure how to interpret it. Actually, it's quite similar to the inconjunct, because the semisextile links together signs of two different elements, modalities and polarities. With the semisextile between Aquarius and Pisces, you have a yang sign and a yin sign, a fixed sign and a mutable sign, an air sign and a water sign thrown together. Even though these signs are next-door neighbors, they are very different from one another. As an air sign, Aquarius could be afraid of slipping into the disorder and chaos suggested by Pisces. Venus in Aquarius might say, "I am not yet in Pisces, but I already sense that I'm heading that way, so I feel a pull in that direction even though it's quite different from how I am now." Venus in Pisces, on the other hand, turns around and says, "I am no longer in Aquarius, and I don't want to slip back into that kind of detachment and that kind of airy overview."

Seen in this light, planets in semisextile often reflect each other's unconscious qualities. The man with Venus in Pisces could be looking for an idealized, perfect madonna figure, and he would want to project this image onto his lover. She, however, has Venus in Aquarius, which would make her more cool, detached and distant than he would like her to be, so he may end up dissatisfied. This dissatisfaction could be a good thing, because it might make him aware that what he is looking for is an overidealized projection that no one could live out on a mundane and everyday basis. The woman with Venus in Aquarius could be doing something similar. She is with a man with a Neptunian-type Venus in Pisces, but she is really looking for a man who is a Uranian or Aquarian type. Both of them are looking for some kind of magic in their relationship, but the magic he wants is a merging magic, and the magic she wants is a more Uranian, separating and observing magic.

Audience: My son is an Aquarian, and his Sun conjuncts his father's Venus and Ascendant in Aquarius. What do you make of that?

Richard: This would mean that your son's developing ego identity (his Sun) would pick up on his father's persona (the Venus rising in Aquarius). If the father is uncomfortable with his own mask or persona, then he won't like to see his son living out these qualities. But if the father feels all right about his Venusian and Aquarian persona, then he would feel very closely identified with his Aquarian son. This could be a nice thing, but it might also create difficulty when the time comes for the son to separate from his father and become his own person.

Audience: What if a woman's Venus is in aspect to a man's Mars?

Richard: Everyone always raves about Mars-Venus contacts in synastry as an indication of a great sexual rapport, but I think these aspects are overrated in this respect. I've found that the aggressiveness and abrasiveness of Mars can raise the hackles in Venus, which then makes her resist his advances. And when Venus withdraws, it will probably provoke Mars into pushing even harder. He'll probably blame their problems on her for being too uptight and skittish, and she'll blame their problems on him for coming on so heavy. Venus and Mars can be too polarized, especially if they're in square or opposition. Venus conjunct Mars is a better interaspect—at least they're in the same sign and therefore operating under the same energy. I would go so far as to say that Venus-Pluto contacts (which we discussed earlier) offer more promise of a good sexual relationship than Venus-Mars aspects.

Audience: How come identical twins can be so different when their charts are almost exactly the same?

Richard: The reason for this is that the twins, in order to differentiate themselves form each other, may live out different parts of their charts. One twin may side with the father and take on his qualities, while the other may side with the mother and take on her qualities. To do this, each twin favors those particular aspects in his or her chart that fit the differing qualities each is taking on. If they have the same Ascendant, one twin often will live out certain qualities of the ascending sign in an extreme way, while the other twin, in the name of differentiation and self-definition, will actually take on the opposite qualities of the ascending sign with which the other twin is identified, and therefore more openly express the qualities of the descending sign. I recently worked with triplets, two females and a male. We discovered that the contract between them was that the male triplet should live out all the animus planets and signs in his chart, while the two remaining females were left to battle it out over the feminine or yin planets and signs in their charts. The three charts were almost exactly similar, but each of the triplets favored different parts of the chart.

Audience: Can you say more about someone born with Uranus on the Ascendant?

Richard: Yes, briefly. Any transpersonal planet making a close aspect to the Ascendant—in particular, a conjunction, square or opposition—indicates that you are constellating or expressing something from the collective unconscious via your mask or persona. This usually makes you an unusual or charismatic type of person, but it can create problems feeling comfortable within yourself. People may project something magical or larger than life onto you, which could make you feel special or different from the masses, and yet, you are not at peace inside yourself. Parents who have a child born with Uranus, Neptune or Pluto in close aspect to the Ascendant often have trouble understanding that child. Most parents want their children to be normal and to be able to adjust easily to life, but a child with Uranus on the Ascendant will be anything but normal. Parents need to learn to love these kinds of children enough to let them be who they naturally are.

Audience: Do you use the asteroids?

Richard: No, because I prefer to work with an uncluttered chart. I'm not saying that the asteroids don't have any significance, but I find that if there are too many bits of information all over the chart, I have more difficulty seeing the overall picture or the *gestalt* of the chart. I feel the same way about using the east point, or the vertex, or Vulcan or Lilith or any of the hypothetical trans-Plutonian planets. You can get so many added bits of information that you end up being able to read anything you want into the chart. All I need is the meat and potatoes of the chart, and that gives me what I want to know.

Audience: What house system do you tend to use?

Richard: The question of house systems is one of those areas about which astrologers often get very dogmatic. I can't understand what all the fuss is about, because each house system is based on its own particular kind of logic and is consistent within its own logical system. I go for Placidus, and sometimes Koch, and I've even experimented with Campanus. The only one that really doesn't interest me is Equal House. I'm not saying it's wrong, but I just don't find it very interesting. What you might do is to set up the same chart in a couple of different house systems, and see what you think. But I don't believe that there is any definite answer to the question of which house system is right or best. It's a matter of personal choice.

Audience: I'm still not clear about the distinction you make between planets and the Ascendant.

Richard: I call the Ascendant "an outlet point"; it's a kind of front door to the world, a way into and out of the world. The planets, however, are entities or beings; they're gods, and represent living, active psychodynamic forces. Although the Ascendant is very important psychologically, it is not a psychodynamic force, but rather a point in space, which is very different from being an energy. Planets are energies. If you have a Mars-Jupiter aspect, for instance, Mars is sending the nature of its energy to Jupiter, which, in turn, is sending its type of energy to Mars. Aspects between planets indicate a mutual exchange of energies, a mutual exchange of the nature of the planets involved. The Ascendant, however, is a neutral point. It's like a door that opens and shuts, and, although it has its own archetypal qualities, I don't think it's an energized type of archetypal quality in the same way that a planet is.

Audience: Can you say something about natal Venus in aspect to the outer planets?

Richard: Venus in connection with the other planets exhibits a tendency to look for magic and for the divine through love and relationship, and, in this way, a Venus aspect to an outer planet is an attempt to mix or blend the transpersonal with the personal. These aspects bring a heightened awareness and sensitivity, and work best when they are channeled into something creative. Venus aspects to Uranus, Neptune or Pluto cause the most trouble and pain for people who insist on looking for a transpersonal experience through personal love—because another person is not a "transperson," to coin a word. One human being cannot embody the collective, unless you are that rare kind of person like Elizabeth Barrett Browning, who patiently waited for a magical poet to come along on whom she could project the transpersonal, and lived happily ever after with that projection. It's not for me to say whether what she did was right or wrong. But I am saying that many of us are continually waiting for something numinous to transpire within a personal relationship, something that would open our channels to the collective. And the plain fact is that we will experience a lot of pain, disappointment and frustration, unless we learn to let go of that agenda and make peace with the fact that no one other person can be everything for us.

We're getting into the last few minutes of the conference, and I want to use the time left to look at how you've been affected by what you learned this week. What feelings has the conference left you with? I feel as if we've opened a can of worms, and the little things are now wriggling around in the open, and the question remains, what should we do about all this? Now that we know more about the scripts, myths and agendas we carry around and project in relationship, how do we fix it all? Is there some key or solution that would heal us and make us whole? It should be clear by now, however, that there are no definite answers . . . there are only questions. We still may be looking for the wizard who can give us the right answers and solutions, but as I said in the opening lecture of this conference, the Wizard of Oz is not the wizard he is cracked up to be. He's not there for us, and if any of you think you have found him, sooner or later he'll prove to be a fake and a humbug. I know a lot of stuff has been stirred up in you this week. All of us have relationships, and all of us have problems with them. I've been going on and on about the kinds of problems people encounter in relationship, but this doesn't mean that I've solved my problems in this area. I'm still struggling with all of this myself.

One thing I do suggest is that you tread gently with what's happened to you this week. You need time to process and work with the feelings that the course has stirred up. It's as if we've dropped a stone in a pool of water, and the ripples haven't yet stopped rippling. I think it's extremely important to be very gentle with yourself for the next couple of weeks, and to give the process started this week more time to develop before you do anything too drastic with your life. You may find it hard to just sit on what you've learned or what you're feeling as a result of the things the course has touched in you. Be especially careful in the next few weeks not to keep hitting yourself on the head with the hammer of Saturn. In his own harsh way, Saturn may be accosting you with something like, "You're such a dumb idiot. Why haven't you seen all this before? Why haven't you realized sooner what you've been setting up in your life? Why has it taken you so long to track down and name the myths which have been shaping your life? You had better get off your backside right now, buddy, and start doing all that you can to change your life and your patterns." Don't get into punishing yourself or judging yourself too harshly. It's not necessary for you to be overly hard on yourself in this way—it won't help you, and could even harm you. This would be a good time, however, for you to invoke your inner, gentle, nurturing mother—a good chance to prove to yourself that she is there for you in the right way. My philosophy is, "everything in its own time." You will have learned things this week that challenge your belief systems and basic ground, but give everything a chance to settle before taking action. It's more important than ever to be good and kind to yourself now.

You may be thinking to yourself that you know what you need to do to change for the better, but, for some reason, you still aren't taking the necessary action to bring about change. You may be wondering when in the world are you ever going to change? I told you before about the quote from *Hamlet* that I have on the wall of my study, which says that readiness is all. Pluto is the planet that has the most to do with transformation, and Pluto knows that a critical mass of energy must be compiled before we can take those first few important steps out of our basic ground. To step beyond the boundaries of your basic ground is an act of heroism and courage, and you have to be very gentle with yourself about taking this step. I keep getting an image of a still pool of water, and you may be looking into this pool and wondering how many rocks and pebbles you have to drop into it before something major happens and the pool begins to overflow. I can't tell you how long it will take you to change or how much energy has to be amassed before you change. But I can urge you to trust in change, because change *is*, and change will come, and change is on its way to you. I also urge you to enlist an ally—a good friend or therapist can be your helper and guide, someone who'll be there to support you in your efforts to take the first little step beyond your basic ground. Remember the jackrabbit, who goes racing round and round the perimeters of his border and territory, constantly doubling back on itself. You don't want to be like the jackrabbit for the rest of your life, going round and round the same territory, perpetually looking for more answers before you initiate a major shift in yourself, perpetually pursuing "Why?" After a point, "why" is not the question you need to ask, and "why" will not give you the answers.

It all eventually boils down to the fact that there is a line that you have to step across. This is where dragon-slaying comes in. This is when the courageous part of you needs to come to the fore, the part of you that is not afraid to confront death, because letting go of old patterns and taking a step into something new feels like confronting death. Confronting major change is as terrifying as dying. And as Jung said, we don't necessarily change until we've suffered enough. We don't change until we are really motivated to change. We will encounter a great deal of resistance to change from inside ourselves—this is our Taurean part, Gaia herself, pulling us back and insisting that we don't bite into the apple. And yet, Gaia is in conflict with another part of us that is urging us to bite into the apple, that is urging us to change and grow. The tension between maintaining the status quo and disrupting what's existing for the sake of something new is an inner conflict that is always going on inside us. This is why we need a friend or ally by our side, someone who says, "I can't take that step over the line for you, but I'll be here by your side when you've finally reached that point of stepping outside of the magic circle surrounding you." Along with a friend or ally, you also need patience. It takes time. It just takes time.

The play, *Death of a Salesman*,[1] keeps running through my mind. At some point in the drama Willy Loman—this modern, tragic hero—cries out that attention must be paid. We too need to pay attention, not only to what we do within our relationships, but also to what is going on inside ourselves. And by this, I don't mean a perpetual examination of yourself in front of a mirror. Paying attention to yourself means paying attention to your inner voice. Paying attention to yourself means becoming still enough to hear your inner voice. Astrology can actually be dangerous if we start thinking that a chart is going to give us all the answers and solve all our problems for us. Charts can't do that. And, as I've said before, don't rush to your ephemeris too quickly when you first start a relationship. Let the relationship be what it is for awhile, before imposing the special language of astrology onto it. Give the relationship time to be whatever it is before you start analyzing it astrologically.

Jung once said that the process of individuation consists of three parts or phases—insight, endurance and action. Psychology is only needed during the first phase, the insight phase. In the

---

[1]Arthur Miller, *Death of a Salesman* (New York: Penguin, 1976).

second and third phases, it is moral strength that plays the predominant role. And I think this is the bottom line. Change comes out of moral strength, which I would also define as the courage to take action. Only Cronus, Time himself, knows when we are ready to do that. The apple will fall from the tree when it's ready.

ABOUT THE CENTRE
FOR PSYCHOLOGICAL ASTROLOGY

The Centre for Psychological Astrology provides a unique work-shop and professional training programme designed to foster the cross-fertilisation of the fields of astrology and depth, humanistic and transpersonal psychology. The programme includes two aspects. One is a series of seminars and classes, ranging from beginners' courses in astrology to advanced seminars in psycho-logical interpretation of the horoscope. The seminars included in this volume are representative of the latter, although the same seminar is never given verbatim more than once because the con-tent changes according to the nature of the participating group and the new research and development which is constantly occurring within the field of psychological astrology. All these seminars and classes, both beginners' and advanced, are open to the public. The second aspect of the programme is a structured, in-depth, three-year professional training which awards a Diploma in Psychologi-cal Astrology upon successful completion of the course. The main aims and objectives of the three-year professional training are:

- To provide students with a solid and broad base of knowl-edge both within the realm of traditional astrological sym-bolism and techniques, and also in the field of psychology, so that the astrological chart can be sensitively understood and interpreted in the light of modern psychological thought.

- To make available to students psychologically qualified case supervision along with training in counselling skills and techniques which would raise the standard and effec-tiveness of astrological consultation.

- To encourage investigation and research into the links between astrology, psychological models and therapeutic techniques, thereby contributing to and advancing the already existing body of astrological and psychological knowledge.

The in-depth professional training programme cannot be done by correspondence, as case supervision work is an integral part of the course. It will normally take three years to complete, although it is possible for the trainee to extend this period if necessary. The training includes approximately fifty seminars (either one-day or short, ongoing weekly evening classes) as well as fifty hours of case supervision groups. The classes and seminars fall broadly into two main categories: astrological symbolism and technique (history of astrology, psychological understanding of signs, planets, houses, aspects, transits, progressions, synastry, etc.), and psychological theory (history of psychology, psychological maps and pathology, mythological and archetypal symbolism, etc.). Case supervision groups meet on weekday evenings and consist of no more than twelve people in each group. All the supervisors are both trained psychotherapists and astrologers. Each student has the opportunity of presenting for discussion case material from the charts he or she is working on. At the end of the third year, a 15,000–20,000 word paper is required. This may be on any chosen subject—case material, research, etc.—under the general umbrella of psychological astrology. Many of these papers may be of publishable quality, and the Centre will undertake facilitating such material being disseminated in the astrological field.

Completion of the seminar and supervision requirements entitles the trainee to a certificate of completion. Acceptance of the thesis entitles the trainee to the Centre's Diploma in Psychological Astrology and the use of the letters D. Psych. Astrol. The successful graduate will be able to apply the principles and techniques learned during the course to his or her profession activities, either as a consultant astrologer or as a useful adjunct to other forms of psychological counselling. Career prospects are good as there is an ever-increasing demand for the services of capable astrologers and astrologically oriented therapists. In order to complete the professional training, the Centre asks that all students, for a minimum of one year, be involved in a recognized form of psychotherapy with a therapist, analyst or counsellor of his or her choice. The rationale behind this requirement is that we believe no responsible counsellor of any persuasion can hope to deal sensitively and wisely with another person's psyche unless one has some experience of his or her own.

The seminars offered in this book are just six of the fifty or so workshops offered by the Centre. Previous volumes in the Seminars in Psychological Astrology Series are *The Development of the Personality*, Volume 1, *Dynamics of the Unconscious*, Volume 2, *The Luminaries*, Volume 3, and *The Inner Planets*, Volume 4. As stated earlier, these seminars are never repeated in precisely the same way, as the contributions and case material from each individual group vary, and as there are constant new developments and insights occurring through the ongoing work of the seminar leaders and others in the field. If the reader is interested in finding out more about either the public seminars or the in-depth professional training offered by the Centre, please write to:

The Centre for Psychological Astrology
BCM Box 1815
London WC1N 3XX
England

Your request for information should include a stamped, self-addressed envelope (for United Kindom residents only) or an International Postal coupon to cover postage abroad.

ABOUT THE AUTHOR

Richard Idemon gained a world-wide reputation for his highly provocative and original teaching style. For more than 20 years he counseled, taught, and lectured on astrological techniques for psychotherapists and psychology for astrologers, speaking on the synthesis of psychology and astrology at numerous conferences throughout Canada, Europe, South America, Africa, and the USA. He spoke at universities, medical schools, and clinics around the country, taught astrology at Sonoma State College in California under the Humanistic Psychology program and counseled prisoners in the California State Prison System. He established the School of Astrological Studies and Pegasus Tapes, which distributes audio cassettes of his and other world-class astrologers' work, and served as a consultant to therapists in both private practice and clinical settings. Richard was a founding member of AFAN, and was affiliated with NCGR, the Jungian Society. He died in 1987.